African Americans Confront Lynching

The African American History Series

Series Editors:
Jacqueline M. Moore, Austin College
Nina Mjagkij, Ball State University

Traditionally, history books tend to fall into two categories: books academics write for each other, and books written for popular audiences. Historians often claim that many of the popular authors do not have the proper training to interpret and evaluate the historical evidence. Yet, popular audiences complain that most historical monographs are inaccessible because they are too narrow in scope or lack an engaging style. This series, which will take both chronological and thematic approaches to topics and individuals crucial to an understanding of the African American experience, is an attempt to address that problem. The books in this series, written in lively prose by established scholars, are aimed primarily at nonspecialists. They focus on topics in African American history that have broad significance and place them in their historical context. While presenting sophisticated interpretations based on primary sources and the latest scholarship, the authors tell their stories in a succinct manner, avoiding jargon and obscure language. They include selected documents that allow readers to judge the evidence for themselves and to evaluate the authors' conclusions. Bridging the gap between popular and academic history, these books bring the African American story to life.

Volumes Published

African Americans Confront Lynching

*Strategies of Resistance from the
Civil War to the Civil Rights Era*

Christopher Waldrep

ROWMAN & LITTLEFIELD PUBLISHERS, INC.
Lanham • Boulder • New York • Toronto • Plymouth, UK

ROWMAN & LITTLEFIELD PUBLISHERS, INC.

Published in the United States of America
by Rowman & Littlefield Publishers, Inc.
A wholly owned subsidiary of The Rowman & Littlefield Publishing Group, Inc.
4501 Forbes Boulevard, Suite 200, Lanham, Maryland 20706
www.rowmanlittlefield.com

Estover Road
Plymouth PL6 7PY
United Kingdom

British Library Cataloguing in Publication Information Available

Library of Congress Cataloging-in-Publication Data:

Waldrep, Christopher, 1951–
  African Americans confront lynching : strategies of resistance from the Civil War to
the civil rights era / Christopher Waldrep.
    p. cm. — (The African American history series)
  Includes bibliographical references.
  ISBN-13: 978-0-7425-5272-2 (cloth : alk. paper)
  ISBN-10: 0-7425-5272-1 (cloth : alk. paper)
  eISBN-13: 978-0-7425-6483-1
  eISBN-10: 0-7425-6483-5
  1. Lynching—United States—History. 2. Hate crimes—United States—History. I.
Title.
  HV6457.W347 2009
  364.1'34—dc22   2008025180

Printed in the United States of America

Contents

~

Chronology

1856	T. Thomas Fortune is born a slave in Florida.
1862	Ida B. Wells is born a slave in Mississippi.
1863	John Mitchell Jr. is born a slave in Virginia.
1866	Ku Klux Klan is organized in Pulaski, Tennessee. Congress passes the first civil rights act in American history and writes the Fourteenth Amendment, making blacks citizens and guaranteeing equal protection and due process of law for all American citizens. Monroe Work is born in North Carolina.
1868	Three-fourths of the states ratify the Fourteenth Amendment, and it becomes part of the Constitution.
1870 and 1871	Congress passes enforcement acts based on the Fourteenth Amendment, including the 1871 Ku Klux Klan Act, targeting violently racist individuals acting "under color of law."[1]
1883	*Chicago Tribune* begins annual report on lynchings, listing lynchings from the previous year.
1886	Ida B. Wells wins lawsuits against a discriminating railroad in Tennessee.

---

[1]"Under color of law" means acts done by authority of state law. The Fourteenth Amendment says, "No state shall" treat its citizens unequally or deprive them of due process of law. It does not explicitly say individuals cannot do so.

1892	After three of her friends are lynched in Memphis, Ida B. Wells moves to New York and publishes *Southern Horrors: Lynch Law in All Its Phases*. The University of Chicago establishes the first American sociology department.
1893	Walter F. White is born in Atlanta, Georgia.
1904	Monroe Work goes to Tuskegee, Alabama, to establish the Department of Records and Research, dedicated to documenting the accomplishments of black people.
1910	National Association for the Advancement of Colored People (NAACP) begins its campaign against lynching.
1912	James Weldon Johnson publishes *Autobiography of an Ex-Colored Man*.
1916	NAACP hires James Weldon Johnson as a field secretary.
1918	Walter White joins the NAACP staff and investigates lynching of Jim McIlherron in Tennessee and Mary Turner in Valdosta, Georgia.
1920	James Weldon Johnson becomes the first black NAACP executive secretary and takes charge of the organization.
1921	Tulsa race riot.
1922	House of Representatives passes an antilynching bill that then fails in the Senate.
1931	Walter White becomes executive secretary of the NAACP and takes charge of the organization.
1932	Franklin D. Roosevelt is elected president.
1937	House of Representatives again passes an antilynching law that again fails in the Senate.
1940	Department of Justice begins to investigate all lynchings in America. House of Representatives again passes an antilynching bill that again fails in the Senate.
1944	Supreme Court decides the case of *Screws v. United States*, ruling that the federal government can investigate and prosecute lynchings when carried out "under color of law."
1953	Dwight Eisenhower is elected president. Department of Justice no longer routinely investigates lynchings.
1954	Supreme Court declares school segregation unconstitutional, igniting a wave of racial violence.
1955	White Mississippians murder Emmett Till.
1960	John F. Kennedy is elected president.
1963	Martin Luther King leads protests through Birmingham, Alabama. Kennedy is assassinated.

1964	Barry Goldwater runs for president of the United States by campaigning against crime. Congress passes a new civil rights law.
1965	Black Panthers organize in Oakland, California. Congress passes the Voting Rights Act, guaranteeing blacks' right to vote. Malcolm X is assassinated in New York.
1968	Martin Luther King is assassinated in Memphis.
1976	Leon Ralph, an African American Democrat from Watts in the California state legislature, writes a state law designed to protect people from violence based on their race, color, religion, ancestry, national origin, political affiliation, sex, or position in a labor dispute.
1981	The states of Washington and Oregon pass laws aimed at crimes motivated by prejudice.
1990	Congress passes the first federal hate crime law, the Hate Crime Statistics Act.
1993	The Supreme Court rules hate crime laws constitutional.
1994	Congress enacts the Violent Crime Control and Law Enforcement Act, requiring the U.S. Sentencing Commission to enhance sentences for persons convicted in federal court of hate crimes.

~

Acknowledgments

I have now been actively researching American lynching for ten years, and in that time I have accumulated many more debts than I can ever repay. For this project I asked my colleague Eva Sheppard Wolf to read an early draft at a time when she was very busy with her own important work. She nonetheless graciously consented and gave my manuscript a very careful and helpful reading. My graduate assistant Mike Caires also read the manuscript and offered his reactions and suggestions. Mike and Christina Speidel helped with the research at the National Archives. When I first wrote this book my daughter Janelle was an undergraduate, and I asked her to read it to identify words and concepts that might be unclear to a student audience. She found many terms and ideas that I had to rework. As always, my wife Pamela provided support and encouragement. She also read an early version of this book and offered useful comments. Numerous librarians and archivists helped me locate the material necessary for this project. The University of Chicago and the Library of Virginia helped with the photographs. Thanks as well to Niels Aaboe and Asa Johnson for their great patience. Jacqueline M. Moore and Nina Mjagkij edited this volume with astonishing energy.

~

Introduction

The word lynching cannot be defined. It is rhetoric, and because it is rhetoric, almost any act of violence can potentially be a "lynching." Since white people have quite often lynched other white people, we cannot say that lynching only means racial violence. The word has a terrible power of its own, and crowds or individuals have used it, or its symbol, the noose, to terrify and frighten people even without actual bloodshed. As sometimes happens with emotional language, the victims of violence have turned the tables and used it to criticize their tormentors. Opponents of racial violence have recognized the word's flexibility and relied on that flexibility to carry on their fight against prejudice. In the twentieth century, the word lynching became an important tool used by the National Association for the Advancement of Colored People (NAACP) and other civil rights groups to denounce white racism. The NAACP has warned that an overly precise definition of lynching could promote violent racism by making it seem as though the problem of lynching has been solved when, in fact, the violence really continues in some new form. Thus, an exact definition could actually damage the fight against racial prejudice and violence. It is not a good tool for separating which acts of racial violence should "count" as a lynching and which should not.

The meaning of lynching is so flexible, and emotionally charged, that a nominee for the Supreme Court could use it to fend off critics. In 1991, President George H. W. Bush nominated Clarence Thomas to be an associate justice on the Supreme Court. Under the rules set down by the U.S.

Constitution, the Senate has to approve a president's nomination to the Supreme Court. In this case, Senate Democrats resented Clarence Thomas, a black man, for his very conservative views and vigorously challenged his nomination. In the course of their investigation, a former employee of Thomas's, Anita Hill, emerged to testify against him, claiming he had sexually harassed her.

Clarence Thomas came from a wooded peninsula in Georgia called Pinpoint, ten miles from Savannah. Born in 1948, Thomas missed the worst of racial violence that plagued the South in the nineteenth century and earlier in the twentieth century. But he saw Ku Klux Klansmen and heard frightening horror stories about white violence from older members of his family. He said later that he grew up feeling afraid and vulnerable, fearful that he might be attacked or even killed at any moment just because of the color of his skin.[1]

Anita Hill's accusations excited the news media. Journalists clamored to take pictures or interview Thomas, his friends, and his associates, anyone with information about what happened. Thomas later claimed that his enemies formed a howling mob that would not be "satisfied until it tasted my blood." Thomas fought back by appearing before the Senate committee investigating Hill's allegations. In his testimony, Thomas accused the Senate committee of carrying out "a high-tech lynching for uppity blacks." Thomas later compared his use of the word lynching to setting off a bomb. The word stunned and shocked his critics. Thomas and his allies thought the word appropriate because his critics had charged him with sexual misconduct, the same crime sometimes alleged against black men in the late nineteenth century to justify the more violent kind of lynching. "The mob I now faced," Thomas later wrote, "carried no ropes or guns. Its weapons were smooth-tongued lies spoken into microphones. . . . But it was a mob all the same." Thomas testified on Friday, October 11; over the weekend, public opinion turned decisively in his favor. The public judged Thomas's use of the word lynching as plausible, and it got him a seat on the Supreme Court. It also demonstrated the power of the word as rhetoric.[2]

Thomas, of course, never faced death. He said later that he felt as if his life was threatened, but he certainly never risked being hanged, shot, or knifed by his political opponents. Reporters trampled his yard, but no one bombed his house. Yet, his story is part of the history of lynching. For one thing, many Americans began paying attention to lynching, and its meaning, in new ways after the Thomas hearings. Remembering that lynching is rhetoric, a powerful tool available to criticize or chastise conduct before an audience, it becomes impossible to dismiss Thomas from the history of American lynching.

At the same time, thousands of people faced death not at all metaphorical and died by hanging, shooting, drowning, knifing, burning, bombing, and almost any other murderous method the human mind can devise. Although many people still associate lynching with hanging, in fact, the word has been used to describe many methods of death. For at least a hundred years, newspapers described lynchings of people of all colors and ethnic groups. While the word lynching is rhetoric, a word that cannot be objectively defined, it is not *only* rhetoric. Real people suffered, dying in acts of violence that newspapers, reformers, and Americans generally called lynchings, using the word loosely, not wanting to define it in any limiting way.

For African American victims of lynching, though, the meaning was nonetheless clear. Lynching was the word that most effectively criticized the white violence that made life so precarious and terrifyingly uncertain. If we understand lynching from the perspective of the people who experienced it, much of the horror came in not knowing exactly how whites might shape their violence. The victims of racial violence understood lynching not only as a killing by a crowd with a rope, not only as a hanging, but also as the authority to kill without fear of punishment. Lynching more effectively controlled black people by being so terrifyingly unpredictable, so beyond any single definition.

The structure of power in America allowed community-sanctioned violence to flourish. Lynching finds legitimacy in community approval. Lynching emerged from communities and neighborhoods, a fundamentally local act, usually carried out in isolation from scrutiny by outsiders in defiance of the rule of law. The Constitution limited the national government in Washington and protected the powers of state and city governments. As senators and congressmen from the lynching-prone states tirelessly pointed out, in the American federal system the national government had no power to prosecute ordinary crimes, like murder or lynching. (Only after the assassination of President John Kennedy in 1963 did Congress pass a law against killing federal officers.) That job belonged to the states, even in states with governments dominated by racist white Southerners who refused to punish lynching. Lynchers took refuge from scrutiny within this federal system the Constitution endorsed. Thus, the American political system shielded the most lawless from prosecution.

While the Constitution protected local power, it achieved greater symbolic power for guaranteeing the personal liberty and safety won in the American Revolution. The authors of the Constitution admired much about the British system, but they disliked Parliament's power to change the law of the land at will. Creating a written Constitution promised permanency, unchanging values such as the right to trial by jury and due process. Individuals should be safe in their homes, the framers believed. Accused persons should have a fair trial, the ability to confront witnesses against them, and a calm weighing of evidence by a competent jury. Lynching violated those constitutional principles. As journalists, especially African American journalists, began pointing this out, an evolving tension developed between national commitment to the rule of law and the nation's prejudices and commitment to local power. Even at its most widespread, community-sanctioned racial violence could not survive a fair testing against the nation's ideals.

This brings us to the thesis of this book: opponents of lynching sought certain protection from violence from the government and made political appeals based on constitutional principle. Constitutionalism is an ideal, one that means accepting some principles as governing the whole nation, without debate. The constitutional precept that accused persons are *always* entitled to due process of law should not be subject to political debate, though it sometimes is. After the Civil War, black Americans used constitutional principles to defend themselves against white violence.

This book examines the interplay between politics and constitutionalism after the Civil War. Its aim is to focus on how African Americans used politics and constitutionalism to fight lynching. The first chapter argues that in the nineteenth century most white people believed that lynching was an appropriate and constitutional approach to crime control, when courts proved too corrupt or incompetent to handle the problem. Since many whites believed blacks too animalistic for the courts to control, they always viewed lynching as an appropriate response to alleged or real black criminality. Since the Constitution protected the right of local government to control crime without any outside scrutiny or supervision, it also protected the custom of lynching.

The second chapter argues that black leaders countered lynching with constitutional principles. The journalist T. Thomas Fortune championed the Constitution, while another journalist, John Mitchell Jr., seemingly followed a political approach. Ultimately, though, both depended on constitutional principles. Political struggle became one with enforcing constitutional ideals.

The next chapter looks at the lives of Ida B. Wells and Monroe Work, two of the most determined opponents of lynching, who battled lynching with numbers and statistics. Both struggled to break the localism that shielded lynchers from outside scrutiny. They compiled statistical information about lynching. Instead of telling local stories as Fortune and Mitchell had done, they used statistics to provide a national story.

The fourth chapter traces the rise of the NAACP and its long battle against racial violence. The NAACP lobbied Congress to pass antilynching legislation so its lawyers could fight lynchers in the courts, by enforcing not just the law but also American constitutional principles.

The fifth chapter explores how whites turned to dynamite to defend their communities against "invading" African Americans. When lynchers turned into bombers, the same impulse guided their killing as when they used ropes or guns. It matters little whether violent white racists used a rope to hang their enemies or dynamite to blow them up. Their intent was the same—ethnic intimidation.

The final chapter examines the last strategy of resistance. After 1980, new concerns with victims of crime led state and federal legislatures to pass hate crime laws. By the end of that decade, few states lacked some kind of hate crime law. Politicians discovered they could advance their political careers by promising to protect crime victims. This led them to reconfigure the meaning of racial violence from lynching to hate crime. Critics accused hate crime law proponents of acting politically, carving out special privileges for particular groups.

Careful readers of this book should note that often events are narrated with explicit references to the written texts that originally described those events. Instead of simply saying a lynching happened, I often say that a newspaper said a lynching happened. In all history writing, it is important to remember that history is not the past but rather a representation of the past based on available sources. This is especially important to keep in mind when reading about lynching because virtually everything we know about lynching comes to us through popular culture, most often journalistic reports. Only for a few decades in the twentieth century did investigators employed by the NAACP visit the scenes of lynchings to verify newspaper reporting. When they did, the NAACP almost invariably found errors in the newspaper accounts. Since so much of lynching scholarship depends on newspaper reporting, most of it not validated by the NAACP, this is a sobering reality. This book is as much about representations of lynching, people's ideas about lynching, and arguments over how to respond to lynching as it is about the lynching itself. To remind readers of this important fact, I *privilege* its sources, calling them to readers' attention.

Finally, here is a note on the scope of this book. While lynching touched every segment in American society, racial violence directed by whites against blacks defines the essence of lynching for most Americans. This book follows lynching at its most notorious, beginning after the Civil War and focusing on lynching directed at African Americans. Many groups, including whites as well as blacks, perished at the hands of lynch mobs. Most notably, Clive Webb and William Carrigan have completed path-breaking work on the lynching of Mexicans and Mexican Americans. It is at least possible that lynchers killed more Mexicans and Mexican Americans than African Americans. Stephen Leonard argues that western lynchers killed more whites, when calculated on per capita basis, than southern lynchers killed blacks.[3]

Such mathematical calculations, though, miss the point. White Southerners hanged, burned, clubbed, shot, tortured, and dynamited black Americans for more than a century. This horror story rewrote the meaning of the U.S. Constitution, and it was this terror campaign that challenged the basic meaning of what it meant to be an American. It raised questions about who protected the rights of American citizens. It forced Americans to consider whether the evil of racial violence could be best conquered by applying constitutional principles or by political negotiation. In other words, opponents of lynching challenged Americans to define the meaning of their national character.

Notes

1. Clarence Thomas, *My Grandfather's Son: A Memoir* (New York: Harper, 2007), 268, 279.

2. Thomas, *My Grandfather's Son*, 217, 257, 271.

3. William Carrigan and Clive Webb, "The Lynching of Persons of Mexican Origin or Descent in the United States, 1848 to 1928," *Journal of Social History* 37 (2003): 411–38; Stephen J. Leonard, *Lynching in Colorado, 1859–1919* (Boulder: University Press of Colorado, 2002), 7.

~

Prologue

Henry Adams

In the aftermath of the Civil War, black Americans discovered that white Southerners intended to continue slavery as best they could, chiefly through violence. Blacks resisted the continuing threat to their lives. A former slave named Henry Adams kept a record of the horrors he experienced. Adams's writings and his testimony before Congress in 1880 revealed how former slaves worked through a variety of strategies to resist, or escape, white violence in the late nineteenth century. Adams's narrative offers a unique and unusual alternative to the newspaper accounts that most often dominate our understanding of lynching.

Born a slave in Georgia in 1843, Adams came to Louisiana at the age of seven. Two years after that, Adams, the son of a preacher, discovered he could heal the sick when he cured a toothache. News of his remarkable skills spread rapidly, and Adams developed a reputation as a faith healer able to cure cases medical doctors could not. Adams explained that his patients put their faith in him and he put his faith in God. He could do nothing for nonbelievers. Soon white as well as black people brought particularly stubborn cases to him, ailments medical doctors had pronounced hopeless, and paid him handsomely, sometimes one or two hundred dollars. With the exception of his army service, he lived in and around Shreveport for the next twenty years.[1]

Adams and all other freed people received their first constitutional promise from the nation in 1865. Congress proposed the Thirteenth Amendment to the Constitution on January 31, 1865, and by December it became part of the Constitution after twenty-seven state legislatures had ratified it. The

After the Civil War, whites often killed African Americans with impunity. The scene shows white "Regulators" shooting blacks near Trenton in Gibson County, Tennessee. Sketched by W. Webb Metz. Library of Congress.

amendment ended slavery by declaring that neither slavery nor involuntary servitude, except as a punishment for crime, could exist in the United States. Many of the legislators understood that those words would end not just slavery but also all the prejudices and violence associated with slavery. The first signs that white Americans might not live up to that expansive hope came just months after the nation ratified the Thirteenth Amendment. It was in 1866 that Henry Adams found the body of a black man hanging from the limb of an oak tree about six miles south of Shreveport. On another road, Adams encountered the severed head of a black man, displayed on a stump by his white murderers. At the Red River, Adams saw ten or fifteen bodies of black men floating, some shot, some with their throats cut, and some with ropes still around their necks. Looking across plantation fields, Adams could see white men riding about with bullwhips, just as they had done before emancipation. To escape such horrors, Adams decided to join the U.S. Army.

The army provided no refuge, and Adams continued to encounter white hostility and brutalities. Adams became a quartermaster sergeant, assigned to the Twenty-fifth Infantry, stationed at Fort Jackson, Louisiana. In Fort Jackson, a white woman set up a school for the soldiers, and Adams learned to read and write in the space of one month. It was the only schooling he ever had, but it gave him the skills he needed to create a written record of his experiences. Assigned to escort prisoners, Adams rode steamboats, where whites abused him, disrespecting his uniform and refusing him access to the accommodations offered white passengers. Passing plantations, he continued to see whites whipping their black field hands, just as they had under slavery. Mates on steamboats kicked and struck black men. Black passengers paying for first-class tickets got third-class accommodations.

In July 1868, the Fourteenth Amendment became part of the Constitution. It defined citizenship: any person born or naturalized in the United States was a citizen. This meant that all African Americans, including Adams, were citizens. It also required every state to treat its citizens equally and instructed them not to deny citizens their life, their freedom, or their property without a fair court hearing. On September 25, 1869, when Adams, discharged from the army, returned to Shreveport with a group of veterans, he learned that southern whites had no intention of honoring the amendment. Shreveport whites buzzed with the news that the discharged black soldiers had landed in town, that the former soldiers could read, write, and figure, and whites feared they might expect respect for their citizenship rights. Some whites said they would just have to kill all the discharged soldiers for fear they would "spoil" all the other blacks in town. Whites worried that local blacks might ask the former soldiers to examine their contracts and accounts with white people. Adams learned that whites had good reason to fear any kind of audit of their contracts with black laborers. Using the skills he learned at Fort Jackson, Adams sat down and refigured the accounts, finding that whites regularly cheated black laborers. Adams urged the blacks to get lawyers and demand their rights. Most of the black laborers refused to get a lawyer or go to court. The few that did came back telling Adams that going to court was not a good idea. Some faced a whipping from their landlord when they came back from court. Whites singled out Adams. "My life was threatened," Adams wrote, and "the white people of the parish said no d——n negro that soldiered against his master should come in that parish." Whites thought Adams put "devilment" in the heads of his fellow blacks, and they wanted to exorcise the source of the devilment.

To escape, some blacks fled into the woods. In 1869, Billy Scrapp and John Dunlow told Adams they had been living in the woods for seven years and said they had seen more than two hundred black men hunted down and killed by crowds of whites in the woods. Adams wrote that thousands of black people told him they had been driven from their homes and crops and had lost all that they possessed.

Riding on a public road with a young black woman, Adams encountered a crowd of whites. They said the girl was too pretty for "such a damn black negro as me" and told him to leave. White men still raped black women, just as they had done under slavery, and Adams feared these white men would rape the woman if he left, so he refused to leave her. Kill me if you will, he told the whites, but he would not leave. Somehow, both Adams and his companion escaped.

For Adams, such violence raised the obvious question: could freed people live in peace with their former masters? With other African Americans, Adams organized a committee to look into this question. Some five hundred blacks joined Adams's committee, which never took a name. "We just called it a committee," he explained later. The committee sent about one hundred of its members into every southern state. "We just wanted to see whether there was any state in the South where we could get a living and enjoy our rights," Adams said. Members of the committee went from state to state, working with the people in the fields. With a few exceptions, the committee raised no money for the expenses of its investigators. Truly learning the realities of life and labor in any locality required working alongside resident blacks, members of the committee believed. The investigators paid their own way. For four years, information filtered back to committee headquarters in Shreveport. The reports were grim, confirming what Adams had already observed in Louisiana. It was bad everywhere. Whites still whipped their black laborers and worked them like slaves; landlords cheated tenants out of their crops with little or no recompense from the law.

While members of his committee fanned out across the South, Adams continued to study realities in northwest Louisiana. He saw whites bully black voters at the polls. Most blacks did not want to vote Democratic for fear the Democrats would make them slaves again. But the Democrats threatened and intimidated any black voter casting his ballot for the Republicans, sometimes cutting off essential financial support. Before elections, mobs of white men broke up black churches and terrorized blacks.

In the face of such brutality, blacks around Shreveport came to Adams. What should we do? they asked. By this time Adams had become an articulate stump speaker and a Republican stalwart. Given an opportunity to speak, he always began by saying he just split rails and he chopped wood for a living and did not know anything about politics. He was, he said, a plain man and an honest laborer who just happened to have an outsider's opinion about politics. This was a tried and true formula white writers had used for generations to give their opinions more force for coming from a down-to-earth, upright citizen. Adams warned that voting Democratic would lead to a restoration of the slavery-era pass system requiring all blacks to present a pass to any inquiring white person. "I told them as to our freedom, our rights, and our votes that no Southern [white] man was our friend." Black Southerners, Adams said, could only trust Northerners and members of the U.S. Army. White Southerners would be against blacks for as long as they lived because they never really accepted emancipation and still wanted to continue slavery, Adams said.

To whites, Adams was a particularly dangerous troublemaker. They again accused him of "spoiling" the other Negroes. Adams told them they should allow blacks to vote Republican, pointing out that no black person ever tried to tell a white person how to vote. "Let us Republicans advise Republicans, and the Democrats advise Democrats," Adams said. Whites responded that all black Republicans had to be killed. Adams had an answer for that, too: "Kill me, only give me my rights while I am living."

Adams continued to review the contracts black tenants brought him. In 1870, twenty-five blacks brought their contracts and accounts with white employers and merchants. Adams recalculated the accounts and found that whites had swindled the twenty-five farmers out of $1,790. Some of the blacks filed lawsuits, but once again it did them no good. Whites killed some of the plaintiffs and whipped others.

In 1871, a crowd of whites came to Adams's house and warned him to leave. The men intended to kill all discharged black soldiers in the area, they said. Adams would not leave. "I had made up my mind to face the battle," he said. Again, whites complained that Adams "ruin[ed] the other negroes." When whites attacked other ex-soldiers, "they got as good as they sent," Adams recalled with satisfaction. Whites had the blacks arrested for daring to shoot at them, even though they had done so to defend themselves. The black men, however, had so clearly acted in self-defense, Adams said, "they came out clear" even in Shreveport's prejudiced courts.

In 1872, Adams and a cousin pooled their money to buy a house and two lots in Shreveport for one thousand dollars with another thousand dollars worth of improvements. Whites waited until Adams was away from home and built a street through his property. Adams and his cousin went to court, yet "they would not allow either one of us to have a word to say in court, nor allow us to pick a jury, nor let a colored man serve on our case." Adams wrote later that whites said they intended to leave no black ex-soldiers living in Shreveport. There was no justice for the colored man in southern courts, Adams concluded.

A year later, though, Adams served on the grand jury for his parish, an experience that only confirmed his suspicions about local courts. Whites on the jury thought every black man accused by a white man should be charged with a crime and put on trial. "I saw little colored boys in there for stealing one can of oysters." Little girls came before the grand jury accused of stealing thimbles and scissors. Adams saw that the judge, the lawyers, the district attorney, the grand jury foreman, and the clerk of court all favored whites over blacks. "That is my opinion," Adams wrote, "however preposterous it may seem." Only one white man went on trial for killing a black man, and he was acquitted. The grand jury investigated the jail, and Adams found black prisoners shivering in misery with inadequate blankets in their drafty cells, but whites did nothing to improve those conditions.

In 1873, Louisiana whites massacred blacks in Colfax, and the next summer whites fielded a new terrorist organization in north Louisiana, the White League. Adams and other blacks responded by forming a new organization, the Colonization Council. Meeting in secret, Adams and other members of the council worked out a plan. First, they would appeal to the president, writing resolutions so they could stay in the South. They took this step in September. When that failed, they would ask Congress to protect their rights and privileges. If Congress would not protect their rights, Adams and his fellows planned to ask for a separate territory in the United States where they could live in peace with their families. Failing that, they planned to ask for an appropriation to pay for all blacks to migrate to Liberia. If that failed, the council intended to ask other governments for help in getting away from the United States.

Often the council did not dare meet, for fear of white violence. "We was scared to hold meetings then—afraid to meet—though we met on the sly sometimes." Afraid whites would kill them, they met in the woods. Even as the council petitioned the president and Congress, and talked about settling in Liberia, its members still hoped to remain in the South. "We had much rather staid there if we could have had our rights," Adams said later. In response to doubts that Adams really wanted to remain in the South in the face of such violence and depravity, Adams said again, "No sir; we had rather staid there than go anywhere else."

In 1876, the U.S. Supreme Court ruled that federal civil rights acts could not protect black citizens from white vigilantism.[2] Blacks could expect no protection except from state judges and state laws. That same year, Adams campaigned hard for the Republicans only to find stuffed ballot boxes, intimidation at the polls, changed polling places, and registration irregularities. Adams and the Republicans lost that election, and in 1877, the most violent white racists took control of Louisiana's state government. Reconstruction ended, and Adams and the other blacks in his organization lost hope, realizing they could never live in the South. In May the council met and thoroughly discussed their options. Adams decided to leave northwestern Louisiana and move to New Orleans; he never really found work there, though he did find brief periods of employment at the U.S. Mint and the Customs House. He continued to travel, going to Texas and other states, learning more about the plight of rural black people.[3] It is not certain when Adams died.

By the end of 1877, every southern state had fallen into the hands of "the very men that held us slaves." Hands that wielded the slaveowners' lash now formally held the reins of power. They no longer had to act outside the law; white racists were the law. And yet, this did not mean that whites abandoned their vigilante ways. Indeed, the age of lynching began in 1877, after whites ousted the Republicans from power in southern statehouses. Now lynchers could act openly, without masks and with no fear of prosecution. Many whites did not believe blacks could be properly controlled through law or legal process. They believed they could fully maintain their place at the top of the racial hierarchy only by acting violently outside the law.

After emancipation, Henry Adams sought institutional protection for his freedom. He joined the army. He urged others to go to court and went to court himself. When that proved ineffective, and even dangerous, he petitioned the federal authorities, the president and Congress for his rights to be protected by some institutional authority, state or federal. He campaigned for the Republicans in the hope that his political efforts would result in the election of a Republican president who would enforce the Constitution and protect the rights of freed people. A Democratic victory, he feared, would allow the Democrats to seize total control of state governments in 1877. He lost hope when he finally understood that no governmental authority would ever protect his rights against the rampaging sea of white hatred. Some blacks shared Adams's despair and left the South. For the African Americans remaining behind, the quest for institutional protection continued for decades. They developed a variety of strategies of resistance. Some spoke out boldly, demanding protection from the government. Others went to court, filing lawsuits and invoking the equal protection of the laws. And some would turn away from law and government, seeking to build protections from within, by organizing the black community.

Notes

1. U.S. Congress, Senate, Select Committee, *The Removal of the Negroes from the Southern States to the Northern States*, 46th Cong., 2d sess., 1880, part II: 101–214. Except as otherwise noted, all that follows comes from this source.

2. *U.S. v. Cruikshank*, 92 U.S. 542 (1876).

3. Nell Irvin Painter, *Exodusters: Black Migration to Kansas after Reconstruction* (New York: Knopf, 1977), 104–7.

~

CHAPTER ONE

White Constitutionalism

"The Demon's Rage"

Throughout much of American history, black Americans understood that whites felt they had a right to kill them. In 1907, the African American poet Lizelia Augusta Jenkins Moorer complained that white men "will often raise a riot" and "butcher up the Negroes" to enforce segregation. She continued,

> If a Negro shows resistance to his treatment by a tough,
> At some station he's arrested for the same, though not enough,
> He is thrashed or lynched or tortured as will please the demon's rage,
> Mobbed, of course, by "unknown parties," thus is closed the darkened page.[1]

To understand the brutal violence African Americans faced throughout American history, this chapter asks how whites could justify racial lynching. The answer is that, through the nineteenth century, white Americans believed that their right of self-governance vindicated such mobbing. The crowd in the street seemed democratic. Great thinkers, including the natural rights theorist Hugo Grotius, the political philosopher Samuel von Pufendorf, and the English writer John Locke, all justified crowd violence as a last resort against tyranny. More than that, habit and custom sanctioned the crowd, which for centuries had controlled crime in the absence of effective criminal justice. This was popular constitutionalism, the idea that the Constitution guaranteed majority rule. Ultimately, this meant the majority decided what was right and wrong and punished wrong. After the American Revolution, many Americans, white and black, believed republican institutions had displaced any need for crowd violence. Some stood heroically for principle against the tides of public tumult.

The word lynching has never been satisfactorily defined. Although most Americans today envision a lynching as a large mob hanging its victim, in fact, lynchings have not always been fatal and some have occurred secretly with perhaps only one or two involved. Any definition must include not only southern whites' lynchings of African Americans but also westerners' informal executions of cattle rustlers and other criminals as well. Nineteenth-century Americans often considered a killing, carried out or sanctioned by a community, to be both a lynching and legitimate. Lynchers often saw themselves as law enforcers, even when they acted outside the law. The Ku Klux Klan certainly saw itself that way. An early—and entirely sympathetic—history of the Klan conceded that normally what the Klan did would be unjustifiable. But given the supposed nature of "black criminality," early defenders of the Klan said, vigilante violence served a good purpose, deterring freed slaves from theft and lawlessness. Such deterrence could only be accomplished outside the law—or so the Ku Klux Klan and its defenders said, showing how little faith they had in the government to maintain order.

The word lynching originated in the American Revolution, when Virginia "patriots" hanged or whipped captured Tories—"lynching" them—rather than escort prisoners long distances to faraway courts, as the law required. Up and down the East Coast, Revolutionary-era crowds challenged English authority in the street. But crowds had captured and punished criminals outside the law long before the American Revolution. Eighteenth-century mobs in both England and America claimed legitimacy because their members believed they enjoyed widespread community support. In eighteenth-century London, crime victims expected to summon and did summon assistance from the crowds of pedestrians that thronged the streets. A call for help, a shout of "Stop thief!" led ordinary citizens, passersby, to make a quick seat-of-the-pants judgment about who was in the wrong and then render prompt street justice without waiting for constables or official authority. This practice continued in the colonies, where residents of the rural "back country" generally found courts and sheriffs too few and too distant to be of much help. Like the Klansman, these vigilantes believed themselves to be the law. By the time the first Ku Klux Klansmen donned a sheet in 1866, the Atlantic world had a long history of popular violence. Americans did not automatically judge mob violence illegitimate; in fact, they leaned the other way.

Though personally opposed to mobbing, President Andrew Jackson's emphasis on majority rule reinforced the existing idea that local majorities could punish crime outside formal law. In 1839, an anonymous writer in the *Southern Literary Messenger* recalled that he applauded the lynching of a white man guilty of abusing his wife. At this time "lynching" meant a whipping. With hardly an exception, the entire neighborhood approved, the *Messenger* writer said, continuing that some crime seemed beyond the reach of the law. When residents of Vicksburg, Mississippi, hanged five gamblers in 1835, the local newspaper defended the killings in much the same way. The community supported the violence, thus making it legitimate according to the newspaper. The hanged men had become intolerable, it seemed, because they had plotted the vilest criminality right in the heart of society. People had to excise such evil and, when the law proved ineffective, they had to act outside the formal institutions of government. After the Vicksburg hangings, other cities and towns rushed to mob their gamblers as well. The white gamblers' deaths seemed to authorize crowd violence against blacks. In 1836. a crowd of thousands burned Francis McIntosh to death in St. Louis. Afterward a state judge told an investigating grand jury it could not touch the lynchers because such a large crowd represented the people at large. The whole of the population could not be punished for breaking the law because the people *made* the law, Judge Luke Lawless explained.

Those seeking legitimacy for such violence most often found Americans receptive to two arguments: that mob action was politically justified or that it was necessary to maintain order. The classic example of the politically justified mob was the American Revolution, but for lynchers, the more plausible model came when vigilance committees seized control of San Francisco in 1851 and 1856, after criminals seemed beyond the control of city officials. The violence got so out of control, some in San Francisco claimed, that criminals dominated city elections, putting people in office friendly or indifferent to the corruption. In both those years, residents of San Francisco formed vigilance committees and seized control of their city, ousting the existing city government and policing crime with militarylike patrols. The fall of city government in a major American city to a mob, twice in the space of five years, inspired controversy and debate across the entire nation. Many Americans thought the vigilantes plausibly defended themselves by saying they acted because corrupt politicians had tolerated crime to a point beyond the ability of courts and institutions to control. The *New York Times* opened its front pages to articles written by San Francisco vigilantes justifying their actions as legitimate revolution, one they expected historians would record with approval. The vigilantes promised to change the California politics by ousting from power those who cheated by stuffing ballot boxes or intimidating voters and derided their governor for calling their "revolution" an "insurrection," a word implying a less-than-legitimate uprising or mutiny. It was a lot more than that, they insisted.

Slavery authorized all whites to police blacks as a part of its ordinary system of control. Any white person encountering a black person in a public place, on a rural road, for example, could demand to see the black person's pass, proof that he or she had permission to be off his or her owner's property. Uncooperative blacks, those that fled rather than present their pass or explain themselves, could be shot. Some African Americans expected the election of Abraham Lincoln in 1860 to end such arbitrary power outside law. Lincoln and his fellow Republicans centralized power in ways that alarmed whites who were comfortable with slavery as a system that not only produced wealth but also disciplined supposedly savage African Americans. When the Republican attack on slavery came, it seemed all the more worrisome for coming as part of a general program to permanently centralize power. In addition to ending slavery through military force, the Republicans passed an income tax, instituted a military draft, centralized banking, and financed a transcontinental railroad. Republicans seemed to present a whole new way of governing.

Reconstruction, the Republican plan to remake southern society after the Civil War, began in 1863, after General Ulysses S. Grant's mighty army swept down the Mississippi Valley, giving the North control over a significant portion of southern territory, which it had to "reconstruct." The U.S. government had to formulate policies to govern thousands of liberated African Americans and a hostile population of whites, all with no functioning police or legal system. Historians call the first phase of Reconstruction, from 1863 to 1867, "Presidential Reconstruction," a time when President Abraham Lincoln and then President Andrew Johnson created largely lenient policies toward the conquered South, allowing southern states that had once seceded from the Union and treasonously disavowed any loyalty to the Constitution back into the Union, forgiving past sins. Conservative white men governed again, as they had before the Civil War. They chose to bar blacks from voting or serving on juries and subjected them to harshly discriminatory laws that mimicked slavery. For example, African Americans had to have proof of employment, much as slaves had to produce a pass when challenged by any white person. Blacks could not testify against whites in court. Disgusted with this situation, Congress wrested control of Reconstruction from President Andrew Johnson in 1867.

To call Congressional Reconstruction "radical," as many historians do, repeats a racist label once trumpeted by white Southerners. Southern whites condemned as "radical" all Republicans, even the most moderate and conservative. Truly radical Republicans wanted to seize plantations, break them apart, distribute the land to freed people, and then protect their civil rights with federal power. In the nineteenth century, such policies never happened. Radical Republicans never constituted the majority of the Republican Party and certainly never had a Reconstruction they could fairly call their own.

While the Radical Republicans would have created a system in which federal officers readily intervened against racist lynch mobs, the more powerful moderate faction of the Republican Party expected the states to handle such violence. Whereas radicals would have aggressively used federal power against violent white racists, moderates wanted to preserve the states' powers. This does not mean that moderates expected the states to have all the powers they had possessed before the Civil War. The Republican-controlled Congress betrayed its suspicion of state courts by passing a series of laws aimed at allowing the victims of discriminating state courts to transfer their cases into federal court. In addition, moderates required the southern states to write new state constitutions in conventions elected by all adult males, regardless of race. Blacks turned out to vote in these elections, which whites often boycotted. As a result, Republicans governed the South for a time, writing state constitutions and laws that pledged to protect citizens' civil rights. It seemed a new day had dawned in the South, with formerly oppressed people enjoying at last the bountiful fruits of true citizenship.

Nonetheless, despite all these innovations, moderates still expected the states to continue policing crimes, much as they had done before the Civil War. They underestimated white Southerners' skill at circumventing the new laws and state constitutions. Radical and moderate Republicans disagreed over whether to police relations between the races with federal forces or leave the states in charge, and thus tolerate mob rule. Moderates did not favor mob rule, but they probably did not fully understand just how much white Southerners had traditionally relied on informal vigilante justice to maintain order.

Every moderate effort to protect the lives and rights of freed people stirred up stern protest that the moderates had acted unconstitutionally. The Civil Rights Act of 1866 represented a moderate effort to encourage the states to treat their citizens fairly, regardless of race, making any federal intervention unnecessary. White Southerners saw even this moderate law as a threat to their power. To white Southerners, the Republicans' Reconstruction policies challenged the Founding Fathers' vision and betrayed fundamental American principles in the Constitution. They focused on the founders' protection of local government against scrutiny or intrusion by the central government. In contrast, Congressional Republicans claimed to more truly represent the founders' vision when they encouraged black voting and overturned the white-run state governments that took root across the South under President Andrew Johnson.

As Congress passed civil rights laws, blacks organized themselves to assert their own rights. During the summer of 1867, the Union League, a political club established in the Civil War to favor Abraham Lincoln, sent organizers South, recruiting thousands of southern blacks, encouraging them to act politically, to stand up for their rights, and to take up arms. The Union League provided a forum for black voters to debate issues, read Republican newspapers, pick candidates, and organize for election campaigns. League members invoked the Declaration of Independence and the rights of labor to steel themselves with the belief that they represented America's most fundamental values. League meetings encouraged members to assert themselves, something that frightened and alarmed white people.

Whites organized as well. In 1866, the Ku Klux Klan began life secretly in an obscure Tennessee village near the Alabama border. When the Union League began its organizing effort, the Klan expanded into a national fraternal organization that terrorized its enemies. White people began calling the Klan the Invisible Empire. White Southern newspapers and ordinary citizens alike claimed to know little or nothing about Klan violence. A former Confederate army general named Nathan Bedford Forrest supposedly directed operations nationally as Klansmen learned secret grips and code words so they could recognize members from around the country. In fact, much of this vision of the Klan as a nationwide, centrally controlled empire had little connection with reality. Local vigilante gangs governed themselves, deciding what to do with no central direction whatsoever. Local Klan units planned their violence carefully, calling on the expertise of local Confederate army veterans to carry it out with military precision. In the space of just a few years after the Civil War, the Ku Klux Klan challenged and undermined the Republican-led southern governments that black votes had helped to elect.

Many white Southern Democrats saw violent white men, acting outside the law, as more legitimate than elected government officials. The Klan also counted on a general understanding among Americans that a majority of citizens had the right to take over crime control when the courts failed. After all, many Americans put majoritarian local politics ahead of national principle. That belief empowered the Klan to claim that it represented the majority of white citizens. In a sense, the Klan challenged not just the Republican Party but also the idea of government itself. Of course, white racists wanted to control the government themselves one day, but that did not mean that most Klansmen ever expected government to fully discipline black people in the way they wanted.

Unlike the Union League, the Klan waged a campaign of terrorism and violence, which white newspapers did not fully report, giving the impression that lynching occurred only decades later, at the end of the century. Through the 1860s and 1870s, American newspapers regularly reported lynchings but found them just as likely in the West and North as in the South. From 1867 through 1869, the *New York Times* reported only fifty-five lynchings, roughly half in the South (The *Times* considered Missouri a southern state) and the rest spread across the other states. Supposedly, lynchers only killed eight blacks during this time. Obviously, this low number documents the paper's unwillingness to count the lynchings the Ku Klux Klan carried out. "A gang of desperadoes" in and around Lawrenceburg, Kentucky, further rendered statistics meaningless by shooting and killing uncounted numbers of African Americans for reasons neither the *Times* nor newspapers in Kentucky explained. The *Times* did not describe the "desperadoes" as Ku Klux Klansmen, and, in fact, no newspapers called Klansmen "desperadoes." If we took the absurdly low number of eight seriously, then we would also have to note that every black person killed for an identifiable crime, all eight, stood accused of rape. So, rape explained lynching for 100 percent of blacks lynched in incidents the *New York Times* reported from 1867 through 1869, according to that newspaper. Obviously, this was not true, and yet most historical studies of lynching rely on exactly this kind of newspaper evidence that so inadequately explained the 1867 to 1869 time period.

Even if newspapers had accurately reported every mob killing in the first years after the Civil War, they would not have fully documented how thoroughly the punishment of crime outside law had become part of American culture. Americans used the word lynching to describe actual killings, but there were near lynchings, anticipated lynchings, and rumors of lynchings. The word developed a frightening power of its own. The word alone, without any actual violence, could intimidate and frighten. The newspapers did not often identify the race of the person lynched, so, presumably, these lynched persons were white. For ordinary Americans, lynching always seemed a plausible response to serious crime, a legitimate option on the shelf when confronted with outrageous misconduct. Every serious or sensational crime enraged public passions, leading at least to tremendous pressure for a lynching if not an actual lynching. Villages and communities engaged in clamorous public debates over whether to lynch or not. In 1869, many in Greenville, Illinois, wanted to lynch John W. More after he allegedly murdered a woman, but others did not, and, after a public debate, the would-be lynchers lost the argument. In New Jersey, an enraged public threatened to lynch a wandering man charged with the murder of three boys, but opposition formed, preventing the violence. In Virginia, some people threatened to lynch a man accused of assaulting his stepchild, but others stepped in and stopped the move toward mob law. Even in Pulaski, Tennessee, where the Ku Klux Klan first organized, opinion divided. Citizens rallied for law and order, passing resolutions in a mass meeting designed to condemn lynching violence. The lives of prisoners charged with the most serious crimes depended on the skill with which opponents of lynching could dissuade mobs intent on death.

Through the 1870s, newspapers continued to report lynchings, never suggesting that white Southerners lynched any more often than their counterparts in other parts of the country or that blacks might be victimized more than whites. However, newspaper writers often excused the violence by emphasizing strong neighborhood support for particular lynchings. This, however, proved a flimsy excuse. The papers themselves often disagreed over whether the public supported particular killings. In 1871, California lynchers killed a man identified as Malaysian who was accused of rape, and most citizens approved, according to the *New York Times*. The *San Francisco Chronicle*, much closer to the actual incident, doubted the approval was so widespread. Most papers reinforced assertions that widespread popular support within a neighborhood excused lynching. In 1874, a Kentucky mob shot and killed Robert Beckett, not identified by race, accused of murder. In newspaper parlance, they "riddled his body with bullets." His crime had filled the community with great indignation, according to the local press.[2] However, when Virginians lynched a horse thief, also not identified by race, the press reported that the entire community condemned the lynching. Newspapers sometimes frankly announced approval for lynch mobs, allegedly composed of all the people enraged by slow-performing courts. Talk of such mass movements inevitably meant the mass within a small locality. Reporting on crime in Kansas, the *New York Times* really trumpeted vigilantism when it felt obliged to question, "Why did not the citizens rise *en masse* and thrust out the evil doers?" The answer was not that the "good" citizens hesitated to act outside the law but rather that there were too many evildoers in the neighborhood and too few good citizens.[3] After a California mob lynched a particularly heartless murderer, the people unanimously approved, the *Times* reported, meaning unanimous within one small locality. The *San Francisco Chronicle* praised another lynch mob for acting quietly and decisively in the case of Matthew Tarpey, who had murdered a woman in Monterey. In fact, the *Chronicle* could hardly find enough superlatives to cover the horror.

Tarpey's crime was the worst ever seen in the county. The funeral procession for Tarpey's victim was the biggest in the county's history. Excitement in the neighborhood ran higher and higher, the crowd increasing from a hundred to hundreds. Finally, no one on the scene could deny the force of public outrage, overpowering the helpless sheriff. The lynching may have violated the law, the *Chronicle* conceded, but very few—perhaps no one—would criticize it. A large crowd earned legitimacy through the sheer force of its numbers.

Sometimes journalists actively collaborated with the lynchers, or wanted their readers to think they had done so. In 1874, a *St. Louis Republican* correspondent complained that U.S. officers in Arkansas had done such a bad job controlling crime that the citizens might have no choice but to take the law into their own hands and form a vigilance committee. A couple of weeks later, the writer confessed that he had known that the citizens had already organized a "Committee of Safety" but had chosen not to reveal all he knew. When the writer did report on the committee, he openly propagandized on behalf of the vigilantes, saying that, since the government protected the thieves, the people had to protect themselves. He reassured his readers that the lynchers would never make a mistake. The innocent need not fear the judgment of the mob, and the guilty had no hope of escape.

In the late nineteenth century, Southerners also justified lynchings as the legitimate will of the people. Arkansas whites accused a black man of murdering and raping a white child. A biracial crowd of two hundred attacked the sheriff, seized the accused "fiend," and hanged him from a tree. The local newspaper reported that the people all regretted having to kill the man but said they had acted justly. The *Edgefield Advertiser*, a South Carolina paper, tried to connect the Ku Klux Klan's violence with legitimate but extralegal crime control practiced by westerners. The Klan exists, the *Advertiser* admitted in 1871, but it is a vigilance committee, and in nearly every case, had organized only because the law seemed unable to properly punish the guilty.

In 1871, Congress passed a law often called the Ku Klux Klan Act, which authorized the president to use military force against insurrections that deprived any class or portions of people their constitutional rights when state governments refused to act. Six months later, President Ulysses S. Grant declared nine South Carolina counties to be in a state of insurrection and used the army to arrest members of the Ku Klux Klan. Grant's forceful action broke the back of the first Ku Klux Klan. For the moment at least, Grant had destroyed its effectiveness.

The Klan, though, ultimately survived Grant's crackdown because it could plausibly—in the minds of whites—present itself as manifesting fundamental

American values of neighborhood self-governance. Nineteenth-century Americans recognized crowd violence as legitimate when it controlled crime in the absence of effective crime control by the authorities, and the Klan claimed it had to suppress crime because Republican governments would not do so. It was a racially charged argument because the Klan claimed the Republicans did not properly appreciate what all whites thought they knew to be true: African Americans could not control their appetites for rape and plunder. Klansmen claimed black arsonists destroyed barns and other structures and black rapists attacked white women. Whites told each other that the courts would not administer justice to blacks arrested for arson and rape. The Klan hanged arsonists and rapists because the courts would not, or so the Klansmen claimed. In public, Klansmen said they had nothing against black voting but had to organize in self-defense and to protect those weak and helpless in the face of savage black barbarisms. Something *had* to be done, whites insisted to each other. Generations of historians accepted this apology for Klan violence so thoroughly that only with the beginnings of the 1960s civil rights movement did younger scholars begin to question the old view. It is hard now to understand how any scholar could ever have considered seriously the Klan's justification of itself. Even the most casual scrutiny of crime in the South reveals that violence and crime ran rampant across the South well before the Republicans took control. The conservative white Southerners who controlled the South immediately after the end of the war had also proved singularly inept at handling crime.

That lynching went beyond race measures the great difficulty opponents of the violence would face. Through most of the nineteenth century, lynchers very often said they fought crime and did not target any particular group out of prejudice. Such statements, which seemed plausible in areas where courts seemed absent or hopelessly delinquent, firmly rooted mob violence in the right ordinary people had to create and control their own government and to define and punish crime. Communities could say that their survival depended on the willingness of citizens to step forward and act outside the law. White newspapers reported that African Americans themselves lynched, sometimes joining whites in biracial lynch mobs and sometimes forming all-black mobs.

Anyone opposed to lynching ran the risk of seeming to side with criminals. For decades before the Civil War, when crowds lynched, the lynchers usually claimed that they acted with universal public support in response to some particularly heinous crime committed in the absence of effective law enforcement. In fact, grisly crimes so aroused public passion that the government could not stop it with all the force it might muster, those sympathetic to lynching said. The Ku Klux Klan took full advantage of this argument, already well established in the press, racializing it and politicizing it. Blacks committed the crime that ordinary citizens needed to control, Klansmen said, when the Republican-controlled courts could not effectively control their criminality. President Grant only temporarily put the Klan out of business. The Klan's idea of extralegal violence as legitimate lived on. At the end of the nineteenth century, African Americans faced a tidal wave of racial violence that many white people—in the North as well as in the South—considered absolutely legitimate.

Notes

1. Lizelia Augusta Jenkins Moorer, "Jim Crow Cars," in *Witnessing Lynching: American Writers Respond*, ed. Anne P. Rice (New Brunswick, N.J.: Rutgers University Press, 2002), 118.

2. "A Murderer Lynched and his Body Burned," *Chicago Tribune*, June 12, 1874; "Mob Law in Kentucky," *Chicago Inter Ocean*, June 14, 1874.

3. "Lynch Law," *New York Times*, March 10, 1872.

CHAPTER TWO

⌒

Black Constitutionalism

T. Thomas Fortune and John Mitchell Jr.

The first black voices to publicly oppose whites' racial violence spoke on the pages of newspapers published by and for African Americans. This chapter looks at the antilynching strategies pursued by two of the most important black journalists working at the end of the nineteenth century, T. Thomas Fortune and John Mitchell Jr. These two writers seemed to have worked out rival arguments for countering white oppression, one Constitution based and one political, but any modern reader will naturally ask how much these two approaches really differed from each other, if Fortune really managed to rise above politics or if Mitchell really avoided rights-based constitutional rhetoric in his own writing.

African Americans had published newspapers for decades before either Fortune or Mitchell started writing. In 1827, two African Americans named Samuel Cornish and John Brown Russwurm began publishing *Freedom's Journal*, dedicated to moral and religious uplift and American democratic ideals. Cornish and Russwurm sought to elevate the race to make themselves worthy of white respect and equal protection under the law. Twenty years later, in 1847, Frederick Douglass, who had escaped slavery in Maryland, started his own paper, the *North Star*, which he also dedicated to self-help. Recognizing white racism as the greatest single obstacle to the abolition of slavery, Douglass expected his newspaper to combat whites' low assessment of blacks' mental and moral capabilities. To attack such assumptions, Douglass called on blacks to prove themselves through their own reservoirs of mental energy. Within a decade, black papers had appeared across the nation.

This early generation of black journalists drew their arguments against white violence from the ideology of the Republican Party, ideas with roots in the Whig Party's opposition to Democratic president Andrew Jackson. In 1838, when Abraham Lincoln spoke in favor of perpetuating political institutions in the face of mob law, he advanced a rhetorical strategy to oppose Jacksonian appeals to popular self-government. Jackson had ingeniously positioned the Democratic Party as the champion of majority rule, the powerfully attractive idea that ultimate power must rest in the hands of ordinary people. Jackson's political opponents, including Lincoln and other Whigs, found it hard to oppose such democratic notions. Lincoln's great contribution lay in his brilliant idea that the Whigs should champion law, the Constitution, and the political institutions created by the Constitution against public tumult and misguided passion. Lincoln's ideas carried forward into the Republican Party, and when Lincoln confronted southern secession and rebellion in 1861, he fell back on his familiar formula. Rather than taking a moral stance against slavery, he argued that the federal government had to uphold law and order, the Constitution, and the existing political institutions that southern secession threatened. The Republicans added Lincoln's idea that public institutions were the bulwark against public disorder, against public passions and tumults, to their rhetorical arsenal. During the Civil War, many Republicans found that they could no longer argue for a strict construction of the Constitution. Instead of abandoning the Constitution, they simply embraced Alexander Hamilton's idea that the Constitution implied great powers for existing institutions. One author even argued that the president's war powers, "hitherto unused," represented a great reservoir of national power that could be used against treason. The Constitution *implied* the president had great power in wartime.

In their darker moments, some Republicans took a gloomier view, fearing that the Constitution fatally limited the government's power to defend itself against rebellion. Important Republican newspapers, like the *Chicago Tribune*, argued against allowing the Constitution to render the national authority powerless against slavery and oppression. The Radical Republican congressman Thaddeus Stevens complained that only the rebels and their supporters invoked the Constitution. Senator Lot M. Morrill of Maine declared he would not construe the Constitution in order to obstruct efforts to defend its creator, the Union. Another Republican, Congressman James M. Ashley of Ohio, said that the law of war superseded the Constitution. Supreme Court Justice James M. Wayne privately declared the Constitution a failure in 1864.

But wartime Republicans also insisted that the Constitution's broad principles warranted their fight for freedom. Senator Charles Sumner of Massachusetts aggressively fought to expand Congress's power to protect citizens' rights, pioneering new powers that disrupted old ideas about the Constitution. He wrote in 1861 that he would yield to no one in honoring the Constitution, adding that he accepted it as a guide. While Republicans like Sumner believed the Republicans in control of Congress did not have to follow the exact text of the Constitution while expanding federal power to protect civil rights, they also knew that they could more easily expand their power to protect rights if they based their actions on the Constitution's most fundamental principles. This position became the intellectual heart of black journalists' campaign against lynching.

A founder of the Republican Party, Sumner served as a U.S. Senator from Massachusetts for twenty years, ardently fighting against slavery and, after slavery ended, for equal rights. Sumner drew inspiration from the American Revolution. In his greatest speech, delivered in 1852 against the Fugitive Slave Law, Sumner declared slavery merely sectional and freedom national. And it was the Constitution that nationalized freedom. The Constitution should be understood as carrying out the Declaration of Independence with its guarantees of equality and liberty, Sumner said. Every word of the Constitution, he urged, should be interpreted as promoting liberty. Sumner argued that the nation had committed itself to sacred principles that admitted no political challenge or debate. When Sumner deployed those national principles in his speeches, he presented himself as a constitutionalist. He argued that the fall of slavery allowed the nation's equal rights principles to triumph.

When black journalist Philip Bell established the *San Francisco Elevator* in 1865, he demanded equal treatment under the law, adding that he wanted nothing more and would settle for nothing less. Like Sumner, Bell argued that national constitutional principles protected black citizens at a time when the nation embraced racism and slavery. While the Supreme Court and other courts insisted that the Constitution endorsed slavery, Bell, like other black journalists, argued that slavery and prejudice violated the nation's "true" ideals and urged enforcement of foundational principles, including justice, due process, and equal rights. He campaigned against legal as well as extralegal disabilities. California had a law forbidding black testimony in court. Since blacks could not testify, Bell pointed out, African Americans could be robbed, beaten, and even murdered with no legal recourse, unless a white person happened to witness the crime.

Bell hoped constitutional principles would make the end of slavery permanent, but he feared that whites might try to reenslave black people. To prevent such a catastrophe, he wanted to make freedom an irreversible principle. Citizenship cannot be annulled, Bell said, except for crime. He also found protections for freedom in the Fifth Amendment's double jeopardy clause, "No person shall be subject for the same offence to be twice put in jeopardy of life and limb." White slaveowners had regularly put black people in jeopardy of life and limb for the "offence" of being black. The Fifth Amendment also said that "no person shall be deprived of life, liberty, or property without due process of law." Slavery, Bell correctly pointed out, deprived black people of their lives, their liberty, and their property outside the law. He also observed that Americans under slavery had pretended to believe that all accused persons are innocent until proven guilty. Yet, whites assumed every black person to be a slave until that "accused person" could prove otherwise. For Bell, slavery contradicted the Constitution time and time again and asked if these great American principles would be acknowledged in the future. He wanted to know if the American people had truly embraced the sprit of freedom generated in the Civil War. The alternative, he warned, was anarchy.

Senator Charles Sumner lived long enough to see black journalists like Bell begin their own fight for the ideas he championed. Sadly, Sumner also lived long enough to see his own hopes for nationally guaranteed citizenship rights imperiled. He saw race riots and massacres in Memphis, New Orleans, Colfax, Louisiana, and other places. In 1874, Sumner neared death. His commitment to equal rights, already legendary, reached mythological status among civil rights advocates when the news spread that the old man had pleaded with his friends not to give up the fight for civil rights even as he lay on his deathbed. At least for a moment, champions of civil rights could take heart that the senator had not died in vain. Congress did pass Sumner's civil rights law in 1875.

Thereafter, the situation rapidly declined. After Sumner's death, racial violence accelerated. In one swift-moving decade after Sumner's death, the equal rights ideal he had championed vanished into the fires of sectional reconciliation, segregation, and racism. In December 1874, whites in Vicksburg, Mississippi, ousted the black sheriff, and African Americans converged on the courthouse, hoping to restore their man to office. Armed whites waited. In the resulting massacre, whites killed nearly one hundred fleeing blacks, shooting most in the back. Such sensational events grabbed headlines, but in some ways the day-to-day violence against individuals proved even more invidious. Newspapers regularly reported with satisfaction the lynching of "negro desperadoes," "mulatto villains," or "brutal scoundrels." Even blacks not remotely guilty of any crime faced violence. African Americans sitting in the white sections of theaters could expect a storm of indignation, cries of "put him out!" and drawn pistols. Theater owners ushered such interlopers out of their buildings to avoid riots. White newspapers justified the violence. In 1878, after reporting the murder of a merchant, a crime not remotely sexual, the *Memphis Daily Appeal* nonetheless said that white men feared that black savagery threatened their wives and daughters. In 1879, the *Baltimore American and Commercial Advertiser* quoted a citizen as predicting that the coroner's jury would not identify members of a lynch mob, and if they did, no grand jury would indict; if somehow one did, no trial jury would convict. When an 1880 South Carolina lynching prompted a white person to condemn the state as bloodthirsty, the *Charleston News and Courier* responded that any black criminal deserved lynching because blacks put themselves outside the law when they committed crimes. The *News and Courier* compared southern lynchings to those long common to the West and insisted that the same forces were at work, which was a public determined to punish crime in the absence of competent courts.

In November 1879, racial trouble erupted in Danville, Virginia, when a white man and black man jostled each other on a crowded sidewalk. Enraged whites turned their guns on the blacks indiscriminately. Initial reports put the number of dead at seven, but the true figure probably doubled that number. The *New York Times* explained that blacks were overeager for their rights, walking around with chips on their shoulders, while whites felt powerless and outnumbered, wholly at the mercy of brutal black savages. Far from offering a sensible explanation for the violence, the willingness of the *New York Times* to excuse white brutality shows the depths to which white lawlessness had taken the country. Many despaired and with good reason. African Americans in 1884 could not know it, but they faced nearly one hundred years of unchecked racial violence.

In January 1884, a group of black and white Civil War veterans and political leaders assembled in Hartford, Connecticut, to honor Charles Sumner, dead for just ten years. They did not know it when they sat down for dinner, but they were about to hear one of two models for black resistance to lynching. Their speaker, twenty-seven-year-old newspaper editor T. Thomas Fortune, had crafted a strategy of resistance that championed law and constitutionalism.

Born a slave in Florida in 1856, Fortune encountered the savagery of white racism at an early age. His parents had fled Reconstruction violence. Fortune went to Delaware, where he briefly worked as a customs inspector.

T. Thomas Fortune. D. W. Culp, Twentieth Century Negro Literature of A Cyclopedia of Thought on the Vital Topics Relating to the American Negro *(Naperville, Ill.: J.J. Nichols & Co., 1902), 227.*

He then went to Howard University, an all-black school in Washington, D.C., before returning to Florida. In 1881, Fortune left Florida and the South forever, finding life there just too degrading for a person of color. He went to New York and founded the *New York Globe*, which later became the *New York Freeman* and then the *New York Age*. When he made his Hartford speech, Fortune had been a newspaper editor for only three years but had already established a reputation as an eloquent speaker. Fortune's speech, and the gathering in Hartford, came a year after the Supreme Court had struck down the civil rights law that Sumner had pleaded for as he lay dying. For most black Americans, though, the heavy, smothering blanket of lawless violence settling across their lives suffocated their rights more than any Supreme Court decision. White violence took race relations out of the courts and legislative halls, as whites intended.

Fortune began his speech by reminding his audience that when Sumner had entered politics the slave power cast its shadow over Americans' claim to stand for liberty and freedom. In that dark moment, Fortune continued, the Supreme Court enforced prejudice as it still did in 1884. Fortune compared Sumner to Moses, leading people to freedom on the Constitution's solid foundation. After praising Sumner's accomplishments, reminders of what had been done, Fortune turned to the "great work" ahead. Continuing Sumner's quest would be no easy task, and here he painted a grim picture. Using violent intimidation, whites squelched black voting in defiance of the Constitution's Fifteenth Amendment. Courts closed their doors to blacks, Fortune said, and suspended the usual processes of law. Mob violence posed the greatest evil, one local courts would not or could not control. He condemned the white South for imposing a reign of terror on blacks but found the situation in the North only a bit less ominous. In the same states where soldiers once volunteered to fight the forces defending slavery, Fortune said, black citizens lurked about the doors of theaters, schools, and restaurants, afraid to enter for fear whites would deny them their constitutional rights to equal treatment. He charged that America drifted backward, toward the old states' rights arguments Sumner had fought against. The Supreme Court had curbed and limited the great Civil War amendments, declaring unconstitutional acts of Congress designed to protect black people. The states denied African Americans protection from lawlessness, and the national government denied that it had jurisdiction.

Fortune insisted on action. "I affirm it to-night," he orated, "as Charles Sumner did a hundred times upon the floor of the Senate, that the citizen of the United States is greater than the citizen of the State."[1] The Civil War, he said, had permanently changed the balance of power between the states and the federal government, making federal law paramount over state law. To validate his stance, Fortune appealed to the Fourteenth Amendment to the U.S. Constitution, which he quoted verbatim for his audience: "No state shall make or enforce any law which shall abridge the privileges or immunities of citizens of the United States."

Fortune wanted no special favors for his race and had a good reason for stressing this point. In 1883, the Supreme Court had struck down the civil rights statute Sumner had supported in the *Civil Rights Cases*, alleging that Congress had been extending special and undeserved favors to blacks by passing civil rights legislation. Fortune denied this charge but did not play the role of humble supplicant. "We ask simply for justice, we demand justice, pure and simple, and though it has been delayed a quarter of a century, *justice we will have!*"[2] As Fortune's speech built toward its climax, his audience waited to see where he would go with his appeals.

Fortune urged black ministers to use their pulpits to thunder against oppression, black newspapers to defend African Americans, and every individual to demand civil rights. "Let us agitate! *Agitate!* AGITATE!"[3] He saw potential power of a black revolution as a wakening force, ready to explode. In earlier speeches, he had begun to compare white Southerners to the French aristocracy standing at the edge of revolution, oblivious to the coming storm. The Constitution offered hope for the oppressed, but whites ignored it at their peril. Fortune warned that they could not trample on blacks' constitutionally protected rights without a violent backlash on a scale matching the French Revolution. He stoked the emotional reserves of his audience, appealing to "the grand sentiment evolved out of the fires of the French Revolution: 'Liberty! Fraternity! Equality!'"[4]

No transcript of any oral presentation can truly capture the speaker's body language, emotional timber, his facial expressions, or his tone and volume. Nonetheless, the dry text of Fortune's speech, with its italics and capitalizations, suggests a powerful orator making an emotional appeal. Another clue about Fortune's style comes from his white critics. In 1892, the *New York Times* published an unflattering portrait of his speaking style, saying he spoke intemperately and waved his arms wildly. According to his own newspaper, Fortune spoke in a steady but forceful voice. Reading his powerful words convinced the aspiring journalist and antilynching crusader Ida B. Wells of his manliness, an assessment she abandoned when she saw his picture with long hair and spectacles.

Though Fortune did not invent the constitutional argument against lynching, he articulated it with a crackling passion. While his warning of a race war if whites insisted on their extralegal violence recalled Bell's predic-

tion of anarchy, Fortune nonetheless carried his predictions to a new oratori-
cal level. More than Bell, Fortune made a name for himself as a lecturer and
orator, following the example of Frederick Douglass. More importantly, by
the time he entered journalism, printing technology had become extraordinarily efficient, wood pulp made paper cheap, and the post office subsidized
the mailing of newspapers. Those factors made it possible for Fortune's generation of journalists to aspire to a national audience.

Fortune knew both W. E. B. Du Bois and Booker T. Washington, the two
great icons of black thought at the end of the nineteenth century, usually
portrayed as polar opposites, irreconcilably opposed to each other. Du Bois
developed a reputation for combative in-your-face resistance as opposed to
Washington's more conciliatory approach. So it is surprising that Fortune
and Washington collaborated. Unlike Washington, Fortune was a protestor,
a brawler, and a hard drinker who did not believe in appeasing whites. He
was more likely to take them to court if they would not serve him in their
restaurants or cut his hair in their barbershops. Nonetheless, Fortune closely
allied himself with Washington, even ghostwriting some of Washington's articles. Washington became famous for favoring black self-improvement, although some critics have charged that he wanted to make blacks worthy of
equal rights rather than demanding those rights.

But Fortune did agree with Washington that African Americans should
better themselves. To satisfy whites, he was willing to say that, after emancipation, blacks were unprepared for the responsibilities of freedom. But he
chided whites for their criticisms of blacks' alleged backwardness. When the
New York Sun condemned blacks as savages, Fortune rose to the defense of
his people. It took whites centuries to emerge from barbarism to civilization,
he pointed out, yet white people thought that blacks had to be inferior because they had not fully shaken off the effects of slavery in just eighteen
years. Conceding that blacks had a long way to go, Fortune echoed Booker
T. Washington.

Many blacks agreed with Washington, and Fortune attracted little criticism when he advocated self-improvement for his race. But he also dared
criticize the Republican Party, something few African Americans found attractive, since they associated the party of Lincoln with the abolition of slavery and the Democrats with white Southerners, slavery, and the wrong side
of the Civil War. When they thought of the Republicans, Abraham Lincoln
came to mind, along with emancipation and all the civil rights legislation
Congress passed in the 1860s and 1870s, laws the Democrats bitterly opposed. Fortune agreed that the Democrats had done nothing to earn the
votes of black people; he just doubted white Republicans were much better.

Fortune revealed his politics most clearly when he took on the venerable Frederick Douglass, a virtual icon of the freedom struggle. Born a slave in Maryland, Douglass had escaped to freedom and made himself an abolitionist leader by indicting the slave system with powerful autobiographies. Through his lectures and writing, Douglass inspired thousands. In 1883, Fortune nonetheless wrote that Douglass was a hopelessly partisan Republican, incapable of change. Fortune pronounced himself "strictly non-partisan" and announced that he had never had any faith in the Democratic Party and had lost confidence in the Republicans after the "treachery" of 1876 and 1877.⁵ He meant the disputed 1876 presidential election when, according to the traditional story, the Republicans and Democrats compromised, allowing Republican Rutherford Hayes to become president in exchange for abandoning Reconstruction. By this account, Hayes's "retreat" from Reconstruction allowed white lynchers a free hand to kill and intimidate blacks with no federal policing.

No doubt the standard story is exaggerated. The Republicans had already begun to abandon their black allies in the South before November 1876, and Hayes believed federal forces actually stirred up racial antagonisms, but from Fortune's perspective, white Republicans had sold out their black friends twice: first, by not standing up to the Democrats' violent tactics aimed at suppressing the black vote and, second, by retreating from Reconstruction, stopping their enforcement of the civil rights laws Sumner had labored so long to enact. Fortune respected the Democrats no more than white Republicans. He believed white politicians all put race before their ideals, no matter which party they claimed. White Republicans, he alleged, preferred a white Democrat over a black Republican every time. He would not leave black rights— including the right not to be lynched—to political campaigning.

With no confidence in political appeals, Fortune had to look elsewhere for a source for rights. He found the answer in natural law. Blacks, he wrote, may not have all the formal attainments of education, but they were nonetheless the children of God. This natural law argument suggested that all humans have a natural right to life. On another occasion, he declared that lynching, in fact, outraged the commands of God. The Declaration of Independence, a foundational document in American civic life, also made a natural rights argument, and Fortune argued that governments exist to protect life, liberty, and the pursuit of happiness. He observed that at no time since the Civil War had blacks enjoyed such immunities.

Fortune criticized the Constitution, echoing the Radical Republicans' arguments of the 1860s. He believed his nation had not accorded blacks their rights because the American system yielded too much power to the states.

The U.S. Constitution divided powers between the central or national government and the states in a way that gave the states free rein to govern most of their citizens most of the time. In nineteenth-century America, the federal government had very little authority, in great contrast to what would happen throughout the twentieth century, when national power expanded exponentially. By giving so much power to the states, Fortune complained, the Constitution left the U.S. government helpless and put citizens at the mercy of local government. He understood that this decentralized system emerged from the colonies' experience with Great Britain. After fighting the American Revolution, the new nation understandably wanted to keep power localized. As Fortune observed, the resulting federal system curbed the tyranny of a central government but left no check on the tyranny of individual states. Fortune asked his audience to consider whether such a system best protected the rights of individual citizens, producing the most liberty possible. He doubted it did and said that experience with such a system proved it did not.

Fortune, thus, had serious doubts about the basic structure of the American constitutional system. American federalism meant that local courts sometimes permitted or even authorized assassination by signaling to the assassins they need never fear prosecution. State laws offered blacks no protection. In the states, the machinery of government gave mobs immunity. All too often, he charged, local law enforcement officers had joined the mobs. Even when they did not actually ride with the Ku Klux Klan or march with the lynch mob themselves, they would not arrest racist killers. A white man charged with killing a black man could count on his grand jury refusing to indict him, the local district attorney refusing to prosecute him, or the jury refusing to convict him. The machinery of justice, Fortune said, endorsed mob violence.

But he also thought the Constitution could protect blacks from violence. Believing passionately in the great principles of the Constitution that promised the rule of law, Fortune had no doubt that when white Southerners turned to violence and mobbing, they defied the Constitution of the United States. When claiming rights, he cited the Fourteenth and Fifteenth Amendments and accused white Southerners of defying the majesty of the law. He acknowledged that the Supreme Court had ruled in favor of states' rights but thought the Court lacked either wisdom or fairness when it effectively sanctioned mob violence.

Fortune had his critics. The black-owned *Troy (New York) Daily Times* doubted he really wanted more law. Blacks already had plenty of law, the *Daily Times* concluded, but whites had perverted it to serve their own ends.

Blacks did not need more law; they needed justice. Fortune acknowledged that whites deliberately framed their laws to oppress black people but argued that when whites used the forms of law to victimize blacks, denying them impartial justice, it was not true law. He did not think that the biased law whites practiced, laws that sanctioned lynching and mob violence, deserved to be called law. This was not an argument over mere words. For Fortune, justice lay in law and due process, not politics. People seeking justice outside law filled the ranks of the KKK and swelled lynch mobs.

Fortune preferred law over politics or violence, but he warned whites that black people did not have infinite patience. Whites had chosen violence over law themselves. Whites denied black people the right to vote and attacked them when they tried to form political organizations. Whites needed to know, he said, that blacks had little choice but to respond with their own violence. He warned again and again that whites sat atop a volcanic force ready to erupt at any moment. Lynchers, he warned, should not count on servile submission indefinitely. Fortune exhorted blacks to fight back. Whites could only be convinced with their own weapons, brute force. There is more honor in dying like a freeman than in living like a slave, he said. If black men have to turn themselves into outlaws to assert their manhood, then let them do it. Blacks must meet white violence with violence. Nonetheless, he opposed killing innocent bystanders, as anarchists were doing in the 1880s using dynamite, and maintained his faith in the Constitution.

In addition, Fortune never shrank from reporting white racial violence. In 1886, a particularly sensational lynching occurred in Carrollton, Mississippi. Fifty white men rode into Carrollton, entered the courthouse, and gunned down thirteen black men inside. The black victims had not aroused the white community into a fever pitch of outrage by committing some horrid crime. Later reports revealed that the trouble had started with the attempted assassination of a white man named James Liddell. Some white writers tried to make it sound as if the thirteen victims had all been involved in a plot against Liddell, but it soon became apparent that only one of the thirteen had even been accused of the crime. The other twelve men were just spectators, attending the trial. White newspapers described the killings as "a tragedy" and, for once, found it difficult to excuse the bloodshed. But after the initial shock passed, some whites began to pardon even this act of violence. The *Memphis Avalanche* admitted that innocents had been killed but charged that blacks had been incited to riot by "vicious" men, their own leaders. Ultimately, the *Avalanche* recruited the not-yet-famous Mississippi demagogue James K. Vardaman to excuse the massacre. Carrollton blacks, Vardaman explained, had become so impudent that whites really had no choice but to shock blacks with a sharp and swift response—a decisive if bloody solution to blacks' refusal to submit to whites' claims of superiority. This was too much for even many whites. Other white papers continued condemning the killers, admitting they acted without provocation.

The Carrollton massacre story appeared in Fortune's newspaper in an article headlined "Mississippi Cutthroats."[6] He had no trouble seeing the affair for what it was and thought it remarkable that so many white papers saw it the same way. Even white people, it seemed, put some limits on what they could tolerate. Whites needed at least the patina of crime control to justify obviously racial killing. Fortune continued the story in later issues, criticizing the governor of Mississippi for not enforcing the law and calling on President Grover Cleveland to intervene. He also quoted the *Vicksburg Herald*, which took the usual white position that blacks had "exasperated" whites so much that they had to act. "What right," Fortune impatiently demanded, "had the whites to get exasperated?"[7] Fortune refused to drop the story, printing later articles from other newspapers as well as letters from correspondents.

Fortune's stalwart persistence in holding whites to constitutional standards provided a clear argument in favor of law that influenced most leading black journalists at the end of the nineteenth century. He was one of the first black men W. E. B. Du Bois respected outside his own family; the Memphis schoolteacher Ida B. Wells, already learning to be a writer, read Fortune's papers and considered him a mentor. Another aspiring black intellectual to get his start in Fortune's paper, John Mitchell Jr. became a columnist for Fortune's *New York Globe* at age twenty. Like Fortune, Mitchell aspired to a national audience. Also like Fortune, Mitchell urged the national government to act against lynchers. Lynching, he wrote, was a national problem, therefore the national government should solve it. Like Fortune, Mitchell urged blacks to resist white lynch mobs with violence.

Despite his beginnings as a columnist for Fortune's *Globe*, Mitchell soon developed a different strategy than Fortune. Whereas Fortune invoked lofty constitutional principle, Mitchell took a more obviously political approach by adopting a heroic persona, becoming a manly figure who defied white racists by boldly striding into dangerous situations. John Mitchell Jr. was born in the waning days of slavery, in 1863. Unlike Fortune, he did not leave the South, staying in his native Virginia. Mitchell attended Richmond Normal School, where he learned French, Latin, history, and science. His classical education did not get him into a college, but he was nonetheless better educated than most Virginians, white or black. Not long after he began working for Fortune's *Globe*, Mitchell observed that a group of black Richmonders

John Mitchell Jr. Library of Virginia.

had started a weekly newspaper. It promised to be lively, Mitchell reported, and would be called the *Richmond Planet*.

A year after the *Planet* commenced publication, its first editor, Edwin Archer Randolph, departed, leaving behind a printer's bill and a list of delinquent subscribers. This setback did not kill the *Planet* because the newspaper represented not Randolph alone but also Richmond's black community. Black Richmonders had organized it and recruited the first editor. Now they met again, and Mitchell, who attended the meeting, emerged as the new editor. Mitchell reflected the will of his patrons by enthusiastically supporting the Republican Party, earning himself a gentle rebuke from Fortune, his former editor. Like Fortune, he immediately plunged into the war against lynching. His stern denunciations of mob violence earned him recognition in the white *New York World*. Even Fortune, himself accused of lapsing into theatrics, thought young Mitchell sometimes overly emotional.

During the *Planet's* early years, Mitchell lived in an attic, personally hefting heavy stacks of newspapers to the post office at a time when he received no salary. His determination and self-sacrifice paid off. After a while, the stockholders lost interest, convinced the struggling editor would fail, and withdrew from the project. The stockholders should have been more patient. By 1890, Mitchell had made enough money to buy his own electric press and employed five young men in his job department and a foreman to run his press. Two years later, he needed more space and had the money to buy newer and better equipment. Fortune visited Mitchell in 1891 and expressed surprise that a black editor could make so much money by printing stationery, church programs, invitations, pamphlets, small books, and all sorts of printed matter for black organizations. It is also possible that Mitchell's loyalty to the Republican Party paid off. Mitchell's paper was so strongly Republican that it seems likely he received a stipend from the party, as did other loyal editors.

Like Fortune, Mitchell aspired to a national audience. He followed Fortune's model, recruiting columnists from around the country. In 1891, the famous white novelist and attorney Albion Tourgée praised him for "nationalizing" himself, pronounced himself a regular reader, and called the *Planet* the best-known black newspaper in England. In 1888, Mitchell could boast that New Hampshire's senator had inserted the *Planet's* list of lynchings into that year's *Congressional Record*.

Mitchell joined Fortune to urge that blacks defend themselves in the absence of help from white-controlled courts. The way to stop lynching, he said, was to put Winchester rifles in the hands of nervy black men. In 1886, though, Mitchell took his fight against lynching in a different direction. In

Mitchell's success allowed him to attack lynching with modern printing presses. Press room of the Planet *newspaper, Richmond, Virginia. Courtesy of the Library of Congress.*

May, a white mob had lynched Richard Walker near Drake's Branch in Charlotte County, Virginia. The white press quickly hurried their single-paragraph stories onto the back pages, but Mitchell wrote a blistering editorial. Within a week, he received a threatening letter, ordering him not to show his face in the county. Such a challenge could not be passed over. Mitchell printed the letter, armed himself with revolvers, and took the train into Charlotte County, where he walked five miles from the train station to the lynching site. Making himself as visible as he could, he toured the jail where Walker had been abducted and walked through the neighborhood where the mob had assembled. Nothing happened. Of course, Mitchell's "manly" journey into the heart of darkness was a gendered performance, typical newspaper grandstanding in some ways. He acted out what Fortune could only recommend from afar and thus began his reputation as a truly fighting editor based on ideas of masculinity whites usually kept for themselves.

Mitchell also sought political influence, establishing relationships with white officials at the highest levels of state government. He negotiated with governors, forging a particularly helpful connection with Governor Charles T. O'Ferrall (1894–1898). The governor needed no convincing that lynch law poisoned his state. A Confederate veteran and determined conservative, he nonetheless had no taste for mob violence. Like other southern governors, he tried to suppress lynchings by dispatching troops and exhorting against anarchy. No lynchings occurred in Virginia during O'Ferrall's first two years as governor, and Mitchell hailed the end of lynch law in the commonwealth. Mob law had ended in Virginia, thanks to O'Ferrall, Mitchell crowed. He used the columns of his paper to heap praise on the governor and arranged to have the *Planet* delivered to the governor's mansion. O'Ferrall confided later that he read the papers Mitchell sent him. Mitchell and the governor had dinner together in the governor's mansion, a social meeting that violated a strongly held racial taboo and subjected O'Ferrall to criticism from his white constituents, who resented any white man, especially their governor, breaking the color barrier.

In 1895, Mitchell and O'Ferrall collaborated to save three black women falsely convicted of murder. The murder occurred some seventy miles from Richmond, in rural, isolated Lunenburg County, a place with no professional police force. Neighbors found a white woman, Lucy Jane Pollard, dead in her yard, her skull horribly mangled with an axe. Some thought the killer had to be a woman. The victim's husband said the killer had stolen some of his wife's clothing, and anyone examining the body could see that the killer had flailed away with the axe at least a dozen times. A man, the amateur investigators believed, would have killed with a single stroke. So, Lunenburg County authorities started randomly rounding up black women living in the neighborhood for the crime. They also arrested a black man named Solomon Marable after he spent twenty dollar bills that looked like they might have come from the murdered woman's house. Marable told a variety of stories but implicated Mary Abernathy, Mary Barnes, and Pokey Barnes. Countless lynchings have proceeded on far less evidence than the townsfolk had marshaled against Marable and the three women. Angry crowds gathered. All four escaped lynching only because O'Ferrall dispatched two companies of Virginia infantry to guard the courthouse and jail. Nonetheless, in four trials, juries with both black and white members found all four prisoners guilty. The four went to Richmond for safekeeping until they could be legally hanged.

In Richmond, Mitchell found out about the trials and verdicts and went to the jail, where he interviewed the convicted defendants. As he sat listening to the prisoners' stories, he decided that the women sounded credible and became convinced of their innocence. The fight to save the lives of Mary Abernathy, Mary Barnes, and Pokey Barnes began. After interviewing the prisoners, the *Richmond Planet* headlined "Women Innocent," and Mitchell assembled a team of lawyers for an appeal. He mobilized law against lynching, working to persuade some whites to put the rule of law ahead of their racism. The women would have been hanged, either by one of several mobs that gathered during their trials or legally by the state after sham trials, had Mitchell not saved the day with his connections to O'Ferrall. This affair also set local autonomy against an increasingly assertive state government led by Governor O'Ferrall. Other Richmond newspapers sided with the state over local justice, began questioning the verdict in their columns, and printed stories critical of Lunenburg County's idea of justice. Mitchell published halftone photographs of all the prisoners, using a technology more advanced than any white newspaper in Richmond.

Amid this onslaught of publicity and legal talent, Virginia's Supreme Court of Appeals granted new trials. At first it seemed the courts made little progress toward a fair verdict. The second round of trials convicted Marable and Mary Abernathy again. But after the prosecution made its case against Pokey Barnes, one of the government's lawyers stood up to say that he found the evidence unconvincing and asked that the prosecution be voided. A circuit judge threw out Mary Abernathy's conviction for the same reason, the evidence was just not persuasive. A few days before Abernathy's third trial was to begin, the prosecution dropped her case and she, too, went free. O'Ferrall pardoned Mary Barnes, the last of the Lunenburg prisoners to gain freedom.

O'Ferrall's dedication to the same kind of abstract principles of law Fortune promoted on the pages of his newspaper led him to use troops to forestall the lynching of Mary Abernathy, Mary Barnes, and Pokey Barnes. Credit for winning the three women's freedom, though, must largely go to Mitchell. Mitchell trekked to the Richmond jail, interviewed the women, and then organized a campaign that raised funds, generated newspaper coverage, and hired the lawyers that would win the women's freedom. Had he not done so, Mary Abernathy and Pokey Barnes might well have anonymously perished on a Lunenburg County gallows.

Mitchell's friendly connections with gubernatorial power ended when O'Ferrall left office, as did his hopes that the rule of Judge Lynch had been broken in Virginia. James Hoge Tyler succeeded O'Ferrall as governor. While Mitchell heaped praise on O'Ferrall, he sharply criticized Tyler. In March 1900, a mob in Emporia, Virginia, threatened two prisoners, a white man named Brandt O'Grady and a black man named Walter Cotton, both charged with murder. Local authorities realized they could not protect O'Grady or Cotton from the mob. Under Virginia law, the governor could not dispatch troops without the request of the sheriff. Both Judge Samuel Goodwyn and the sheriff united in making the request to prevent further mob violence. One company of Virginia state troops, sixty men, arrived in

Emporia at 4:15 p.m., March 23. When the soldiers surrounded the jail every-thing seemed quiet, but soon a crowd assembled, threatening and menacing. Mitchell observed that whites seemed incensed that the militia had arrived.

At 10:00 p.m., the commander of the state troops attended a meeting at Goodwyn's home. According to Major Sol. Cutchins, influential citizens and the sheriff were also in attendance. Cutchins had already warned that he would have his men shoot to kill if the crowd tried to rush the jail. He asked for reinforcements, and another company prepared to depart for Emporia. As those troops packed their gear, the town's leading men convinced Goodwyn and the sheriff to ask the troops to leave, promising that the citizens would assist the sheriff in guarding the jail. One might imagine that a meeting ne-gotiating such a life-or-death decision as to whether the troops should guard the jail or depart would be lengthy, but in fact this seems to have been a re-markably brief meeting. By 10:40 p.m., not only had the judge and the sher-iff agreed to ask the soldiers to leave, but they also had prepared written in-structions formally asking Cutchins to leave. Governor Tyler approved the troops' departure. Mitchell printed the telegraphic correspondence between Cutchins and the governor. Cutchins understood exactly what the soldiers' departure would mean. The first message from Cutchins went out at 7:30 a.m., March 24, the day of the lynching: "Hold company at Armory. Every-thing quiet this morning. We will soon be discharged, without protection, the prisoner will be lynched tonight. Shall I obey order and leave?" Although Cutchins told his governor that "the prisoner will be lynched," Tyler telegraphed back: "The sole responsibility is on the Sheriff. If he orders you to withdraw you can do nothing but obey. We have done everything possible to uphold law and prevent mob violence."[8] Not implausibly, Mitchell com-pared Tyler to Pontius Pilate, washing his hands of Christ's blood. With no access to the governor, Mitchell had no political connections he could call on for help. Perhaps for that reason, he now turned to the U.S. Constitution, particularly the Sixth Amendment, guaranteeing that, in all criminal prose-cutions, the accused shall enjoy the right to a speedy and public trial with an impartial jury. However, in 1900, the Sixth Amendment applied only to fed-eral prisoners and federal trials. Mitchell was on firmer ground when he quoted the Virginia state constitution, Art. I, sec. 10, which guaranteed all state prisoners due process rights. Mitchell also said that the governor, the sheriff, and the judge had all violated their oaths of office, swearing to en-force the law. Mitchell charged that, by agreeing to the troops' withdrawal, Tyler had made himself a party to murder.[9]

According to Mitchell, the mob that hanged Cotton included blacks as well as whites. Lynching had become so widespread, so much a part of the culture, that even blacks, usually the victims of lynching, sometimes joined the mobs. After Cotton had been hanged, black men insisted whites had to be lynched as well. They pointed out that blacks had been lynched and blacks had joined the mob; now, they said, you must give us the white man. A leading white citizen tried to talk the black lynchers out of it but finally acquiesced. You should not do it, this citizen supposedly said, but if you must, then take him. The black mob then rushed the jail, taking O'Grady out into the "court-green." Mitchell described the scene: "A white man climbed the tree to adjust the rope over the limb for the colored men and then, with a mighty whop, they caught the other end of the rope, and O'Grady was dragged in the air."[10] On April 2, Judge Goodwyn asked a grand jury to indict the black and white lynchers of Cotton and O'Grady. Mitchell approved Goodwyn's charge to the jury as thoroughly competent but characterized Goodwyn himself as oddly pitiable. Goodwyn, after asking for the troops, saying he needed them to prevent a lynching, then reversed himself, Mitchell explained, unable to resist public pressure and frightened that his own home might be dynamited. When that pressure abated, Goodwyn tried to compose himself, recover his dignity, and make some show at doing his duty. Mitchell reported that Goodwyn felt so humiliated that he believed he would have to resign his position.

The nail in the coffin of Mitchell's hopes that he might derail white lynchers with his political connections came in 1900. That year whites opened a conference in Montgomery to discuss what they called the "race problem." This was strictly a white man's conference, and Mitchell wrote little of it in his columns. If he followed its proceedings in detail, he learned that some of those in attendance condemned lynching. But he could not have missed the meeting's racism, the determination of those present to exclude blacks from politics. Hillary Herbert, a former Secretary of the Navy, captured the sense of the majority present when he expressed satisfaction that public opinion, he meant white opinion, had progressed to the point where the public generally understood that the experiment of allowing black voting had failed. Other speakers promoted segregation and demanded the repeal of the Fifteenth Amendment. A white statistician from the Census Bureau reassured the white audience that African Americans would soon be extinct.

Mitchell published an article about the conference that had originally appeared in the *Richmond Times*, a white paper. The *Times* complained that most Northerners knew nothing about southern whites except what they heard from agitators for civil rights. It wanted everyone to know that none of the whites attending the Montgomery conference advocated lynching.

This was progress. Whites had begun to understand, the *Times* intimated, that while lynching might seem necessary in one place, even unavoidable, nothing could prevent copycats from spreading the violence generally, leading to anarchy and a general disregard for law. Mitchell published the *Times* story without comment, but it is easy to see why he wanted to share the article with his black readers. The *Times* thought that the country had turned a corner, against lynching. Mitchell had been overly optimistic about the impact of Governor O'Ferrall, and he had just opened the columns of his paper to lengthy accounts of the Cotton and O'Grady lynchings. Tyler clearly frustrated him, but he still hoped that the lynching of a white man by blacks represented an opportunity to convince even the most ardent racist that mobbing had gotten out of control and had to be repudiated.

In this, Mitchell was soon disappointed. Many more lynchings followed, although the *Richmond Planet* did not report them with lengthy articles and excerpts from official documents, as it had the Cotton and O'Grady lynchings. The regular drumbeat of racial violence that followed the Montgomery race conference appeared in the *Planet* as brief articles under modest headlines. Mitchell seemed worn down and disillusioned. In February 1901, Mitchell's frustrations reached a new level. In an editorial headlined "Horrible! Horrible!! Horrible!!!"[11] he reported that a white mob in Louisiana had killed not only an aged black man, guilty of no crime, but also his five-year-old daughter, wounded another daughter, and then "criminally assaulted" another young girl. Victorian newspapers did not like to say the word "rape"; they preferred language like "criminally assaulted." Mitchell complained that the community where this outrage had occurred showed no indignation. No bloodhounds had been unleashed to track down the criminals; no one would be burned at the stake. Instead, whites just dismissed the matter. Mitchell wanted to know why the American people did not realize the full extent of the injustice his people suffered. He asked why African Americans could not see that united action was necessary. Mitchell's response also documented that he had not entirely cooled his rhetoric. He again called on every black person to arm themselves. Blacks should put their prayer book and their Bible in their pockets, he said, and pick up a gun to defend their womanhood. He recognized that some would see his language as inflammatory but asserted that no other alternative course of action existed. Every black funeral, Mitchell insisted, should be accompanied by a white funeral. And then he repeated what he always said, African Americans should be polite and respectful but should never back away from their rights. He instructed African Americans to smile when going about normal business, but when confronting a mob, take out as many as possible.

Both Fortune and Mitchell intended their appeals for militancy to send a message to whites: stay within the law or you will spark a violent reaction. And both editors *campaigned* for black militancy. Fortune and Mitchell cajoled their readers to fight back, hoping to change the structure of power through their appeals. Mitchell hoped to inspire his readers with examples of heroic blacks resisting white racism. In April 1902, an Alabama sheriff tried to arrest a black man named Will Reynolds for obtaining goods under false pretenses. Rather than be arrested, Reynolds shot the sheriff and his deputy. Every white man in town armed himself and rushed to the scene. A squad riddled the house with their rifles but missed Reynolds. Whites then tried to blast Reynolds out with dynamite, failing in that as well. Eventually, the whites killed Reynolds, but by then he had slain seven of his attackers. Mitchell praised Reynolds, publishing his admiration in large headlines that applauded his accurate aim.

The white press condemned Mitchell's editorial. Black people, men, women, and children, he responded, have been tortured and brutalized, sometimes while on their knees begging for mercy. They should die fighting rather than trapped and killed while whites blubbered that they could not protect their prisoners. Mitchell insisted he believed in law but then added that he also believed in manhood. Whites had earned a place in history through their bravery and courage in the face of overwhelming odds. All men, white and black, must admire Reynolds's courage in facing off his attackers. Just to be sure no one misunderstood his insistence on law, Mitchell made sure his column of editorial admonitions that day took on a decidedly legalistic tone:

> Lawless colored people, must be sent to the rear with the lawless white people.
> We should be careful to retain the respect and good will of the better class of white people.
> Colored men who assault white women should be legally hanged, and the colored people should have no sympathy for them in their undoing. This rule should also apply to white men who assault colored women.[12]

On August 2, 1902, after a mob in Leesburg hunted down Charles Craven with dogs and killed him, Mitchell observed that mobs seemed to be gaining the upper hand in Virginia, becoming more common, not less. At the end of August, he repeated his tactic of walking into the heart of violent white racism. Hearing reports that a white man had raped a black woman in Henrico County, Mitchell made his way to the scene of the crime, to highlight the contradictions in the white mind between blacks accused of rape and whites. Mitchell made a flamboyant gesture with his march into Henrico County, and he covered the front page of his newspaper with the story, but his effort failed to impress local whites. A month after he strode into Henrico County, a jury acquitted the white rapist, and a subdued Mitchell wrote that the times seemed gloomy. There is one law for whites and another for blacks, he grimly observed. In October, he thought the white violence against blacks increasing rather than decreasing. A few days later he despaired that his nation had entered one of the bloodiest periods in its history. Respect for law waned, he said.

Other black journalists added their voices to that of Fortune and Mitchell. Edward E. Cooper, of the *Indianapolis Freeman*, also called for national law enforcement, denied that black people had any tendency toward criminality, and heralded blacks that violently resisted racist lynch mobs. Charles H. J. Taylor became editor of the *Kansas City American Citizen* in 1890, making it one of the largest black newspapers in the West. More than Fortune, Taylor sided with the Democratic Party rather than the Republicans. But his politics did not sway him from angrily and repeatedly denouncing lynching. He sometimes took a natural law or religious approach, asking how churchgoing people could tolerate such awful violence.

Both Fortune and Mitchell suffered terribly in their final years. Fortune got the worst of it; real demons plagued his final decades as he battled alcoholism. In 1907, he incorporated his *New York Age* for the first time, with Booker T. Washington as a principal but secret stockholder. The same year he gave Washington a stranglehold on his finances, Fortune confessed in a letter that he had begun to see the work for freedom as so hopeless that it might be best to just end it. In 1907, he wrote that the hopes of his youth had perished, destroyed by the racial realities he had to live with every day of his life.

Mitchell's biographer attributed his success to his uncanny ability to balance his own ambitions, both entrepreneurial and racial, against the realities white America imposed on him. Mitchell was a genius at advancing his race while carefully identifying and recognizing the limits whites put on his life. The death of Booker T. Washington in 1915 ended an era for both Fortune and Mitchell. In the case of Mitchell, Washington's passing apparently changed his life. Washington and Mitchell had engaged the benevolent paternalism of white elites while gingerly and carefully asserting their rights when they could do so safely. In the racial world after Washington's death, whites became less generous and Mitchell less willing to avoid offending white sensibilities. After World War I, he seemed to have lost interest in checking his own ambitions against white racism. In 1919, he offended Richmond whites by buying a luxurious white theater and converting it to black use. Things took an even more serious turn two years after that, when he ran for governor and imprudently, and publicly, praised the founder of the Universal Negro Improvement Association, Marcus Garvey, a black Jamaican separatist who frightened and alarmed many whites. Ironically, the most violently racist whites basically agreed with Garvey's campaign against cooperation across racial lines. Garvey, organizer of various business enterprises, had the kind of aggressive independence Mitchell respected as manly but probably would have resisted in the Booker T. Washington era. Now he enraged whites by endorsing the separatist.

Both Fortune and Mitchell were extraordinarily talented black men, living in a time when whites insisted blacks could not be talented. Black ambition had to be checked. In such a world, there would be casualties. Perhaps because he lost his knack for pursuing his own projects without exciting white anger, Mitchell's fortunes spiraled downward. In 1923, Virginia authorities convicted him for embezzlement after money had disappeared from a Richmond bank Mitchell had organized and directed. He got this conviction overturned on appeal, but financial problems dogged him for the rest of his life. Fortune also faced financial stringencies, often pleading with people he knew for loans. His friends worried that he might be losing his mind, and in fact, he did begin to suffer religious delusions. He himself began to fear that he had begun a descent into insanity. Fortune and Mitchell died within a year of each other, in 1928 and 1929.

Two great talents thus perished, crushed by the wheels of oppression they could not escape. The two followed different trajectories. In his relationship with O'Ferrall, Mitchell had put more faith in the political process than Fortune ever did. But it would be a mistake to see the two as polar opposites. Ultimately, both relied on the great legal and constitutional principles associated with the essence of the American nation. Both understood, better than most, the racial world it fell to their lot to inhabit, but the two journalists had staked what they valued most, their dreams and ambitions, on the hope that even a racist culture could be bound by fundamental rules.

Notes

1. "Charles Sumner," *New York Globe*, January 19, 1884.
2. "Charles Sumner."
3. "Charles Sumner."
4. "Charles Sumner."

5. T. Thomas Fortune, "Complaints of the Republican Colored Voters," *New York Times*, August 14, 1883.

6. "Mississippi Cutthroats," *New York Freeman*, March 27, 1886.

7. "The President and Mississippi Cutthroats," *New York Freeman*, April 3, 1886.

8. "The Story of a Lynching," *Richmond Planet*, March 31, 1900.

9. "Trouble in Greensville," *Richmond Planet*, March 31, 1900.

10. "Trouble in Greensville," *Richmond Planet*, March 31, 1900.

11. "Horrible! Horrible! Horrible!," *Richmond Planet*, February 9, 1901.

12. *Richmond Planet*, April 26, 1902.

CHAPTER THREE

The Power of Numbers

Sociology and Lynching, Ida B. Wells and Monroe Work

At the end of the eighteenth century, Americans had agreed that a constitution should be an agreement among the people to protect the liberty of communities and individuals from the potential tyranny of national power. Local citizens should make the important decisions about collecting and spending the people's money to build a new bridge or courthouse, or so most Americans believed. According to this logic, the neighborhood should have the power to punish crime as well. This idea that a constitution should protect neighborhoods from outside interference persisted through the nineteenth century. In 1879, after some federal judges had allowed blacks to serve on juries, one white newspaper protested that such "absolutism" threatened constitutional "principles dearest of all to the heart of the American citizen": state autonomy, community independence, and home rule.[1] Such commitment to local justice over national principles lingered into the twentieth century, but not without challenge. The rise of a national press led to the wider distribution of ideas and knowledge, raising doubts about the merits of local authority. This did not happen all at once; the technology available in nineteenth-century America did not easily conquer distance. Newspaper printing became more efficient through the nineteenth century, but at the end of the century, few journalists questioned whether rural people lived according to shared American ideals. Newspapers shared information with one another and big-city newspapers had little reason to send their own correspondents into remote areas. Urban editors trusted the small-town reporters to get the facts of sensational murders and hangings right and to make the right moral judgments. This meant that news about how American communities punished crime came from the communities themselves.

Sociologists were some of the first to raise questions about this system of collecting information and moral judgment. At the end of the nineteenth century, as sociology became a recognized field of study, it became fashionable to collect numbers, statistics, and objective evidence from the entire country. Sociologists organized their first university classes and departments to study statistics and objective facts. They gathered their statistics from neighborhoods, but some dared imagine they could compile information from the entire nation to present facts that would represent the whole country, not just isolated villages and hamlets. Expertly collected numbers from across the nation challenged the kind of insider knowledge once the sole preserve of villages and neighborhoods. The statistical assault on isolated communities might seem the logical outcome of better transportation and communication and bigger printing presses, but leading sociologists saw other forces at work. Some traced this new way of gathering information to the bloodied soil of the Civil War and the growth of vast bureaucracies to organize mighty armies and administer the veterans of those armies after the war ended. That war taught some that they no longer lived in a primitive, simple society but rather in a complex network of human association they could scarcely understand and that required expert explanation.

Some people thought the war not only dislodged Americans from the sanctity of their isolated neighborhoods but also destroyed idealistic notions about the greatness of American nationalism. After the Civil War, it seemed to some people more difficult to trust in the power of constitutionalism or law to reform government or improve citizens' lives. Society had become too complicated for that; it was no longer a collection of discrete neighborhoods but rather a gigantic social network, daunting in its complexity. To make America into something that resembled its ideals would require political work based on scientific research. This, at least, is what Albion Woodbury Small, the founding father of American sociology, wrote about its origins.

Small, who established the first sociology department at the University of Chicago in 1892, believed that most of the problems sociology had to solve emerged out of the greater human connectedness the Industrial Revolution produced. Just as people relied on each other more than in previous generations, they also had become increasingly perplexed by their fellows. The Industrial Revolution created poverty, slums, unemployment, and alarming social unrest, complex national problems that challenged the entire nation. At the moment when people most needed good sociological data drawn from across the country, they still had information-gathering tools designed for neighborhoods and small towns. Small saw this as a great opportunity for sociologists; they could develop new tools for gathering statistics and also design the reform strategies based on the new data. Small called for a direct, systematic, and far-reaching remedy. He wanted nothing less than to remodel the American social structure, including race relations.

This does not mean every sociologist eagerly enlisted in Small's cause. Sociologists compiled a mixed record of fighting racism, with some actually excusing and even championing prejudice. Social Darwinist William Graham Sumner believed that subordinate population groups had earned their low status as a result of personal shortcomings. Robert Park took a paternalistic approach toward blacks, whom he considered artistic and effeminate. Edward A. Ross urged whites to the barricades of civilization to avoid being overwhelmed by proliferating blacks. But some sociologists took up Small's challenge. W. E. B. Du Bois defended the moral values of an urban black community and used sociology to challenge stereotypes of African Americans.

While Du Bois did not formally investigate mob violence, some opponents of lynching found that sociology provided an opportunity to challenge local power with national data. Two African Americans, Ida B. Wells, a journalist with no formal education in sociology, and Monroe Work, a trained academic, both believed that publishing information could help change public opinion and take away local power to protect lynchers. Wells's objective, but nonacademic, approach was as much sociology as the efforts of Monroe Work, who had a PhD from the University of Chicago, the center of American sociology. Both publicized information about lynching, taking it from the clutches of the neighborhoods that sponsored lynchings. Wells and Work both wanted to redistribute power in America, moving the authority to judge the legitimacy of violent acts to a national audience. To accomplish this they needed to emphasize the elements of the Constitution that guarded citizens' rights and de-emphasize interpretations that protected local government.

Building a national database required fact-based sociology along more modern scientific lines. Perhaps the most important step leading toward building a national database occurred on January 1, 1875. On that day, the *Chicago Tribune* announced that changes in business required a new and more scientific writing style based on facts, numbers, and tables. The paper wanted to further Chicago's image, to show the city's economic growth. Thus, its 1875 review of commercial statistics counted the bushels of wheat, rye, barley, and corn; the barrels of flour; and the numbers of sheep, cattle, and hogs passing through Chicago. By 1883, the *Tribune* no longer only promoted Chicago; it now boosted itself as a champion of social science, compiling and listing "the more important crimes, casualties, suicides, lynchings, and judicial executions for the year."[2] It assured its readers that it still found Chicago trade healthy and growing, but the newspaper had also decided to tally the unpleasant features of the dead year as well as the good economic news and to do so for the whole country, not just Chicago. It turned to lynching in part because it seemed one more thing that could be counted, along with bushels of wheat, shipwrecks, and suicides. But the *Tribune* may also have had a political motive for including lynchings, a more controversial and politically charged topic than storms and shipwrecks, which the paper also tracked. It was a Republican paper, and its editors saw their scientific data as a tool for civil rights reform.

The *Tribune* had promoted the Union war effort through the Civil War and championed Reconstruction when the war ended. It denounced white Southerners' violence and had long urged Congress to pass civil rights legislation, including the voting rights law. While the paper produced statistics of lynching for a year or two without comment, it made sense that in 1883 it would headline one of its lynching reports "How the Colored Man Has Suffered." White Southern newspapers protested that the *Tribune* had "gone completely daft" with its reports of depraved white people abusing and torturing "honest, patriotic, and intelligent colored gentlemen." So what if southern white Democrats had regained political control of the South? the *Galveston Daily News* asked. "Has not the South as much right to be in the saddle as the North?"; the paper claimed southern elections just as free as in the North. Southerners accused Northern newspapers like the *Tribune* of misusing census data to prove that Southern whites prevented black voting. The presence of many blacks in the South, and the small number voting Republican, proved intimidation and violence, the Northerners said. White Southerners countered that many black Southerners freely voted Democratic and that whites used no violence against African Americans. "The most intelligent negroes in the South vote Democratic or independents in politics, while the great body of the negroes vote as their employers and friends suggest and advise," the *Daily News* explained. The *Tribune's* mistake, the *Daily News* said, was in assuming that blacks voted Republican. The *Tribune's* lynching statistics brought new information to the debate, exploding white Southerners' picture of peaceful elections with blacks happily voting for their oppressors.[3]

Ida B. Wells was one of the reformers who used the *Tribune's* data to improve society. Little in her background explains how she could take on such a daunting task. Wells began life in 1862 as a slave in the little Mississippi village of Holly Springs, where slaves made up one-third of the population. Wells's parents had talents whites valued and had enjoyed that degree of independence common to slaves who had advanced skills. Wells's father, Jim, was a carpenter, the son of his master and a slave woman named Peggy. Jim's owner and father never put his son on the auction block. As a result, he never knew the worst horrors of slavery. Her mother did. Whites had sold and resold Wells's mother, Elizabeth Warrenton, so many times that she had lost track of her original family. Nonetheless, her cooking abilities won her privileges not available to most slaves.

The independence that Wells's parents enjoyed as slaves encouraged them to assert themselves after emancipation, and they provided their daughter with powerful role models. During Reconstruction, Wells's father claimed his political rights that he believed the federal government guaranteed. He refused to vote Democratic even when pressed to do so by his white employer. Jim Wells remained true to the Republican Party until a yellow fever epidemic cut him and his wife down in 1878.

News of her parents' deaths reached Wells while on a visit to her grandmother. She wanted to rush to the side of her six sisters and brothers, now orphans, but friends urged her not to set foot in disease-ridden Holly Springs. No passenger trains ran because train operators feared going into a town ravaged by yellow fever. Wells, though, demonstrated the determination and stalwart courage for which she later became famous. Only fourteen years old, she took a freight train into Holly Springs and helped nurse her family. After the epidemic abated, Wells insisted on keeping her siblings together, finding work as a schoolteacher to support them.[4]

Like most African Americans in the years after the Civil War, Wells embraced the notion of national citizenship rights. Wells condemned the racial segregation local authorities enforced as a sin and aimed harsh criticism at those African Americans refusing to resist. Wells saw national statistics as a tool she could use against the communities that sponsored and excused lynching. Collecting information about lynching on a national level implied the solution should be national, based on principles shared by the entire nation. Using national statistics against lynching would reinforce T. Thomas Fortune and John Mitchell Jr.'s effort to nationalize the conversation about mob violence. But while Fortune and Mitchell remained committed to the idea that the courts could enforce higher principles, Wells lost her faith that law and principle could win over white people. In the winter of 1886–1887, Wells won two lawsuits against a railroad corporation she had charged with discrimination. At first, her court victory confirmed her belief in the power of law working on behalf of the nation's best ideals. But the railroad company appealed to the state supreme court. Wells's lawyer used soaring rhetoric to insist that law must stand above racist appeals. He denounced racial prejudice, which he

Ida B. Wells. Source: Courtesy of the Special Research Center, University of Chicago Library.

characterized as "waves of passion [that] break against the doors of the temple of justice." Race prejudice enforced by law, he raged, was "a startling proposition" that he urged the court to repudiate.[5] The Tennessee Supreme Court nonetheless found against Wells. The judges, all former Confederates except one too young to have served, sniffed that they could find no rule that allowed passengers to pick their own seats on a railroad car. The railroad companies had a right to assign seats to their passengers as they pleased. Through its ruling against Wells, the Tennessee Supreme Court showed itself willing to favor local racial custom over constitutional principle.

The court's decision challenged Wells's faith in legal process. Passion had overwhelmed the temples of justice. She had put her faith in the law, and it had failed her. Wells wrote that she would like to gather her race around her and fly away. The law had promised fairness, but Confederates had manipulated it to create a racist society dominated by the color line. Losing confidence in truly neutral law, Wells hardened herself anew to life in a hopelessly segregated society where power came from politics, not the Constitution. Seven days after learning of her defeat in court, Wells attended a meeting of the Negro Mutual Protective Association. Organizers urged African Americans to find strength in their own people. Racial unity offered the only protection. The energy of the speakers impressed Wells, and she came away from the meeting excited and enthusiastic about the possibilities of a mass movement.

The Tennessee Supreme Court had thwarted Wells's effort to impose national standards on Tennessee railroads, but the case ultimately allowed her to build a career that would take her far from Memphis. Wells published an account of her lawsuit in a magazine and purchased a third interest in the Memphis *Free Speech and Headlight*. The railroads gave free passes to journalists, and Wells traveled up and down the Mississippi valley, selling subscriptions. She was determined to make a living from her new occupation, and her travels paid off. Subscriptions to the *Free Speech* increased all along the spur of the Illinois Central Railroad in the Mississippi River delta. A woman working as a newspaper correspondent and an editor was, Wells wrote later, something of an innovation, but she had found her calling.

Wells became a writer in the 1880s, the same decade when academic sociology began to marshal its forces to become a powerful presence. In 1885, Indiana University offered the first sociology course in the country, followed by the University of Kansas in 1889 and Colby College and Bryn Mawr in 1890. In 1892, the same year Small arrived in Chicago and established a sociology department, Memphis whites lynched three black grocers, friends of Wells. Before the lynching, Wells said later, she had accepted the idea that, although lynching violated law and order, the crime of rape so outraged men that they could not control their anger at the rapist. She accepted Victorian stereotypes of gender that allowed male sexuality its brutish side. Whereas women lacked passion, men struggled to keep their animal passions under control and did so only imperfectly. Wells echoed widely held beliefs when she wrote that perhaps male rapists deserved their fate for having an animal-like mentality that put them beyond the reach of civilized reason. The murders of Wells's friends shook such conventional thinking at its core and changed Wells's identity from journalist to crusader against lynching. Those three grocers had committed no crime against white women; rather, they had been economically successful. One even owned his own home. Their deaths challenged Victorian conventions that accorded respect for virtuous and useful middle-class people. Rather than a response to male brutishness, their murders seemed a calculated conspiracy to eliminate economically successful African Americans. Race rather than gender had motivated the lynchers. The murders also occurred just as some Americans changed their thinking about how to study and reform American society.

In the wake of the lynching, black residents of Memphis were shocked, and many fled to Oklahoma and Kansas. Wells supported this exodus to the West. Those who stayed behind reacted to the lynching by boycotting the streetcars. The superintendent and treasurer of the City Railway Company came to Wells's office in hope she would call on blacks to patronize the streetcars once again. One of the white men protested that his streetcar company had nothing whatsoever to do with the lynchings. Wells coolly responded that she knew full well that every white person in Memphis anticipated the lynchings in advance, consented to the killings, and that her race blamed them all, holding every white person in town responsible for what happened.

Many whites did excuse such violence. Lynching's defenders did what they could to make mobbing seem modern. Wells and the historian Hubert Howe Bancroft both studied human association. Unlike Wells and Work, Bancroft did not believe broad, universal values should trump localized associations of people, neighborhoods, and communities. Modern communities, Bancroft wrote in 1887, practiced vigilance based on Enlightenment ideals of self-governance. Bancroft defined law as the will and voice of the community. According to Bancroft, a "public tribunal" (recognizing that the term had fallen into disrepute, Bancroft avoided the word "lynching") really represented the idea that a small group of neighbors can best set the bounds of moral conduct without guidance from outsiders. The very existence of vigilante committees meant that government was no longer enforcing the law as they should. For all his claims that mob justice represented Enlightenment thinking, Bancroft really defended a truly archaic practice that flew in the face of Wells and Work's more modern sociological ideas.

Other apologists for lynching depicted black males as particularly prone to rape. In the magazines and newspapers that white people read, assertive black males often appeared as rapists. In 1884, a Virginia aristocrat named Alexander Bruce explained that black men found white women so "strangely alluring and seductive" that they could not control their lust. A Georgia woman said that freedom had "retrograded" . . . "our old-time friends, the negro . . . into a dangerous beast." White Democrats sexualized political struggles by suggesting their opponents encouraged black men's sexual aspirations. Some state elections turned on the issue, and when Republicans almost passed a federal voting rights law in 1890, Democrats fought back by arguing that voting aroused the black bestiality and lust that made lynching necessary. Politicians like South Carolina's Ben Tillman sometimes denounced lynching, but at other times pledged to lead mobs to defend the purity of white womanhood against animalistic black males.[6]

Determined to prove black males no more capable of rape than whites, Wells investigated a series of cases in which whites alleged rape, finding every time that the alleged white female victim had willingly agreed to the liaison. Her investigations prompted such an angry white reaction that the antilynching crusader considered a move to Oklahoma herself. She clearly could not go back to Memphis; the Memphis *Commercial Appeal* reprinted her editorial about the lynching of her friends and called for Wells to be lynched. Her friend and fellow journalist Fortune offered a more appealing option, calling on Wells to move to New York. On May 27, 1892, a mob destroyed the Memphis offices of the *Free Speech* while Wells was en route to New York. She took a position at Fortune's *New York Age*.

On June 25, 1892, Wells published a long article on the Memphis lynchings that she reprinted as the pamphlet *Southern Horrors: Lynch Law in All Its Phases*. Three years later, she published another pamphlet, *A Red Record: Lynchings in the United States, 1892–1893–1894*. In all her writing, Wells provided both anecdotal evidence looking at particular lynchings and statistical data drawn from the annual count that the *Chicago Tribune* had published since 1882. Wells refuted white allegations that black criminal acts justified lynching. While whites claimed that black male rapists provoked lynching, Wells demonstrated that white women often cried rape when threatened with exposure for taking a black lover. Wells's examination of the *Chicago Tribune* statistics revealed that only one-third of mob victims had even been charged with rape. Wells nailed her case. She noted that when whites claimed rape, they effectively silenced the press and the ministry, stifling the consciences of those who might otherwise protest lynching. Other black writers, including Robert C. O. Benjamin, wrote similar appeals, using similar evidence.

Working for the *New York Age* taught Wells that merely putting her story in print could not sway the communities where white lynch mobs found sustenance. Wells documented instances where white women fabricated rape charges that led to lynching. In some cases these women felt enough remorse to admit what they had done. Wells quoted one woman as confessing she was strangely drawn to her black lover. When neighbors saw him going to her house she felt she had to lie to save her reputation. Wells mounted an assault on the myth of white feminine purity, and her publisher was determined to bring her words to the attention of white America. The *New York Age* printed ten thousand copies of its issue with Wells's article to be distributed across the United States; they sent out one thousand copies to the streets of Memphis.

In *A Red Record*, Wells argued that whites had always supported lynching, justifying their violence as a necessary response to the threat of black insurrection. During Reconstruction, whites had promoted a second excuse. Blacks had gained the right to vote, and whites believed they had to organize violent militias to maintain the white man's government. After whites successfully suppressed the black vote, they needed a new excuse for their racial violence; only then did they begin talking about "Negro criminality" and black men's alleged predisposition to rape. Wells followed with statistics and a catalog of horrors taken from white newspapers, "Lynching Imbeciles," "Lynching of Innocent Men," and "Lynched for Anything or Nothing." It was a grim picture, but she closed by calling on her readers to spread the truth about lynching. She asked her readers to fight lynching by telling the world the facts. Through scientifically objective data, she insisted, Americans could inaugurate an era of law and order.

The key to Wells's optimistic assessment lay in what she saw as her success in breaking down loyalty to region and neighborhood. Despite her doubts about white-dominated courts, she still believed in universal principles of justice and hoped for law and order. She just understood that the American legal system could not deliver justice or order without prodding from the outside. She now saw that the door in the wall of white indifference lay outside the United States altogether. She wanted to globalize the discussion over lynching. From Scotland, the author Isabelle Fyvie Mayo, outraged by a terrible Texas lynching, offered to pay Wells's passage to England so she could speak against lynching, gaining a foothold in the British press.

Mayo thought an American denouncing lynching in England would arouse public sentiment against extralegal violence in America. White Americans might ignore Wells's writings in America, but they would find it harder to resist an aroused English public. Americans looked to the English as particularly cultured. If the civilized British denounced lynchers as uncivilized, white Southerners would be embarrassed. For Wells, arousing English indignation seemed an opportunity to set a higher legal standard against mob violence. If white judges could not be made to follow neutral law, perhaps a kind of higher law could be established in the popular culture—with the help of the English news media.

On April 5, 1893, Wells sailed for England. She gave lectures in England and Scotland and received good notices in the press. When one English citizen asked why British citizens should take an interest in ordinary policing in American towns, Wells penned a reply saying that in America the pulpit and the press say little against lynching. Since Americans would not mobilize their own religious and moral sentiment, Wells and other opponents of lynching had no choice but to turn to the British as allies. Americans, she wrote, saw the United Kingdom as morally superior, a more advanced civilization, and would be unable to ignore criticism from such an esteemed source.

In 1894, she returned to England, arranging with a Chicago newspaper to hire her as its correspondent. Whereas her first tour had aroused little press coverage in America, the second attracted all the attention she could have hoped for. By June 23, Wells reported that her lecturing and writing in Great Britain had aroused the South. Georgia's governor denounced Wells, urging the English to get their facts from a more reputable source. The *Memphis Daily Commercial* attacked Wells's character. Such criticism meant her campaign had struck a nerve; she had broken the silence imposed on her American criticism. Just as she predicted, criticism from Britain stung, and her campaign convinced at least some Americans to distance themselves from their earlier toleration of lynching. In her autobiography, Wells credited English denunciations of American extralegal violence with also shaming American leaders prone to excuse mob law.

In 1895, Wells married Ferdinand Lee Barnett, a Chicago lawyer. While Mitchell predicted that Wells would continue to do good for her race, other black editors wondered if she would continue her antilynching crusade as a married woman. Wells herself had no such doubts. Just a few days after her marriage, she became editor of a black newspaper called the *Conservator*, and within two months she had returned to the lecture circuit. In 1896, Wells became a working mother when she gave birth to a son, but refused to allow motherhood to curb her activism. She took her son with her when making speeches and lobbying Congress for a federal antilynching law, but she did believe she had to put her family ahead of her career. After the birth of her second child, Wells resolved to give up lecturing and return home. Newspapers criticized her for deserting the cause, and Susan B. Anthony rebuked her for becoming a mother and housewife. Anthony complained that, since Wells's marriage, agitation against lynching had almost completely dried up.

Events in New Orleans drew Wells back into the battle. On July 23, 1900, two black men left their shabby New Orleans dwelling for Dryades Street, hoping to attract the attention of two black women living there. Both blacks and whites lived on Dryades Street, and the sight of two black men lingering in a mixed neighborhood after dark prompted a police investigation. Three officers appeared to question the two men. One of the men, Robert Charles, stood up, in what the police took as a threatening movement. Charles and the three officers exchanged gunfire. After shooting an officer, and getting shot himself, Charles fled, retreating to his room on Fourth Street. Alerted by the news that one of their comrades had been shot, more police turned out to search for Charles. By 7:00 a.m., nearly the entire New Orleans police force had converged on Fourth Street. Charles confronted them, killing two, including a police captain. Despite the presence of so many police, Charles again escaped, finding another hiding place on Saratoga Street. On July 27, tipped off by an informant, large numbers of police and civilians came to Charles's final hideout. Observers estimated that fully one thousand armed white men fired five thousand bullets into Charles's room. Somehow Charles survived from 3:20 to 5:00 p.m., firing his Winchester fifty times, hitting people twenty-four times. Before his own death, Charles killed seven men, including four police officers. Terrible race rioting followed.

Wells published a pamphlet praising Robert Charles, emphasizing that the white officers who originally rousted Charles had no warrant and no reason to believe he had committed any crime. They acted, she wrote, confident they could literally do anything to a black man without fear of any reaction or consequence. Wells explained that in any law-abiding community, Charles should have delivered himself to the authorities for a fair trial, but New Orleans was not such a place, for a black man. Charles knew, Wells explained, that he faced lynching or, at best, a long term in the penitentiary for defending himself. Thus, he courageously decided to defend himself for as long as he could pull a trigger. Wells hailed Charles as a hero, praised his courage, and described him as a quiet and peaceful man. She closed her pamphlet with a count of lynchings from 1882 to 1899 based on the *Chicago Tribune*'s annual tallies.

Despite her family obligations, Wells continued her efforts against white racism into the twentieth century. In this campaign, she confronted not just white opposition but also black provincialism. On the Sunday after the 1908 Springfield, Illinois, race riot, she passionately denounced blacks' apathy and called on her Sunday-school class to organize. At first just three members of her church class responded, but Wells pushed ahead, organizing the Negro Fellowship League to uplift black youth, since the YMCA would not admit African Americans to its programs and facilities. In 1909, she again confronted local blacks' indifference after Cairo, Illinois, whites lynched Will "Frog" James for the murder of a white woman. Illinois law required the governor to remove from office sheriffs unwilling to protect prisoners from lynchers. After the James lynching, the governor of Illinois dutifully removed Sheriff Frank Davis from office. But the law also allowed the ousted sheriff to make his case for reinstatement in a hearing before the governor. In Cairo, Wells found that many blacks had asked the governor to return the sheriff to office. Narrowly local political concerns controlled Cairo blacks' thinking, Wells thought. As one black resident explained to her, the ousted sheriff had been a friend of Cairo blacks and had hired black deputies. His replacement, a Democrat, had dismissed all the black deputies. Once again, politics prevailed over law, and although Wells no longer had much faith in the power of law to reform society, she demanded that Illinois authorities enforce their law against prolynching sheriffs. Wells argued that Cairo blacks endangered the lives of blacks all over Illinois by permitting their local concerns to determine their course. She declared that blacks had to unite against lynchings in Illinois by repudiating the sheriff, and she succeeded in persuading some Cairo blacks to sign a petition. Traveling to Springfield, she made a powerful speech against the sheriff and countered the petitions he produced with her own resolutions. In the end, the governor agreed not to reinstate Davis because he had not properly protected his prisoner. Wells again triumphed over localism. She also confirmed that lobbying, speech making, and petitioning mattered more than abstract legal principle when it came to winning rights.

That same year, the National Association for the Advancement of Colored People (NAACP) formed, partly in response to the Springfield riot the year before. With some reluctance, organizers called on Wells to lend her support to the association, although her fundamental approach to racial problems differed from the organization's commitment to putting race in a broad context of reform. In a 1909 article that articulated the founders' ideas, Du Bois urged that the race problem not be segregated from other reform movements. Poverty and ignorance, he declared, represented a human, not a black, problem. The solution lay in human methods. In her autobiography, Wells judged the NAACP harshly. It lasted longer than other such movements, she admitted, but fell short of its founders' expectations. She blamed the NAACP's troubles on a white woman named Mary White Ovington, chair of its executive committee. Wells complained that Ovington's experience in New York City and Brooklyn had not prepared her for the national stage. Wells's daughter explained that her mother thought the leadership of the NAACP should be entirely black.

Though Wells never studied at the University of Chicago, she made a kind of search for neutral truth that was becoming popular in the late nineteenth century. She began A Red Record by observing that "the student of American sociology will find the year 1894 marked by a pronounced awakening of the public conscience to a system of anarchy and outlawry." In both her publications and public speaking, she attacked lies with objective truth. She made herself into an investigative reporter, an objective speaker of truth. She berated herself for crying when delivering one speech. An emotional display, she believed, betrayed weakness. One writer described Wells's attitude as "controlled outrage." Her claim to recognize "a pronounced awakening" mirrored sociologists' optimism that their research really could reform society. Writing in 1895, a time when there was painfully little reason for optimism, she urged her readers to see her crusade against lynching as "blessed with the most salutary results." She presented evidence that her work had compelled governors, newspapers, members of Congress, and bishops to speak for or against lynching. Wells said this good work did not result from the higher law she once trusted; "latent spirit of justice" had asserted itself. Instead, her reliance on scientific data had forced the subject into the open.[7]

While Wells collected facts as a journalist, Monroe Nathan Work, also a child of former slaves, followed a university-based reform strategy. In contrast to Wells, who relied on the Chicago Tribune for her data, Work fought lynching by compiling his own national database of lynching, building on the Tribune's listings, and continuing and expanding the newspaper's collection. Work was born August 15, 1866, in North Carolina, before his parents migrated to Cairo, Illinois, and then to Kansas. In the 1870s, Work's father staked out a homestead near Aston and raised wheat, corn, and oats. Working on his father's farm prevented him from attending high school until 1889, when his father left his farm to live with one of his married children. At age twenty-three, Work could finally continue his education. He found being so much older than his fellow students humiliating but nonetheless persisted and graduated from high school in June 1892. Still ambitious to advance himself, Work tried teaching, hoping to make enough money to continue his education. When that effort failed, he became an African Methodist Episcopal minister. He preached for a few months in Wellington, Kansas, but his academic sermons, delivered through barely moving lips, convinced his congregation to find another minister. In 1893, discouraged from teaching and the ministry, Work returned to farming, staking out a claim on Oklahoma's Cherokee Strip.

Work next moved to Chicago, where he secured a teaching position in the public schools. In 1897, he entered Chicago Theological Seminary, where he studied for three years but graduated as a sociologist rather than a minister. In 1892, the Chicago Seminary had established a department of Christian sociology that taught the social gospel movement, a Christian reform effort aimed at tackling the problems of an industrialized society. This did not mean merely spiritual concerns. Believing that churches had to study social problems before they could solve them, the Chicago Seminary sent its students into Chicago's slums to study conditions. At the seminary, Work fell under the spell of William Graham Taylor, chair of the seminary's sociology department. Under Taylor's tutelage, Work studied crime among Chicago blacks, eventually producing an article for the *American Journal of Sociology*. Despite his continuing commitment to the social gospel movement, Work switched to the University of Chicago's sociology department in 1898. It was an easy transition to make, since the seminary had close ties to the sociology department. Taylor taught in both.

Led by Albion Small, the University of Chicago's sociology faculty encouraged service, and Work came to believe sociology should be a tool to change social conditions. He became one of the first black sociologists and was one of only four black students at the university. The four formed teams and practiced debating against each other to sharpen their skills. Work remembered later that he learned the importance of facts and the power of factual information in any debate. One issue the four debated was the famed black agriculturalist Booker T. Washington's 1895 speech at the Cotton States Exposition urging blacks to subordinate civil rights protest in favor of accommodation, a view that repelled Work. While at Chicago, he came under the influence of Professor William I. Thomas, who rejected current theories of racial inferiority, arguing that prejudice had its roots in ignorance set in a primitive instinct going back to when society organized itself at the tribal level. Thomas doubted racism could ever be entirely eradicated, but he expressed optimism that better communications and the flow of information between groups and cultures would greatly reduce its significance. Work's reliance on facts made him receptive to Thomas's idea that education and information could defeat prejudice.

In 1903, Work returned to the South, taking a teaching position at Savannah's Georgia State Industrial College. Here the young sociologist continued his research, collecting information on Africa and forming an alliance with Du Bois, with whom he collaborated on a number of research projects. Work contributed an essay critical of white claims that black people had smaller brains than whites to a book Du Bois edited in 1906. As Du Bois increasingly criticized Washington, Work sided with Du Bois. When Du Bois formed the Niagara Movement in 1905, Work attended the first organizing meetings. He then returned home to Savannah's oppressive racism.

In 1908, Washington, seeking to win over Du Bois's allies, invited Work to leave Savannah and join the faculty at his Tuskegee Normal and Industrial Institute. Washington's invitation came after the 1906 Atlanta race riot and the failure of a black boycott of Savannah streetcars the same year. He offered Work twelve hundred dollars a year and a house, a great advance over his meager salary in Savannah. Washington's offer also came at a time when Work and Du Bois had grown apart intellectually. Du Bois increasingly lost faith in objective truth, while Work remained unwavering in his determination to marshal data against white racism. Washington offered Work library facilities to collect and organize his facts and, through his extensive network of political contacts known as the "Tuskegee Machine," connections that would broadcast his facts to America and the world.

Work wanted to document the black experience, and he became the keeper of records at Tuskegee, where Washington learned to rely on him for information and statistics to cite in his speeches. Work developed a reputation for accuracy and reliability. He kept track of Tuskegee alumni; it was thanks to Work that Washington could boast that not one of his graduates had ever been convicted of a crime, that one-third had become teachers, and that most owned their own homes. Work's ambition, though, ran far beyond merely cataloging information on Tuskegee graduates. He acquired and cataloged books, pamphlets, documents, reports, and press clippings about black life. Work disseminated information drawn from his vast archive by answering requests for information and by publishing the *Negro Year Book*. Beginning in 1912, the *Year Book* provided an encyclopedic compendium of facts. Newspapers came to rely on the *Year Book* as a reliable source of information about black America.

Outraged by lynching at least since his student days in Chicago, where he read the *Chicago Tribune*'s annual count of lynchings, Work had tried to collect lynching data while still living in Chicago, but only after he moved to Tuskegee did he have the resources to compete with the *Tribune*'s effort. Work believed other newspapers ignored the *Tribune*'s data because it came from a rival. In 1914, he sent his lynching data to three hundred white newspapers, the Associated Press, and all leading black newspapers. In 1915, the *World Almanac* began reprinting Work's annual lynching count. He initially met hostility from white editors, but his determination to present only facts, untainted by propaganda, won them over. Even small-town, rural white newspapers in the South came to accept Work's data as the reliable "official" lynching count. Work firmly believed that his facts spoke for themselves. His lynching summaries gave a number for lynchings in the previous year and broke down the total count by the nature of the reported offenses. Whites claimed that a black propensity to rape justified lynching; Work, like Wells, showed that only a third of lynchings involved allegations of rape. Most importantly, his statistics painted a national portrait of lynching, his neutral facts implicitly arguing that racial violence posed a national problem requiring a national solution.

Nonetheless, Work's lists were not complete, since he necessarily relied on newspapers for his data. The Tuskegee Institute hired clipping services to collect articles on lynchings from newspapers across the country, thus following the same method as the *Chicago Tribune*, which collected its data by scouring the columns of other newspapers. During the time when it counted lynchings, the *Tribune* never publicly acknowledged the problems its editors ran into defining lynching—if they considered the problem at all. More likely, when neighborhood newspapers counted a killing as a lynching, then the *Tribune*'s editors simply accepted the local judgment. The *Tribune* essentially made itself a prisoner of its own sources, incorporating all the omissions and redundancies of the local papers into its own reporting. Work also became invested in his sources' view of the subject. If local newspapers did not call a killing a lynching, then neither did Work and the Tuskegee Institute. If the local press judged a killing to be a lynching, then Work added it to his tally. His lists of lynchings relied on local whites' willingness to accurately report all lynchings. He also assumed all his sources operated with the same definition of what constituted a lynching.

Work took a sternly conservative approach to collecting lynching data, meaning that if local public opinion did not accept a killing as a lynching, then neither would he. This method led to controversy, but it particularly ran afoul of Americans' determination to distinguish a "riot" from a "lynching." This became an important issue in 1919, when race riots broke out in twenty-five American cities and towns between April and early October. In July, five days of rioting began in Chicago when black swimmers entered a beach whites had reserved for themselves. Whites armed themselves with guns and cruised the streets in cars looking for blacks to murder. Other whites formed mobs to beat, stab, and shoot blacks they encountered. By the time the military had restored order, seven blacks had been killed by police and another sixteen by mobs.

Such brutality shocked, and still shocks, but even more serious violence erupted three months later in Phillips County, Arkansas, when black sharecroppers tried to organize a labor union. When whites attacked an organizing meeting near Hoop Spur, a hamlet near the larger town of Elaine, blacks returned fire. Seeking revenge, whites formed massive posses, and while five whites died, we can never know the number of murdered blacks. Estimates range from 20 to 856, with a member of the white mob admitting that he saw between two and three hundred dead blacks with his own eyes. In both Chicago and in Arkansas, and elsewhere, mobs of whites killed individual blacks but did so in the midst of general rioting. No one has offered a good reason a mob acting in the midst of a riot should be distinguished from mobs operating outside a riot. Since we do not know the number killed in rural Arkansas, even an honest attempt to count all victims of racial violence could not produce a complete count. The problem deepens when we try to distinguish mob killings in the context of a riot from lynchings taking place outside a riot. In Arkansas, newspapers reported four blacks had been "lynched" in the riot, making an arbitrary distinction between those four and the dozens (or hundreds) of others also killed in the same riot. The four blacks supposed to be lynched were brothers, sons of a Presbyterian minister, innocently hunting with no idea that whites had launched their own hunt. Perhaps their innocence made their deaths seem more like lynchings, but even if every other African American killed that day had been involved in union organizing, they were all just as innocent. Accepting the press accounts, Work counted twelve lynchings in the entire state of Arkansas for 1919, well below even the minimum number of deaths journalists attributed to the Elaine riot. Clearly, Work seriously underestimated the death toll, failing to count the victims of rioting as lynchings. However, he did better than the NAACP, which put the toll for Arkansas at just seven. Work included the deaths of the four brothers the NAACP would not count. He also dismissed the Chicago killings from his count. While twenty-three blacks perished in Chicago, killed by white mobs, Work insisted that not a single lynching had occurred in Illinois. The Illinois press would not admit that the killing mobs in Chicago had "lynched" anyone, and Work dutifully followed that local decision. He tried to impose a national standard on local data. Since he did so in the absence of a universally accepted definition of lynching, he achieved only imperfect success, but the most significant point is that he tried.

Wells lived until 1936. She had broken through gender barriers to make herself an international spokesperson for her race and broken into a career previously closed to women. She defined her life by transcending local boundaries. The end of slavery allowed her to leave the plantation South, but she escaped through her own efforts. Defeat before the Tennessee Supreme Court led to her deep disappointment in white-dominated courts. Without truly impartial law to referee relations between the races, it seemed for that moment she could do nothing more than flee. Wells concentrated on survival strategies in a hopelessly brutal, segregated society. Her scheme to attack lynching in America by going to England represented a masterstroke, one that might not have appealed so strongly to someone who did not associate freedom with physical mobility. In England, Wells could make American whites listen to her message in a way they would not had she stayed in the United States. In Britain, she did more than merely survive; her writing helped change the American rhetoric of lynching. Her own research into lynchings, supported by the *Tribune*'s statistical data, made it more difficult for whites to justify their violence as a response to black criminality.

Work lived until 1945. He quietly gathered lynching data, information that became the basis for statistical studies of racial violence for many years. In 1927, the *Chicago Defender* published an article questioning Work's statistical approach. It reported that Work had counted nine lynchings during the first six months of 1927. The *Defender* then explained to its readers that Work's count of nine lynchings only listed the officially recorded deaths. Many more people, shot down on streets, killed on peonage farms, and flogged to death in rural places, die without notice by the outside world. Black people die mysteriously in the South all the time, the paper said, before cautioning its readers to take Work's count with a grain of salt, and continuing, "There is far in excess of nine lynchings in the South during the past six months."[8] But even as it criticized Work, the *Chicago Defender* documented his importance. Work's count of lynchings really had become the "official" count, reported in white and black newspapers alike. Long after the *Defender*'s criticism had been forgotten, scholars relied on Work's listing of lynchings as the basis for their knowledge of lynching.

Wells and Work pioneered the sociological attack on lynching. Both nationalized the conversation over lynching in new ways and brought facts and figures before wider audiences. Work even persuaded white editors, North and South, to rely on his data. Wells and Work took important first steps toward separating lynching from its local legitimacy, making lynching a national priority.

Notes

1. "The Conflict of Judicial Authority," *Danville (Virginia) Daily News*, March 5, 1879.

2. "The Tribune Annual Review," *Chicago Tribune*, January 1, 1883.

3. "1874. Trade and Commerce of Chicago for 1874," *Chicago Tribune*, January 1, 1875; "The Tribune Annual Review"; Christopher Waldrep, *The Many Faces of Judge Lynch: Extralegal Violence and Punishment in America* (New York: Palgrave Macmillan, 2002), 112–145; "Republican Tariff Reformer Hoisting the Bloody Shirts," *Galveston Daily News*, January 2, 1884.

4. Ida B. Wells, *Crusade for Justice: The Autobiography of Ida B. Wells*, ed. Alfreda M. Duster (Chicago: University of Chicago Press, 1970), 11–17.

5. *Chesapeake, Ohio, and Southwestern Railroad Co. v. Wells*, 85 Tennessee 613 (1887).

6. Joel Williamson, *The Crucible of Race: Black-White Relations in the American South since Emancipation* (New York: Oxford University Press, 1984), 111–21; Stephen Kantrowitz, *Ben Tillman and the Reconstruction of White Supremacy* (Chapel Hill: University of North Carolina Press, 2000), 105–6.

7. Ida B. Wells, *A Red Record: Tabulated Statistics and Alleged Causes of Lynchings in the United States, 1892–1893–1984* (Chicago: Donohue & Henneberry, 1895); Shirley W. Logan, "Rhetorical Strategies in Ida B. Wells's 'Southern Horors: Lynch Law in All Its Phases,'" *Sage* 7 (Summer 1991): 3–9.

8. "Lynching Report Fails to Cover Many Outrages," *Chicago Defender*, July 16, 1927.

~

CHAPTER FOUR

NAACP

Organized Resistance

In the twentieth century, the National Association for the Advancement of Colored People (NAACP) built on the work of Ida B. Wells and Monroe Work to launch the first organized attack on lynching. The NAACP organized after a 1908 spasm of racial violence in Springfield, Illinois. From its beginnings, the NAACP had to confront violent racism in many forms. Whites in Springfield "rioted," but they also "lynched" their black victims. Since the NAACP chose to follow a legalistic, court-based approach, based on constitutional law, the confusion over the definition of lynching challenged the organization in its struggle against racist bloodshed. To write a law, lawmakers would have to define the thing they wanted to outlaw.

The Springfield violence differed from a mass lynching only in that the intended victims fought back. The trouble started in August 1908, when authorities arrested George Richardson for allegedly raping a white woman. Around seven in the evening, on Friday, August 14, a crowd gathered outside Richardson's jail cell. Angry groups of men had clustered around the county jail throughout the day. Richardson was not the only black prisoner likely to attract the attention of a white mob. Another African American, Joe James, already sat in the county jail charged with murder in connection with attempted rape, when authorities hustled Richardson into his cell. At two o'clock, one group cornered a black man and attacked him with baseball bats. By four o'clock it looked like Sheriff Charles Werner's small force might not be able to defend the jail in the face of a mob attack. In 1908, cars were a rare and expensive novelty for most people, and the sheriff had to borrow one of the few in town to drive Richardson and James to Bloomington, sixty-six miles away. The police chief and the sheriff calculated that, once the mob realized that the prisoners were beyond reach, most of the public anger would dissipate.

They miscalculated. The crowd had swelled to one thousand by eight o'clock and kept growing, reaching eight or ten thousand. The mob vented its frustration on the automobile used to transport the prisoners out of town, and then turned on the auto owner's business, a restaurant. Startled diners scrambled to safety as the mob threw bricks and rocks before invading the restaurant and wrecking the building. A stray bullet struck and killed a bystander near the restaurant. After demolishing the restaurant, the maddened crowd surged into Springfield's black district, looting and destroying black-owned businesses. The mob lynched Scott Burton when he tried to defend himself. Burton's daughters later said their father had blindly fired his shotgun into the mob after men had invaded his house and threatened him with an axe.

According to the *Chicago Tribune*, by five o'clock the next morning African Americans living in Springfield had started fleeing the town. The *Tribune* painted a vivid picture of African Americans packing every outbound train while four thousand National Guardsmen crowded the inbound trains. Guardsmen patrolled the entire town, posting sentries on street corners, but four thousand troops proved inadequate for the task. The violence continued, unabated. Guardsmen ran from one part of town to another, trying to stop erupting violence. At nine o'clock that night, a mob of five hundred marched down Spring Street, stopping at William Donnegan's house. Donnegan, an aged black man, some reports put him at eighty years old, had married a white woman, which may account for why the mob came to his house.

Donnegan sauntered out to the street and innocently greeted the crowd only to be knocked down with a brick. Half a dozen rioters swarmed over the fallen man, yelling for a rope. As the old man pleaded for his life, piteously begging for mercy, the crowd turned a deaf ear, repeatedly hoisting him up and stabbing him with knives as they did so. His family remained in his house, cowering in fear, but the mob showed them no mercy and torched that refuge as well. Then the crowd departed, leaving Donnegan sprawled on the ground, still alive, his throat pumping blood. He died some hours later. Eventually, the troops restored order.

The history of the NAACP traditionally begins with the Springfield violence, which historians have said surprised and shocked all of America. Writers have described the riot as especially shocking and disturbing because it occurred in the North and in Lincoln's hometown. The argument that the Springfield bloodshed precipitated the NAACP focuses on an influential article the socialist William English Walling published shortly after the riot, urging the creation of such an organization. The article did support the work of those people founding the NAACP even if it is unlikely that the fact of a Northern riot shocked or surprised anyone. Walling, who took the train down to Springfield from Chicago, walked the still-smoldering streets, talking to the citizens he encountered. The riot, he decided, proved that violent white racism had metastasized like a cancer, demanding an answer from Congress, because it now affected the whole nation. The violence seemed especially gratuitous, he wrote, because blacks made up only 10 percent of Springfield's population, posing no possible political threat to whites. Northern public opinion seemed to tolerate the lynchings, excusing the mob with "mitigating circumstances." Springfield was a Northern town associated with racial progress, Abraham Lincoln, and the Emancipation Proclamation. Walling interviewed several white Springfield residents who said, "Why, the niggers came to think they were as good as we are!" Walling closed his account by asking who among his readers understood the seriousness of lynching and saw that a "large and powerful body of citizens" must intervene to stop the violence.[1]

It seems unlikely that Northern racial violence could have shocked anyone by 1908. In 1900, it took one hundred New York police officers to subdue rioting whites after a black man killed a police officer. In that year—eight years before Springfield's violence—the *New York Times* published an anonymous letter saying that the New York episode taught Northern people that racial violence was not confined to the South. On July 5, 1903, violence erupted in Evansville, Indiana, when a white mob tried to lynch the alleged black slayer of a police officer. Shortly after, rampaging whites in Danville, Illinois, killed two, injured twenty-two, and required four companies of militia to restore order. Just a few weeks after the Danville riot, a mob of 150 white men hunted through the Bronx, looking for black people to lynch. The New Yorkers shouted, "Kill him! Kill that nigger! Shoot him! Shoot him!"[2]

Such violence had become too routine to shock anyone. Neighborhood racial tensions had simmered all over America, close to the boiling point. In 1903, the fiery South Carolina senator Ben Tillman had observed that the extent of northern rioting proved that the race problem belonged to the whole United States and not just the South. Tillman warned that the nation faced a race war in its near future. In 1905, after five thousand rioters took to the streets in New York, the *New York Times* briefly noted that there had been bad feelings between the races ever since blacks first arrived in the neighborhood. According to the *Times*, the violence occurred around Amsterdam Avenue, the borderland between the races, a place where police officers at the West Sixty-eighth Street Station had learned to expect a riot at least once a week. Hostile feelings predominated in a tense atmosphere, according to the *Times*. The only surprise was that this week's violence came a little earlier than the usual time and involved larger numbers of rioters. In 1906, the most spectacular racial violence took place in Atlanta, but rioting also broke out in Delaware and in Springfield, Ohio.

African Americans had made numerous attempts to organize themselves to better assert their rights before the Springfield violence. As early as January 1884, T. Thomas Fortune envisioned a national black organization, an all-black National Afro-American League modeled on the Irish National League. In 1887, Ida B. Wells attended a meeting of the Negro Mutual Protective Association and enthused that African Americans had begun to think for themselves and recognize the power of unifying against white oppression. African Americans had established many organizations; however, they had not created an enduring structure that was truly national in scope. Frederick Douglass and Booker T. Washington were nationally known men, and Washington had an extensive network of contacts and allies that spread across the country, but neither man had organized a mass movement on a national scale. Fortune had built a national reputation but had trouble building an organization that reached across the whole country. In 1894, in an article dismissing Fortune as a minor leader of a small faction based in Brooklyn, the *New York Times* described the black community as too splintered to organize. Whatever Fortune does, the paper explained, it will be denounced by another faction. The *Times* may have been right, at the time, but the demand for a national organization continued nonetheless. In 1896, black newspapers called on Fortune to revive his Afro-American League, but Fortune was too sick to answer the call and doubted enough support existed for a national organization. So, instead of Fortune, Bishop Alexander Walters of the African Methodist Episcopal Zion Church in New York City emerged to lead the National Afro-American Council. For several years the council actively pursued African American rights. In 1899, Walters led a delegation of National Afro-American Council leaders that went to President William McKinley with their concerns about lynching. The council also drafted a model antilynching law. By 1900, Walters's council claimed to represent two hundred thousand black voters. Eight years later, Walters said he spoke for ten million. The council's demands remained consistent over time. Walters's organization opposed mob violence and regularly criticized state laws designed to disfranchise black voters. While its basic message did not change, the council became increasingly militant over time. At the National Afro-American

Council's ninth annual meeting in 1906, speakers warned ominously that while violent trouble all came from whites now, trouble never stayed on one side. The Reverend George W. Lee warned that blacks would soon start some trouble of their own. The Reverend A. L. Gains of Maryland said that, when attacked, blacks should kill as many of their assailants as possible. Booker T. Washington had blessed the council in its early stages, but in 1908, it repudiated Washington's accommodationist strategy. As the ranks of the council swelled, Walters felt increasingly powerful, coming to believe he and it could influence the national election. In March 1908, Walters presided over a meeting of two thousand African Americans that hooted and hissed Theodore Roosevelt and William Howard Taft and called on Republicans to nominate Charles Evans Hughes rather than Roosevelt or Taft. Delegates attending the meeting paraded with brass bands and torches and heard a telegram from W. E. B. Du Bois. Newspapers reported that, when Du Bois called on delegates to support the Democrat William Jennings Bryan if the Republicans would not nominate Hughes, all of the African Americans in the hall leaped to their feet, cheering and stamping, shouting "We will! We will!"[3] Bryan was an avowed enemy, Du Bois said, but that was better than a false friend, Roosevelt. Hughes was better than either. Walters and his followers hoped to influence both Democrats and Republicans.

A second organization, Du Bois's Niagara Movement, began in 1905 with thirty men meeting in Ontario, Canada. Du Bois rallied the African American professional elite: lawyers, doctors, educators, businessmen, and ministers. He drafted the group's "Declaration of Principles" and steered his group toward a confrontational path, issuing demands and promising protest. Du Bois wrote that he had no hesitation to complain and planned to do so loudly and insistently. His declaration protested the limitations on black suffrage, segregation, and denial of economic opportunity. They demanded upright judges, pleaded for an opportunity to live in decent houses with good schools, free from mob violence. The group urged Congress to pass new civil rights laws to enforce the promises made in the Civil War amendments and spoke of citizenship rights. But Du Bois emphasized political action as a way of achieving civil rights. He expected African Americans to achieve their rights through agitation, by making demands and not as a gift bestowed by the white framers of the Constitution.

In 1909, a group of mostly white intellectuals from an organization called the Constitution League and other white organizations met with members of Du Bois's Niagara Movement to organize what came to be called the National Association for the Advancement of Colored People. The NAACP appeared as an alternative to the all-black Afro-American Council, which could not offer white people a vehicle for protesting the rising tide of racial violence. Walling's article on the Springfield riot had ignored the Afro-American Council and instead called for an altogether new national organization. The most important response to Walling's call came from Mary White Ovington, the socialist white descendant of abolitionists. The pair met and discussed how to form a large and powerful organization to combat racism. Ovington had already been talking with John Milholland, a newspaper reporter turned wealthy inventor. In 1903, Milholland had organized the Constitution League, which he hoped could defeat prejudice using lawsuits based on the Fourteenth Amendment.

The NAACP formed at the intersection of Milholland's organization and Du Bois's all-black Niagara Movement. Milholland had been a *New York Tribune* reporter before making his fortune by inventing a pneumatic tube mail delivery system. Motivated by Christian principles, Milholland wanted to attack discrimination and racial prejudice systematically. Like Ovington, he admired Du Bois, but more than the Niagara Movement, his Constitution League emphasized using constitutional principle against prejudice, as its name implied. Milholland demanded enforcement of the Fourteenth and Fifteenth Amendments. In 1908, Ovington favored both Milholland's Constitution League and Du Bois. She explained that she wanted to continue nationalizing the work of previous activists. She wanted to publicize conditions in the South and to persuade Northerners they bore some responsibility for white Southerners' violent assaults on blacks' constitutional rights.

The most progressive white people in America endorsed the NAACP. Famed social worker Jane Addams joined investigative journalist Lincoln Steffens to sign a call to arms penned by Oswald Garrison Villard, grandson of the famed abolitionist and progressive journalist. Albert E. Pillsbury, a former Massachusetts legislator and state attorney general, author of a model antilynching law and an article in the influential *Harvard Law Review* arguing for a federal law against lynching, enlisted in the effort as well. Pillsbury's presence among the NAACP's founders signaled that the NAACP would dedicate itself to defeating lynching through legislation. But his support also indicated a certain degree of conservatism among the original founders. He had made himself the enemy of the great progressive lawyer Louis D. Brandeis and had little sympathy for feminism, believing that women belonged in the home. When the NAACP organized, Pillsbury, but not Brandeis, stood among its founders.

The Massachusetts lawyer made an essentially conservative argument against lynching: the national government should end lynching not because it threatened race relations but rather because it represented anarchy. He wrote at a time when many in America felt threatened by anarchists, especially anarchists of foreign origin. Pillsbury may well have hoped to exploit anti-anarchist sentiment by linking white racial violence to anarchy, or he may have genuinely believed violent white racists resembled bomb-throwing anarchists.

Pillsbury favored using federal law against lynching. In 1902, he had argued in a *Harvard Law Review* article that the Fourteenth Amendment not only forbade state discrimination but also required the states to fight mobs. If a citizen was put to death by a mob because the state failed to provide the protection it was bound to provide, he argued, then it had effectively denied equal protection. Pillsbury's brief article rested on a handful of precedents and considerable supposition and conjecture. He thought the Constitution implied federal policing powers not actually stated, an argument that might well have worked had the Supreme Court been inclined toward expanding the powers of Congress to control racial violence, which it was not. Nonetheless, the NAACP relied on Pillsbury as its authority for arguing that Congress had the constitutional power to pass a law against lynching.

The meeting that formally founded the NAACP came in May 1910. Organizers named Moorfield Storey, a progressive Boston lawyer, president; William E. Walling, chairman; John Milholland, treasurer; and Oswald Villard, disbursing secretary, all white men. Du Bois became executive committee chairman, in charge of publicity. The meeting set dues at one dollar, a figure that did not change for seventy years.

Though it initially relied on white leadership, from its beginnings, the NAACP used African Americans to serve in bookkeeping, clerical, and field staff positions. A board made up of whites dedicated to racial equality ran the organization while Du Bois edited the NAACP's magazine, the *Crisis*. Du Bois used the *Crisis* to record and report on lynchings. In 1911, when Coatesville, Pennsylvania, lynchers killed Zachariah Walker, NAACP leaders convened an emergency meeting at their New York headquarters to decide how to respond. They decided to gather evidence against the lynchers. Two board members traveled to Coatesville to begin gathering facts, and the NAACP hired the William Burns Detective Agency to more thoroughly investigate. The NAACP organized an antilynching rally that drew some four hundred men and women. In the end, the NAACP effort did not lead to the conviction of any lynchers in court and left the organization with just four hundred dollars in its antilynching fund.

Five white men, New York lawyers, composed the NAACP's National Legal Committee. In 1913, the committee expanded, adding its first African American member, Deborcey Macon Webster, who, unlike most African

American lawyers in 1913, had a Wall Street practice. He worked divorce and estate cases and had once served as Booker T. Washington's lawyer. For the most part, however, the first generation of NAACP lawyers included no blacks. The NAACP initially tied itself to wealthy lawyers with stellar credentials and distanced itself from black trial lawyers it suspected might be interested in using the organization for pecuniary gain.

The death of a white man spurred the NAACP to redouble its efforts against lynching. In 1915, a mob broke into the Georgia penitentiary to hang Leo Frank, falsely accused of killing a young white woman employed in his pencil factory. This lynching prompted Boston philanthropist and lawyer Philip G. Peabody, the wealthy world traveler and son of a Supreme Court justice, to propose donating ten thousand dollars to the NAACP to fund a campaign against lynching. Peabody asked the NAACP to write a proposal, and the organization went to work, producing a document dated May 22, 1916.

If the lynching of a white man helped inspire Peabody to propose funding a campaign against lynching, the lynching of a black man convinced him of the hopelessness of the effort. On May 8, as the NAACP worked on its draft proposal for Peabody, the family and neighbors of a Texas farm wife discovered her dead body, bludgeoned to death with a hammer. Authorities quickly identified Jesse Washington as the murderer and hustled him off to the Dallas City Jail to prevent a lynching. While in Dallas, white officers extracted a confession from Washington, and a grand jury indicted him on May 11. Washington went on trial on May 15, one week before the NAACP had scheduled an appointment with Peabody to present their proposed anti-lynching campaign. Over two thousand rowdy white spectators crowded the Waco courtroom and courthouse yard during the trial. Surrounded by disorderly townfolk, Washington's lawyer hardly dared venture a defense, asking just one question on cross-examination. In such an environment, no juror would have voted to acquit, even if any had been inclined to do so, and none were. The jury pronounced Washington guilty. As the judge bent over his docket to record the verdict, the agitated crowd outside stormed into the courtroom, seized Washington, and hauled him outside, where the mob stripped and castrated the black man before dragging him through the streets chained to an automobile. Fifteen thousand spectators stood by as a small group of lynchers hoisted Washington over a fire, watching him desperately claw his chain as he slowly burned to death. Newspaper reports emphasized that women and children joined the crowd to watch the show and that schools dismissed classes so high school students could participate. On May 16, newspapers across the entire United States presented the barbaric spectacle to their readers, including Peabody. For Peabody, the news came as he prepared to meet the NAACP leadership. For a man with money seeking to end lynching, Jesse Washington's death did not seem a good omen.

Roy Nash had prepared the proposal for Peabody entitled "Lynch-Law and the Practicability of a Successful Attack Thereon." The first part of the memorandum simply provided a short history of lynching based on James E. Cutler's 1905 book, Lynch-Law. Nash then tried to meet Peabody's concerns by arguing that agitation by Ida B. Wells and others had already made so much headway against mob violence that another push was bound to succeed. Some governors had already stated their opposition to lynching, and Nash pointed out that several states had passed laws against lynching, including Georgia, South Carolina, Ohio, Tennessee, Kentucky, and Texas. Public opinion was the key, he recognized. The NAACP leader said that lynchers had to have public approval to carry out their violence. In words seemingly belied by the Jesse Washington lynching, just days before, Nash wrote that more reasonable white Southerners had already turned against lynching and that the sentiment against lynching was growing. The NAACP proposed nurturing and encouraging the opposition to mob violence it thought already existed among Southern whites. Instead of directing all the grant money toward investigating and publicizing lynchings as they occurred, Nash first wanted to systematically advertise the virtue and courage of those Southern white men willing to stand against mobs. He suggested turning to white Southerners themselves to lead this effort, financed by money from the grant, hoping to discourage the bad people of the South by rewarding and celebrating the good people. His second proposal urged more lynching investigations, sending researchers to the scenes of lynchings to interview witnesses and gather information. Third, he wanted to finance lawsuits against sheriffs guilty of permitting mobs access to their jails. Nash optimistically predicted that, if Peabody would fund such a campaign, lynching would end within five years.

Although Nash devoted the bulk of his narrative to preventing lynchings, he proposed spending most of the money investigating lynchings that had already happened and suing white sheriffs and counties that tolerated lynchings. If the budget exposed Nash's true priorities, then it seems he had tilted his narrative toward the positive message he thought Peabody wanted.

Unimpressed, Peabody donated only one thousand dollars, not the ten thousand he had originally offered. Nonetheless, the NAACP forged ahead and soon raised almost as much money from other sources. The Jesse Washington lynching in Waco discouraged Peabody, but the NAACP turned it into the centerpiece of its publicity campaign against lynching. Nash had already recruited an English suffragist named Elizabeth Freeman to investigate the Waco incident. Despite Peabody's rebuff, Freeman devoted herself to the investigation, interviewing town officials and other witnesses to write a detailed narrative of the whole affair. The NAACP published her findings in the July 1916 issue of *Crisis* and circulated the article—with illustrations—to seven hundred newspapers.

In the fall of 1916, the board hired the talented African American educator, novelist, journalist, and diplomat James Weldon Johnson as field secretary. Author of *Autobiography of an Ex-Colored Man* (1912), Johnson brought something to the job his white predecessors had not, a direct experience with lynching. Johnson had nearly been lynched for the "crime" of talking to a woman journalist in Florida whom an angry mob believed to be white. In his memoir, Johnson describes himself sitting with the woman on the bank of a river, when he heard the noise of dogs barking and men shouting. Johnson found himself face-to-face with death when the crowd grabbed his body, tearing at his clothes, yelling, "Come on, we've got 'im! Come on, we've got 'im!" and "Kill the damned nigger!" Johnson escaped death by convincing the crowd that his companion was not white and by not turning his back on them or taking even a single step in retreat.[4] Nonetheless, he came away from the experience having faced death in a way no white leader of the NAACP ever had. Well respected and sophisticated, Johnson immediately went on an organizing trip, one focused on African Americans. He compiled a directory of black professional leaders and systematically worked through it, making remarkably fast progress. In his first year as field secretary, Johnson organized thirteen new branches in the South. In the three years after he joined the NAACP in 1916, the number of branches increased from 68 to 310 and *Crisis*'s circulation passed one hundred thousand. Johnson developed close connections with black churches and lodges, and regularly addressed black professional organizations. In 1920, he became the NAACP's first black executive secretary and took charge of the whole organization.

Working to increase NAACP membership took Johnson into the South, where he met and hired Walter White in February 1918. White had blond hair, blue eyes, and white skin, but he also had African ancestry and identified himself as black. Like Johnson, White had experienced racial violence firsthand. He could remember seeing the 1906 Atlanta race riot from his parent's house. Years later, White claimed he could still remember the cry of the mob. "In that instant," he wrote, "I knew who I was. I was a Negro, a human being with an invisible pigmentation which marked me as a person to be hunted, hanged, abused, discriminated against."[5]

Walter White, executive secretary of the NAACP. Courtesy of the Library of Congress.

Johnson and White redoubled the NAACP's commitment to fight against lynching. White immediately began the work that would make him famous, investigating lynchings. Two weeks after he joined the NAACP staff, in February 1918, White left for Estill Springs, Tennessee, where a mob of one thousand had chained Jim McIlherron to a tree, tortured him with hot irons, cut his body horribly, and then burned him alive. White arrived in Tennessee with press credentials from the *New York Evening Post* and passed as a white man to gain the confidence of the lynchers. White delighted in fooling racist whites, and he filled his reports with sarcastic comments about the white bigots he encountered who mistook him for a white man. He developed a skill to get such people to talk freely about their violence. In Estill Springs, he found a geographically isolated hamlet of about two hundred people strongly committed to religious fundamentalism. White's interviews revealed that white people living in the area had resented McIlherron for his economic success and refusal to accept racial conventions. He had lived in the North for a while, and local white people thought that experience had ruined him for living in Tennessee. McIlherron had shot and killed two whites when they harassed him, throwing rocks. Even some of the white people White interviewed conceded that he acted in self-defense. Nonetheless, whites had lynched him.

As White began writing narratives of particular lynchings based on his unconventional field investigations, the NAACP collected lynching statistics to use in lobbying Congress for a law against lynching. In April 1918, Johnson and White enlisted two Republican congressmen, Leonidas Dyer from St. Louis and Merrill Moores from Indianapolis. Both Dyer and Moores, though white themselves, had a large number of black constituents in their districts. Working in tandem with the NAACP, Dyer and Moores proposed a law to make lynching a federal crime, invoking the Fourteenth Amendment, which guaranteed equal protection under the laws. The bill promised to guard citizens against lynching when states refused to do so. It stipulated that state officials tolerating lynching could be imprisoned and fined. It also barred members of lynch mobs from serving on juries that heard cases under the act.

Dyer and Moores challenged the idea that prosecuting ordinary crime, including homicide, was solely a state responsibility. They sought to take responsibility for one kind of homicide from the states and give it to the federal government. Their idea of holding communities responsible for mob violence followed well-established common-law precedents. English common law had suppressed mobs in the same way for centuries, and several states had laws against lynching that followed the same formula.

As the NAACP lobbied Congress to pass a law against lynching, White continued his trips into the heart of lynching country. His next trip after the McIlherron lynching took him to Georgia, where rioting rural whites had killed at least eleven people. Still pretending to be a reporter for the *New York Evening Post* (he had never returned the credentials he had used for his Tennessee investigation), White interviewed both black and white witnesses and compiled an narrative of appalling brutality. In May 1918, after the murder of a white farmer, whites rampaged across southern Georgia through one bloodily horrific weekend. On Friday, May 17, lynchers killed two black men, Will Head and Will Thompson. The next day they killed Hayes Turner. On Sunday the crowd killed Turner's wife, Mary, after she protested the death of her husband. The rioters had tied Mary Turner upside down, soaked her clothing with petrol, and set her on fire. The woman was eight months pregnant and the lynchers cut her open, ripping out her fetus before crushing it underfoot. Georgia's white press seemed a bit defensive about killing a woman, indicating that she had made "unwise remarks" and that she had had a gold watch belonging to the murdered man.

Armed with his *New York Evening Post* press credentials, White confronted Georgia's governor, Hugh Dorsey, who blamed the violence on blacks' alleged criminality. Dorsey, though, did declare parts of two counties to be in a state of insurrection and dispatched state troops to restore order. The soldiers were themselves white Georgians and shared the same racial ideology as the lynchers, but local folk resented the troops as "outsiders." The *Valdosta Times* spoke for the embittered locals when it complained that the governor sent the soldiers after hearing "exaggerated reports" from outsiders.[6]

White's reports generated new publicity for the NAACP's fight against lynching. When White went undercover to Shubuta, Mississippi, he tried to expose to national attention a quadruple lynching that had received scant press coverage before he wrote about it. A mob had broken into the county jail, where authorities had jailed the two men and two women for ambushing a wealthy white dentist, Richard Johnston. Local whites at first refused to talk to the NAACP investigator, but finally revealed that the married dentist had been carrying on an affair with two of the black victims. The trouble started when Johnston got into a feud with a black man romantically interested in one of the women the dentist had seduced. The whites willing to talk to White admitted that no evidence existed that black people had killed Johnston, but none of that had mattered to the mob. The district attorney led the mob, White learned, hanging the four blacks from a bridge over the Chickasawhay River.

In 1919, White also documented the inability of state courts to punish lynchers. Across the nation, grand juries refused to even indict members of a mob, so when Alabama authorities took the unusual step of putting eighteen lynchers on trial, White hurried to Tuscumbia so he could attend such anamalous proceedings. He watched the state squander an opportunity to stand up to lynching. The trial grew out of a triple lynching; the mob killed two black men accused of shooting a police officer. The third victim, Will Byrd, had been in jail for a minor offense, and the mob had mistakenly killed him as well. Such misdirected lynchings always generated more criticism than lynchings that hit their target, and perhaps for this reason, the state prosecutor seemed sincere. He introduced black witnesses to identify the lynchers and argued that killing innocent blacks harmed the business climate in Alabama. Despite the eyewitness testimony and the prosecutor's economic argument, White watched in disgust as the trial jury swiftly acquitted the first two defendants. The NAACP leader commented that every white person in Tuscumbia believed all the defendants were guilty but also knew the jury would acquit them all.

While White accumulated evidence in support for a federal law against lynching, some of his colleagues in the NAACP hoped to speed things up by using the World War I emergency to persuade Congress to outlaw lynching. In May 1917, NAACP board member Joel Spingarn had joined the army and used his position to press the president to endorse an antilynching law. Spingarn wanted to base such a law not on the Fourteenth Amendment but rather on the president's more loosely defined war powers. Spingarn's bill would have allowed federal prosecution of lynching only during time of war. Moreover, it would have protected only federal employees and those liable to military service (all adult males, in other words), and close relatives of soldiers and sailors. Spingarn invoked his service in the Military Intelligence Branch, arguing that as an intelligence officer he was in a position to know that German agents would use American lynchings as propaganda. He pointed out that Congress had passed a law against sedition in 1917, authorizing prosecution of a crime already punishable under state law. As a wartime measure, Spingarn argued, the federal government had an interest in suppressing lynching.

"Riots," little more than mass lynchings, erupted in the first decades of the twentieth century, reaching epidemic proportions in the "Red Summer" of 1919, when as many as twenty-five cities, towns, and villages experienced racial bloodshed. Some whites persisted in arguing that a maddened white populace could not be expected to control itself in the face of black "misconduct," as when white rioters killed blacks in Chicago and raged through Phillips County, Arkansas. In some places, white authorities blamed the violence on what they saw as the NAACP's provocative conduct, such as telling blacks they had rights. Sometimes these whites tried to solve their problem with the NAACP by banning the organization from their jurisdiction. In August, John R. Shillady, head of the NAACP, traveled to Texas to implore the governor of that state not to outlaw his organization. Governor William P. Hobby refused to meet with Shillady, but County Judge Dave J.

Pickle did—as the head of a mob that beat the NAACP leader severely. The judge candidly told newspaper reporters he had beaten Shillady because the NAACP incited insubordination among Texas blacks. He not only made no attempt to hide his role in the beating, but also boasted he would not shirk responsibility. In a telegram to the NAACP, Hobby defended Pickle and the other members of his mob, blaming Shillady for his own beating. Shillady, the last white man to lead the NAACP, never recovered psychologically from the beating. Before he went to Texas he had not imagined that any place in America could react so violently to civil rights reform. When he returned to New York, other members of the NAACP thought he suffered from shell shock, what today would be called posttraumatic stress syndrome, a malady common to soldiers returning from a war zone.

In 1920, a few months after Shillady, broken in spirit, stepped down as head of the NAACP, the NAACP began planning its first great legislative campaign to persuade Congress to outlaw lynching. The 1920 election seemed to set the stage for passing a federal antilynching law. During the campaign, James Weldon Johnson had gone to Marion, Ohio, hoping to persuade Republican presidential candidate Warren G. Harding to endorse such a law. Harding expressed concern but refused to issue the public statement Johnson wanted, presumably for fear of losing white votes. The results of the election helped ease those political worries. Before the 1920 election, the Republicans only narrowly controlled the House and Senate; afterward, they had a twelve-seat majority in the Senate and a majority of 113 in the House. Since Republicans still called themselves the Party of Lincoln and celebrated a heritage based on ending slavery and passing the nation's first civil rights laws, such thumping Republican majorities implied strong support for a law against lynching. The new president did call on Congress to end lynching. But most members of Congress considered murder a state responsibility and questioned the constitutionality of a federal antilynching law. Even within the NAACP leadership, some initially doubted the constitutionality of a federal law. To combat such reservations, Harding's Department of Justice endorsed the Dyer bill's constitutionality in congressional hearings, supplying a longer and more convincing case than NAACP-supporter Pillsbury had twenty years before in his *Harvard Law Review* article.

More racial violence made the need for an antilynching bill even more apparent. In Duluth, Minnesota, a young white girl sparked a triple lynching when she claimed to have been raped by African American circus hands. Authorities arrested suspects from the circus train and jailed them. Five thousand whites filled the streets of Duluth, overwhelming firefighters and police who tried to defend the jail. The riotous, rock-throwing crowd of men, women, and children hanged three prisoners from a lamppost. An NAACP investigator easily determined that the girl had fabricated the rape story. If Minnesota proved that Northerners could lynch with the same savagery as Southerners, Tulsa, Oklahoma, made the case for the West. In 1921, ten thousand whites destroyed Tulsa's black business district (some consider this the worst race riot in American history). The South proved its continuing dedication to lynch law when a white mob struck Rosewood, Florida, a year later, killing at least eight in a riotous mass lynching.

Even in the midst of all this violence, white Southerners scorned Dyer's bill. They characterized the Tulsa and Rosewood mass lynchings as "riots" as part of their campaign to minimize lynching. Lynching, white Southerners said, was about to end on its own, without any federal lawmaking. According to this narrative, because whites in Tulsa and Rosewood only "rioted," their violence did not contradict the story white Southerners promoted to resist the NAACP's efforts to fight lynching through law. Republican leaders, white Southerners argued, proposed the Dyer bill not because lynching posed any real threat but only to satisfy "Negro agitators," a reference to the NAACP. Southern congressmen consistently insisted that lynching was over because violence increasingly no longer involved a public act of ritualistic terror carried out in the town square. Even as they denied the problem, Southern whites invoked white womanhood as a justification for the lynchings that did occur. Congressmen James B. Aswell of Louisiana accused Dyer of deliberately protecting rapists from justice. Another white Southerner suggested the sponsors of the antilynching bill just admit they favored rape and put protection of rapists in the title of their proposed law. Aswell made the familiar argument that the lynching impulse was so primal no law could stop it. Mobs result not from conspiracies, according to this argument, but from hysteria. He said that the instinct to protect the female is animal in its origin, too fundamental to be extinguished, a basic instinct. Mississippi Congressman Thomas Sisson declared he would rather kill every black person in the world—presumably including those not charged with any crime—than have just one white girl raped by a black man.

However, the white South's most potent support came from those congressmen making a more reasoned constitutional argument. White Southern congressmen insisted that the Constitution did not allow the national government to intrude into the states' police powers. South Carolina's James Byrnes accused proponents of the legislation of having a moblike spirit in their reckless determination to violate settled constitutional law. Congressman Sisson graphically charged that proponents of antilynching legislation wanted to stab an already bleeding Constitution, destroying the work of the founding generation. Hatton Sumners of Texas attributed the antilynchers' willingness to support what he saw as an unconstitutional measure to the political influence of lobbyists like the NAACP. The bill, he said, proposed powers for the federal government that the Supreme Court had already declared unconstitutional, and he quoted language from Supreme Court decisions calling the constitutional theory of the bill absurd.

Constitutional arguments of the sort Sumners used often seemed to work, killing antilynching bills when first proposed, but the 1920 election had put enough Republicans in Congress to overcome Southern opposition, with the help of a massive, nationwide mobilization effort by the NAACP. The NAACP organized the constituents of wavering congressmen to hold their representatives' feet to the fire with letters and petition campaigns. On January 26, 1922, the House passed the Dyer bill, 231–119. The NAACP was halfway to its goal. All it had to do was persuade the U.S. Senate to vote for what the House had passed.

White Southern senators could use the filibuster to prevent passage, making it a tougher nut to crack. Even a small number of senators could prevent a vote on any measure by giving long speeches. A coordinated and determined group of senators, speaking in rotation, could tie up the Senate for months, preventing anything from being accomplished. At the outset of the NAACP's campaign to win the Senate, the *New York Times* attacked the House antilynching bill as a political stunt and outlined and endorsed the views of conservative white politicians. The article said that black voters' defections from the Republican Party in recent city elections had led Republicans to try to win back their former supporters by supporting an unconstitutional measure. Wholly embracing white Southerners' arguments, the *Times* alleged that Republicans backed the Dyer bill for political rather than constitutional reasons, wanting to win back black voters. The paper pointed out that Dyer, the bill's chief proponent, represented a St. Louis district with numerous black voters. The article quoted Idaho Senator William Borah's charge that by knowingly voting for an unconstitutional bill, Dyer and other Republicans acted as lawlessly as the lynchers. Borah illustrated the difficulties the NAACP faced getting its bill through the Senate. Johnson and other association leaders had harbored reasonable hopes that they could win Borah over to their side. Respected by his fellow senators for his supposed constitutional knowledge, his support would have gone a long way toward assuring passage. Instead, he not only opposed the measure but also began adopting the same harsh language white Southerners used.

The antilynching bill went first to the Senate Judiciary Committee, where it got a chilly reception. At the end of May, newspapers reported that every member of the committee, with the exception of California Senator Samuel Shortridge, considered the bill unconstitutional. As had happened when the House debated its lynching bill, racial violence erupted to challenge white Southerners' claims that lynching was fading away on its own. As the Judiciary Committee debated the finer points of constitutional law, lynching swept four states. Plummer Bernard Young, the *Norfolk Journal and Guide's* African American editor, wrote that a peculiar madness had seized the minds of masses of white men. A few days later, Young predicted that the Senate would reverse course after a white mob killed nineteen white miners in Herrin, Illinois. Young dryly observed that the lynching of white men would lead the white senators to change their tune on an antilynching bill. On June 30, Young's prediction seemed on the mark. Overcoming its earlier reservations, the Senate Judiciary Committee unexpectedly approved the bill.

However, the Herrin lynching had no impact on white Southerners in the Senate, and they prepared to block a vote by filibuster. As they readied their speeches, lynching continued, sometimes becoming so wanton it incensed even federal agents stationed in the South. After the Senate Judiciary Committee reported the bill, and while the NAACP and its allies desperately maneuvered to get it on the Senate floor for a vote, a Department of Justice agent in Florida documented the government's need for congressional action. Agent Leon Howe investigated a case involving an African American named Oscar Mack in Kissimmee, Florida. Mack had been awarded a government contract to deliver mail from a railroad station to the post office, beating out white competitors for the contract. Indirectly, he had become a federal employee. Nonetheless, white Floridians seemed determined that his federal connection would not exempt him from lynching. On July 16, a mob of angry whites converged on Mack's house and shot into it. A white assistant postmaster had anticipated the trouble and felt enough sympathy for Mack to give him a pistol. Mack used the postmaster's gun to fire back at the mob, killing two of the attackers. Whites were enraged that he had defended himself. In the days after July 16, whites combed the area around Kissimmee, searching for Mack. Two hundred black families fled the area. Howe wrote that, if the mob found Mack, there was no doubt he would be lynched.

Alarmed, Howe desperately tried to stop the lynching by wiring the postal inspector in Atlanta and meeting the U.S. Attorney, hoping to persuade some agency of the federal government to do something before the mob found Mack. He understood that Mack's only hope lay in a federal intervention; state officers routinely allowed mobs to execute black prisoners.

To prevent such an outcome for Mack, Howe frantically urged his superiors to contact state officials, thus alerting them that the federal government was watching their conduct. He pleaded for a federal investigation. "This case," he wrote, "appears to offer an opportunity to obtain Federal jurisdiction, as Mack was a government employee." Howe pressed so hard he felt he had to explain himself. "This agent holds no brief for negroes," he wrote, "but from my brief residence in Florida I am convinced that some federal action should be taken in such cases as these." No action occurred, and on July 19 Howe reported that the mob apparently found Mack and hanged him. "Case closed," he wrote on his final report. The Mack affair further illustrated the difficulty of counting lynchings. Newspapers did not report that any lynching had occurred, and Howe could not be certain that Mack had died. The black man simply disappeared into the Florida swamps.[7] Regardless of what ultimately happened to Mack, Howe's narrative, buried in the Department of Justice's filing system, made a powerful argument for congressional action against lynching in the face of the states' indifference to racial violence.

In December, five months after Howe closed the Mack case, the white Southern filibuster triumphed. Senate Republicans closed the book on their effort to pass Dyer's antilynching law when Henry Cabot Lodge, the senior senator from Massachusetts, a Republican with a history of supporting even the most controversial civil rights legislation for voting rights—the senator who should have been the bill's principal proponent—instead offered only limited support. He apparently feared losing white support if he backed a bill of questionable constitutionality that blacks passionately wanted but many white voters disliked. Rather than turning to Lodge, Republicans gave the bill to an inexperienced junior senator, Samuel Shortridge of California, who was quickly outmaneuvered by Mississippi's Pat Harrison. Once Harrison got control of the debate, he and his fellow Southerners could run the clock out with their seemingly endless speeches.

While the NAACP lost the Senate vote, it had educated politicians and the public on the need for reform, and the effort gave Johnson and White valuable lobbying experience. The NAACP perfected its skills at rallying the nation's black population behind its cause. In 1922, as the Dyer bill hung in the balance, one black newspaper reported that every African American church and organization in the country supported the bill. This was an important achievement for the NAACP and a tribute to the tireless work of Du Bois, Johnson, and White, who had made speeches, published articles and brochures, investigated lynchings, written letters, and organized petition drives.

For a time, though, it seemed this valuable expertise would lead to nothing further. Through the 1920s, the NAACP found it difficult to duplicate its effort as the political climate for civil rights legislation deteriorated. During this time, the NAACP found the limits of its political power when it campaigned against Republicans who had not energetically supported the Dyer bill and achieved only mixed results. Through the remainder of the decade the NAACP shifted its legislative priorities, de-emphasizing lynching.

Nevertheless, White remained doggedly committed to the fight against lynching. He still saw public opinion as the great prize and tried to mobilize increasingly powerful urban newspapers on behalf of the antilynching crusade. Recognizing that big-city papers and magazines reached larger and larger audiences, and wider geographic areas, White, like Wells and Work, saw an opportunity to pierce the localism that shielded lynchers from outside scrutiny. He understood that many whites harbored racist views, but he also understood that white toleration of lynching rested on the idea that locals had special insider knowledge and so knew best what was necessary. White wanted to nationalize lynching news to break down that localism.

White's greatest newspaper success came four years after the failure of the Dyer bill, on November 5, 1926, when the *New York World* launched a lengthy expose of a lynching in Aiken, South Carolina, as a result of his efforts. On April 25, 1926, a South Carolina sheriff and his deputies had gone to the home of Annie and Sam Lowman, an African American family, to investigate charges that the Lowmans were illegally selling whiskey. When the officers, traveling in an unmarked car and wearing no uniforms, failed to identify themselves, the Lowmans resisted, and the resulting gun battle killed Mrs. Lowman and the sheriff. Every surviving Lowman suffered gunshot injuries. The deputies arrested Sam Lowman as well as five younger members of his family, Clarence, Demon, Rosa, Birdie, and Bertha Lowman, for conspiracy to commit murder. A jury convicted Sam Lowman for possessing liquor, and the younger Lowmans went on trial in proceedings that the South Carolina Supreme Court later described as unfair and biased against them. The trial judge praised Henry H. Howard as the best sheriff in South Carolina and essentially apologized to the jury for the defense counsel, saying they had been appointed by the court and had no choice but to do their duty. After hearing the evidence, the judge directed the jury to acquit Rosa and Birdie Lowman, but sentenced Demon and Clarence to death by electrocution and Bertha to life in prison. In 1926, the Supreme Court of South Carolina heard an appeal and found that there was no proof of conspiracy and that the Lowmans had a right to defend their home against invasion by men who had not identified themselves as officers. The state supreme court's reversal of the convictions meant that Clarence, Demon, and Bertha Lowman would get a new trial.

In October, South Carolina authorities put the three on trial a second time. This trial never reached a verdict. The South Carolina Supreme Court's decision convinced some whites in the area that they could get the justice they wanted only outside the law, by lynching the Lowmans. Early in the morning of October 8, a mob entered the jail, seized the three prisoners from their cells, and took them out of town. In a pine thicket, the mob shot all three dead. Newspapers reported the news in brief stories on inside pages, hardly noticed and easily forgotten. Most newspaper editors apparently believed that killing guilty people outside the law, while not legal, was not a very serious crime. The victims of lynching had to be innocent for their lynchings to offend many whites.

White hoped to interest the *New York World* in printing more detailed accounts of the Lowman lynching. The paper had a long history of investigative reporting. In 1921, the *World* had depicted the Ku Klux Klan as a national fraud, fleecing its members of their dues behind a facade of "false romance and patriotic bombast."[8] Nonetheless, the paper's editors at first thought their initial news story sufficient and doubted there was anything more to say. To persuade the *World* to launch its own investigation, White needed something sensational, information suggesting that the lynching was more than a routine extralegal execution of criminals. At the end of October, White went to South Carolina, interviewed as many witnesses as he could find, and discovered that the Klan controlled the county and had organized and led the mob that killed the three Lowmans. White had investigated many such lynchings before, his goal always to get his information before a national audience. With the Lowman lynchings, he succeeded.

White lobbied the *New York World*, writing letters and using his research in South Carolina to persuade the editors they should launch their own investigation. At first reluctant, the paper finally bowed to White's pressure and sent its staff writer, Oliver H. P. Garrett, to Aiken. Garrett soon had dramatic news, reporting that he had been menaced by the Ku Klux Klan and threatened by the governor's investigator, who vowed to arrest him if he did not stop his inquiries. For nearly every day through the entire month of November, the *World* ran Garrett's articles, trumpeting shocking revelations. In his articles, Garrett followed White's lead, saying that local officials had collaborated with lynchers.

The *World* boasted that its reporting exposed to national viewing the kind of local violence outsiders usually overlooked or ignored. At one point the paper even ran a cartoon showing its coverage as a spotlight, cutting through the dark, illuminating lynching.[9] The articles stirred South Carolina's governor to order his own investigation. Garrett's stories reached beyond New York as magazines with national circulations commented on the articles. The *Nation* lauded the *World* series and thought the Lowman lynchings tested the sincerity of South Carolina's announced opposition to lynching. The magazine told its readers that, since the governor knew the identity of the lynchers, it would be interesting to see if he acted against them or did nothing, proving the need for a federal law against lynching. White's scheme to use the *World* to nationalize the story worked to perfection. The lynching of three African Americans in rural South Carolina was the sort of small incident that large urban newspapers like the *World* normally covered with a single, modest article often written by part-time reporters from the same neighborhood as the mob. The paper's series was very much a personal triumph for White.

White's investigative efforts won him the confidence of the NAACP board, and in 1930, after Johnson retired to assume a teaching position at Fisk University, White became the NAACP's executive secretary. He took over when the stock market crash of 1929 had plunged the nation into the Great Depression. Millions of Americans lost their jobs as businesses failed and factories shut down. The schoolteachers and other professionals that made up the core of the NAACP's membership found it difficult to continue their financial support, putting strains on the NAACP. Inside the NAACP, though, White wielded considerable power through the Great Depression. Under Johnson's competent leadership the NAACP's board had grown accustomed to deferring to the executive secretary. Johnson had made himself an important spokesman for black America; White picked up his mantle.

As White took charge of the NAACP, it faced a serious challenge from the American Communist Party (CP). Economic hard times led many Americans to look to communism as a reasonable alternative to capitalism, which the stock market crash and the Great Depression seemed to reveal as a failure. The CP championed a very broad definition of lynching, one that would have included almost any act of racial violence. Focused on class struggle, the CP recognized labor violence as lynching, something the NAACP was slow to do. In the 1930s, when white snipers shot black firemen out of the cabs of train locomotives in a labor dispute, the communists insisted that the shootings should be condemned as lynchings. Some black newspapers sided with the CP, the *Baltimore Afro-American* asking why such killings would not count as lynchings. The League of Struggle for Negro Rights, a communist organization, agreed, claiming that the NAACP soft-pedaled racial violence, actually seeking to deceive the black masses.

The NAACP's showdown with the communists came in 1931, after Alabama authorities arrested nine black youths for allegedly raping two white women on a train near Scottsboro. The nine black teens narrowly missed a lynching at the time of their arrests, and authorities tried to hustle them through hasty trials to quick executions. The communists rushed to intervene, claiming that a sham trial before a biased judge and jury amounted to a lynching even if the lynchers followed legal procedures. When the NAACP, miscalculating the incident's importance, did not forcefully intervene on behalf of the Scottsboro Nine, the CP's International Labor Defense (ILD) hired lawyers, staged speaking tours, and generally took full advantage of a case that became a national cause célèbre. As a result, the ILD reaped the benefits for fund-raising and recruitment of new members, while the NAACP faltered. After this setback, the NAACP needed an issue to revive itself. From that perspective, it made sense to refocus on lynching.

White also felt pressure from African Americans normally friendly to the NAACP. The Associated Negro Press urged that the meaning of lynching be broadened to include "any death to an individual or individuals inflicted by two or more privately-organized citizens, who impose such violence with correctional intent."[10] This definition reflected an increasing realization that racial violence not only persisted but increased. The number of lynchings did seem to go up in the Great Depression. In 1933, Robert S. Abbott, editor and founder of the Chicago Defender, announced his paper would launch its own national drive for a federal law against lynching.

The Defender opened its campaign in FDR's first year as president. Roosevelt promised dramatic action not only against the Great Depression but against crime as well. Nonetheless, during his first two terms as president, Roosevelt did little to end lynching. He told his wife and others that he feared losing the votes of white Southern congressmen, votes he desperately needed to pass the New Deal programs he believed essential to revive the economy and save the nation from poverty and starvation. Within a few months after Abbott began his campaign for a law against lynching, it was clear that Roosevelt intended to do little on the issue. Roosevelt's attorney general, Homer Cummings, announced a twelve-point program to increase federal authority in a fight against crime but conspicuously overlooked lynching. Some in the NAACP reacted to this "oversight" with revulsion; nonetheless, in the most general terms, Cummings had proposed what the NAACP wanted. He pointed out that local policing often fell victim to politics, something the NAACP had argued for years. National policing could be political too, of course, but Cummings promised that his agents would be more professional than local police. Black leaders recognized that his plans to expand federal power exactly fit with their ambitions. Since he seemed to be moving in roughly the right direction, toward more national policing, the NAACP hoped to persuade him to move against lynching in the future.

To encourage Cummings along those lines, opponents of lynching marshaled constitutional arguments. In 1933, after an Alabama mob had killed two African Americans and left another for dead, the NAACP's black lawyer Charles Hamilton Houston insisted that the federal government had jurisdiction. Houston, born in 1895, had served in World War I and returned determined to assert his rights. He wanted to use the law and the courts to correct social wrongs. At Howard University's Law School, he taught a generation of young black lawyers to use the Constitution as a weapon against racism. Houston and two colleagues wrote a forty-seven-page brief arguing that the federal government had the power necessary to protect ordinary people against lynching. They later toned down their rhetoric to better appeal to the white men running the Justice Department, but in some of their early drafts, Houston militantly demanded an expanded federal authority. "A Nation whose government can protect its citizens abroad, which can invade the sovereignty of a foreign Nation" should not fail its citizens "through a lack of official courage to enforce the written law," he said.[11]

Houston and his coauthors argued that the government could protect its citizens, based on the Fourteenth Amendment and Reconstruction-era civil rights laws. The Fourteenth Amendment's text seemed to protect citizens from unfair and discriminatory state action, not private action by ordinary people acting outside the law. "No state," the Fourteenth Amendment says, "shall . . . deny any person within its jurisdiction the equal protection of the laws." Such language did not promise equal rights to all, only protection against state misconduct. The Reconstruction Congresses authorized federal intervention when the states discriminated against blacks, but not when private individuals discriminated.

Congress had tried to outlaw private misconduct, as in 1871 when it passed the Ku Klux Klan Act making it a crime for two or more persons to disguise themselves to prevent another person or class of persons from enjoying constitutionally protected rights. The same law more closely followed the Fourteenth Amendment when it also specified that any person acting under state law or custom to deprive another person of their rights had committed a crime. But in a series of decisions starting in 1876, the Supreme

Court ruled that Congress could only use these laws against states, not against private persons. Members of lynch mobs discriminated against blacks in the most brutal way possible, denying their right to live by killing black people on the basis of their race, but they were private individuals. They acted with no authority from their state government at all. In fact, they violated state murder laws, although state authorities often did not enforce their murder laws when whites killed blacks. Houston nonetheless believed he had figured out a way for the federal government to prosecute lynchers under the Fourteenth Amendment. He argued that, when sheriffs assisted mobs by not protecting their prisoners, then the state had, in effect, discriminated in a way that allowed the federal government to invoke the Ku Klux Klan Act without violating the Fourteenth Amendment.

The Department of Justice took a dim view of Houston's argument, claiming that he had reached his conclusions but had not submitted any facts to support such conclusions. Houston and the government lawyers all agreed that a state government, rather than ordinary citizens, had to discriminate before the federal government could intervene. The disagreement came over who should do the initial investigating to determine if a state had discriminated. The Department of Justice insisted that Houston had to prove the state discrimination before it could act at all, even to make the most preliminary investigation to see if a state might have discriminated or not.

In 1934, Houston and the NAACP lawyers felt they had another chance at forcing the federal government to act against lynching. That year, lynchers had crossed state lines to take Claude Neal from his Alabama jail cell before taking him back to Florida for a grisly death. The NAACP thought that the crime clearly violated the federal antikidnapping law passed just months after famed aviator Charles Lindbergh's baby had been kidnapped and killed in 1932. The NAACP's Roy Wilkins compiled a plan of action within twenty-four hours of Neal's death that called for petitioning the president, members of Congress, and the press, and alerting the NAACP's network of branches. Since the lynchers had kidnapped Neal and carried him across a state line, Houston was convinced the Department of Justice should not wriggle out of its responsibilities. The NAACP consulted the leading legal minds of the nation, but in the end the Department of Justice refused to investigate the case, insisting the Lindbergh law only applied when the kidnappers demanded a ransom.

As White had pursued his campaign for a federal law against lynching, the nation's racial demographics had changed. Black Southerners had migrated North in large numbers, largely moving into the great Northern cities of New York, Detroit, and Chicago. As Southerners, these African Americans could not vote, but as Northern urbanites, they could and did. And as they voted, their preferences shifted dramatically, switching from the party of Lincoln to the Democrats, the party of Franklin Roosevelt.

Roosevelt's critics have long complained that he would not risk his white Southern political support by explicitly endorsing the antilynch law the NAACP supported. In 1934, two Democrats in the House of Representatives, Edward Costigan of Colorado and Robert Wagner from New York, introduced a new antilynching bill, one that followed the earlier Dyer bill as a model. White lobbied for the Costigan-Wagner bill, contacting Eleanor Roosevelt and lining up support inside and outside Congress. In 1934, White could not persuade Congress to bring the bill to a vote. In 1935, he tried again. Roosevelt worked behind the scenes, trying to persuade individual senators, but he never publicly endorsed the bill, and it failed again. White complained that Roosevelt's refusal to take a public position in favor of an antilynching law represented the greatest obstacle to getting a law passed.

Nonetheless, black migration to the North probably did influence Roosevelt, especially after his first two terms. The NAACP had a tradition of

Howard University students protesting the Roosevelt administration's failure to investigate lynchings in 1934. International News Photo Co. Courtesy of the Library of Congress.

Walter White, lobbying for a federal law against lynching in 1937. William Hastie, dean of Howard Law School; Walter White; Illinois Congressman Raymond McKeough; and Joseph Gavagan, congressman of New York City and an important NAACP ally in Congress. Courtesy of the Library of Congress.

nonpartisanship, but its sympathies so clearly lay with the Democrats that, by 1936, the organization found it nearly impossible not to take the Democratic side openly. NAACP board president Joel Spingarn endorsed Roosevelt in 1936. Nevertheless, the organization's support for Roosevelt did not lead to success as it continued its fight for a law against lynching. Every year the NAACP's allies in Congress proposed antilynching laws, and every year southern conservatives defeated those efforts.

Though unwilling to publicly take a stand in Congress, Roosevelt nonetheless did act against lynching. In 1939, under pressure from his new black constituents, and lobbied by his wife and White and urged on by labor leaders, Roosevelt replaced Attorney General Homer Cummings with Frank Murphy, the former governor of Michigan and mayor of Detroit. A civil liberties champion, Murphy promptly created the Civil Liberties Unit within the Department of Justice's criminal division. With the defeat of the antilynching law, it was clear that if Department of Justice wanted to promote civil liberties it would have to do so with existing legislation.

The NAACP took to the streets to press Congress for a federal law against lynching. Courtesy of the Library of Congress.

In addition to demands from his new black constituents, Roosevelt also responded to events overseas. War in Europe began in 1939, and the global emergency provided urgency for Roosevelt's efforts to increase federal power against lynching. Once World War II began, federal officials could now say, much as they had in World War I, that lynchers aided and abetted the nation's enemies. Axis propagandists made the most of American lynchings, the U.S. government pointed out, looking to the mobs as evidence that the Americans did not really believe in liberty and freedom for people of color. To prove that Americans did believe in their ideals, Civil Liberties Unit lawyers worked to convert Reconstruction-era enforcement laws into anti-lynching laws to satisfy black voters but also to negate Axis propaganda.

Lawyers in this new civil rights unit adopted, in broad outlines, the legal arguments Houston had advanced in 1933. To justify a federal prosecution, government investigators looked for evidence that state employees had discriminated against blacks by aiding lynch mobs. Based on the legal assumption that the federal government had the right to investigate those incidents, the Department of Justice probed every lynching in America in the 1940s. The NAACP believed their job would be made harder by the changing nature of lynching. In 1940, the organization published a pamphlet entitled "Lynching Goes Underground," arguing that violent white racists had learned to act secretly, killing by stealth rather than publicly, in great crowds. In the pamphlet, an anonymous white investigator said that "countless" blacks mysteriously disappeared every year, quietly and without general knowledge. Using techniques pioneered by Wells and White, the investigator provided detailed narratives of two "underground lynchings." In Mississippi, a large mob quietly killed Joe Rodgers after the laborer questioned a deduction from his paycheck. The mayor of Canton edited the local newspaper, the *Madison County Herald*, and could make sure his paper printed nothing about Rodgers's disappearance, or the subsequent discovery of his body. When local papers successfully suppressed news of a lynching, the larger newspapers almost never broke the story. Since the big urban papers depended on the local newspapers for their information about lynching, they rarely knew about the cases silenced by small-town editors. The investigator commented that the silence signaled the mayor's determination to hide the facts of the case from the public. The second underground lynching involved another Canton, Mississippi, mill worker, Claude Banks. After some person assaulted a white man, an assassin shot Banks for the crime. Once again, city authorities refused to acknowledge the incident. Lynching, the investigator concluded, had entered a new and dangerous phase. Sentiment had turned against lynching, and public opinion increasingly agitated for laws against lynching. Yet, the most determined white racists did not believe it was possible to maintain white superiority without violence. Lynching must continue. So, instead of a vast, howling mob, a few men gathered quietly to handle the work secretly.

Government lawyers sometimes referred to the NAACP as "our clients." One reason the Justice Department sided with the NAACP was that FBI agents and federal prosecutors saw themselves as more professional than corrupt, amateurish local cops all too often in league with the lynchers. Just as federal agent Leon Howe had been genuinely alarmed by the impending lynching of Oscar Mack in 1922, federal officers in the 1940s often expressed real determination to solve lynching cases, especially when they identified white Southern sheriffs as corrupt or incompetent. Federal lawmen generally saw themselves as more professional and capable than their local counterparts.

The Justice Department's first effort to prosecute a lynching came from a case in Missouri. In January 1942, a Sikeston, Missouri, mob killed Cleo

Wright after he assaulted a white woman. The Sikeston lynchers dragged Wright through the streets in a fifty-car, horn-honking convoy. The cheering crowd watched Wright burn, turning out of church and noonday meals for the show. Government lawyers tried to persuade a federal grand jury in Missouri that the Reconstruction laws justified the prosecution of the lynchers. The grand jurors heard the government's witnesses, listened to the lawyers' explanations of the law, and were not persuaded. They refused to indict even one member of the mob.

In October, Mississippi mobs hanged two teenagers named Ernest Green and Charles Lang, accused of attempted rape, and they hanged Howard Wash from a bridge trestle, after a jury convicted him of manslaughter rather than murder. In the Wash case, FBI agents gathered testimony identifying some of the killers. This time a grand jury returned indictments, and the case went to trial. Newspapers headlined the case as the first federal lynching trial in forty years. Lawyers for the defendants attacked the federal government for prosecuting the kind of crime usually handled in state court. The defense lawyers accused the federal authorities of trespassing on Mississippi sovereignty. Such arguments provided only a thin covering for whites' racism. In 1941, many Mississippi whites just did not believe whites should have to stand trial for killing a misbehaving black person. The trial jury refused to convict.

African Americans knew full well that white racism continued, and many doubted Roosevelt would sincerely fight lynching. In 1943, Harry McAlpin, chief of the *Chicago Defender*'s Washington Bureau, went to the Department of Justice and spent an hour interviewing an unnamed official, probably Victor Rotnem, head of the unit. McAlpin began the interview skeptical of the department. He believed the department only investigated cases reluctantly and only if forced to do so by groups like the NAACP and the American Civil Liberties Union (ACLU). In 1942, McAlpin's paper had reported the lynching of Green and Lang, and called the hope for a federal investigation almost hopeless. His interviewee flattered the journalist by sharing information not available for publication. He explained that the Department of Justice was like the army and the navy; it could not reveal its "work-in-progress" without tipping off the enemy. The department had fifty ongoing investigations in eighteen states. Not only that, but the department surprised McAlpin by telling him that the number of cases initiated by pressure groups amounted to only a drop in the bucket compared to the total. Most lynching investigations began with complaints filed by individuals, usually white Southerners. McAlpin thought the interview a revelation and announced that blacks really did have a champion in Washington. The *Defender* provided very positive coverage of the Department of Justice, describing its fight against lynching as uncompromising and even opening its columns to an article authored by Rotnem.

The *Chicago Defender* reported the department's greatest success prosecuting lynchers, following the case against Mack Claude Screws from the initial crime, in early 1943, to its finale at the Supreme Court. Screws, a Georgia sheriff, had arrested Robert Hall and then beaten him to death. Two officers assisted Screws, so the crime could be called a mob killing and not the act of an individual. The NAACP first publicized the murder as a lynching but then backed off at the request of the Roosevelt administration. Government lawyers told them they thought they had a real chance at getting a conviction, even though the trial would be held in Georgia, with an all-white jury. White jurors, the government explained, would be more likely to convict if the case seemed ordinary and not a cause célèbre championed by a civil rights organization hated by many white Southerners. Lynchings attracted national attention; ordinary beatings did not. The NAACP cooperated and stopped calling the incident a lynching. Federal prosecutors pressed the case at trial, and an all-white Georgia jury convicted Screws and his cohorts. The three men then appealed their conviction to the Supreme Court, arguing that the Department of Justice had no jurisdiction to try an ordinary homicide case.

The Supreme Court in 1944 consisted of eight justices appointed by Franklin Roosevelt plus Owen Roberts, a conservative Republican selected by Herbert Hoover in 1930. Roosevelt had an uneven record with his appointments. Some, like Hugo Black, Wiley Rutledge, Frank Murphy, and William O. Douglas, championed civil rights. But Roosevelt also appointed Robert Jackson and Stanley Reed, two men less committed to civil rights for African Americans. By 1944, the chief justice, Harlan Stone, had proven himself a poor administrator and seemed unable to lead his colleagues in any particular direction. Under Stone's leadership, the Supreme Court split into rival factions and quarreled bitterly over sometimes-trivial issues. Roosevelt had created a badly divided Court.

This factionalism was evident in *Screws et al. v. United States.* As they deliberated their decision, the justices divided so sharply that for some weeks it looked like neither side could get the five votes necessary to resolve the case. In their secret deliberations, the justices recognized that, if they approved the prosecution they would, in effect, be passing an antilynching law, something Congress had refused to do. Ultimately, the Supreme Court overturned the convictions but agreed that the government could prosecute lynchers under the Reconstruction-era Ku Klux Klan Act making it a crime to take away another person's constitutional rights under color of state law. But the justices decided that prosecutors would have to scale an almost insurmountable hurdle, proving that the lynchers intended to deny their victims specific civil rights such as the right to vote or the right to due process of law. Judges would have to instruct jurors about this almost impossibly high standard of proof before they began their deliberations.

In a sense, then, the NAACP had finally achieved its goal of federal intervention against lynching. It failed to convince Congress to pass a new law, but it succeeded in persuading the Department of Justice to use existing law against mob violence. The Supreme Court put severe restrictions on the use of the Klan Act, but black America had successfully prompted a federal prosecution of lynchers. As blacks and other opponents of lynching scored modest gains on that front, white racists had already begun to shift tactics, finding new and more terrifying ways to continue their racist violence.

At the same time, there were signs of the violent black resistance Fortune had predicted. In 1955, army veteran Robert F. Williams (1925–1996) joined the NAACP chapter in Monroe, North Carolina, an organization rapidly shrinking in the face of white violence. Dynamite blasts were common around Monroe, and the Ku Klux Klan grew in size and force. Within months, Williams had become chapter president and recruited new members who agreed with him that white violence must be met with black violence, a policy not endorsed by the NAACP. Lynching must be met with lynching, Williams told reporters in 1959. Blacks needed guns, he said, because the Fourteenth Amendment did not exist in Monroe, North Carolina. Martin Luther King's program of nonviolence, Williams said, was "bullshit." In 1961, Williams fled the United States for Cuba, where he operated a radio station, Radio Free Dixie, calling for the overthrow of the U.S. government.

Notes

1. William English Walling, "The Race War in the North," *Independent* 65 (September 3, 1908): 529–34.

2. "Race Riot in the Bronx," *New York Times*, August 16, 1903.

3. "Negroes for Hughes and Hiss Roosevelt," *New York Times*, March 27, 1908.

4. James Weldon Johnson, *Along This Way: The Autobiography of James Weldon Johnson* (New York: Viking, 1933), 166–69.

5. Walter White, *A Man Called White: The Autobiography of Walter White* (New York: Viking, 1948), 11.

6. *Valdosta Times*, quoted in "Lowndes County's Answer," *Augusta Chronicle*, May 26, 1918.

7. Leon B. Howe, reports from Tampa, July 18 and 19, 1922, file 144–10, section 1, serials 1–32, box 10, RG 65, Records of the Federal Bureau of Investigation, Classification 44, FBI Headquarters Files, National Archives, College Park.

8. "Ku Klux Klan's Invisible Empire of Hate Scored by Army Officer who Abandons It; Department of Justice to Make Inquiry," *New York World*, September 7, 1921.

9. The series began on November 5, 1926, see Oliver H. P. Garrett, "Sheriff is Accused of Complicity with the Lynchers of 3," *New York World*, November 5, 1926.

10. Christopher Waldrep, *The Many Faces of Judge Lynch: Extralegal Violence and Punishment in America* (New York: Palgrave Macmillan, 2002), 136.

11. There are numerous undated drafts of the brief in box 163–25, Charles H. Houston Papers, Manuscript Division, Moorland-Spingarn Research Center, Howard University, Washington, D.C.; "Memorandum for the Assistant to the Attorney General," August 30, 1933, file 158260, Department of Justice Central Files, National Archives, College Park; Roger A. Fairfax Jr., "Wielding the Double-Edged Sword: Charles Hamilton Houston and Judicial Activism in the Age of Legal Realism," *Harvard Blackletter Journal* 14 (Spring 1998): 17–44.

CHAPTER FIVE

~

Facing Dynamite

In the twentieth century, violent white racists turned to terrifying new technologies, substituting dynamite for the rope, allowing lynching to take new forms toward familiar goals. Both the purveyors of violence and their victims lost confidence in the government's ability to solve their problems and protect their rights. In a sense, such doubts about the state may have been inevitable. White and black Americans had competing expectations for government: many whites wanted it to protect their property, their racial privileges, and the racial purity of their neighborhoods, while African Americans grasped the founding documents as tools to establish equal rights. Through the twentieth century, these contradictory notions of the state, one conservative and one dynamic, repeatedly clashed, each side invoking the law to accomplish its goals. And both sides lost confidence in government at about the same time.

Bombing became a social and cultural force in the twentieth century. Both world wars involved extensive bombing, but organized crime and social protest by the Left made the dynamite bomb a fact of life in American cities well before the first soldier fell on a European battlefield. The prevalence of dynamite in the culture led lynchers to its use as well. Demographic change also promoted new forms of lynching. Nineteenth-century lynching had been primarily a rural phenomenon, but in the twentieth century, large numbers of blacks migrated into cities. As blacks urbanized, so did the violence against them, both in the North and the South. Bombings in Northern cities became common as blacks moved into previously white neighborhoods.

None of these cultural changes fundamentally altered the nature of white violence or its basic intent to terrorize its victims.

The black population in Southern cities like Birmingham and Miami increased dramatically during and after World War II, and it was a population prepared to buy property. Two federal agencies, the Federal Housing Administration and the Veterans Administration, both financed mortgages that increased the demand for black homes. The cities used racial covenants as a legal defense against black expansion into white neighborhoods. Racial covenants were legal agreements white homeowners signed, pledging not to sell their property to blacks, keeping neighborhoods all white. State governments enforced these contracts.

When local government tried to use its power to protect white neighborhoods, it ran into an expanding black population it could not contain, further demonstrating the limits of governmental power in achieving whites' goals. In Birmingham, Alabama, whites zoned blacks into flood-prone neighborhoods, often near heavy industry. The black population expanded from 108,938 in 1940 to 130,025 in 1950. Yet, the city zoned no new land for blacks to occupy. The burgeoning African American population had to press outward. The most contentious space lay along the frontier between Smithfield, a black neighborhood, and Graymont, a heavily populated white area.

Local government efforts on behalf of whites ran afoul of Roosevelt-appointed judge Clarence Mullins, of the U.S. District Court for the Northern District of Alabama, who was increasingly determined to enforce constitutional principle against narrow prejudice. Little in Mullins's past distinguished him from any other white Alabama lawyer or jurist. Born in Clanton, Alabama, in 1895, Mullins practiced law for years with little distinction or notice other than the time he represented an outfielder for the New York Yankees in a 1928 divorce case. Once he became a district judge, though, Mullins began ruling in favor of civil rights and against local discrimination. The first case he ruled on came in 1946, when the Birmingham Housing Authority evicted some black tenants from its housing projects in Smithfield because the families' incomes were too high to qualify. In the tight housing market, those families had no place to go within existing black areas. In August, the National Association for the Advancement of Colored People (NAACP) tried to relieve the pressure by filing a lawsuit attacking Birmingham's racial zoning laws. Although the Supreme Court had ruled in favor of zoning in 1926, it had also outlawed city ordinances requiring residential segregation. Judge Mullins saw the law as clearly on the side of the plaintiffs. In October, he declared racial zoning unconstitutional in nearby Tarrant City, signaling he would do the same in Birmingham at the next opportunity. Even the potential of a ruling against white privilege sparked violence. The Ku Klux Klan bombed black homes around the white neighborhood of North Smithfield so often that it earned the nickname Dynamite Hill.

The failure of local government to protect white interests accelerated vigilantism, but blacks still pressed for enforcement of the constitutional principle of equal rights. In January 1947, the Klan sent warning letters to NAACP officers, demanding that the lawsuits be withdrawn. Arthur Shores, the black attorney pursuing the lawsuits and the target of the Klan's threats, saw the law and the Constitution as blacks' salvation. He worked his way through law school so he could represent the victims of police brutality and fight for the right to vote in court. In the 1940s, Shores regularly worked for the NAACP, representing teachers in lawsuits demanding equal pay with white teachers. To become more expert in constitutional law, he went to Howard University and studied with Charles Houston.

The authorities' reaction to white violence confirmed Shores's determination to use law against racism. In 1947, a crowd of taxi drivers killed a black man in Greenville, South Carolina, after he had allegedly killed a taxi driver. The FBI launched a major investigation, identifying thirty-one lynchers. The state of South Carolina seemed eager to put the men on trial, even hiring a special prosecutor to make a conviction more likely. Big-city journalists descended on Greenville to cover the trial, including Rebecca West, writing for the *New Yorker*. In the end, the jury refused to convict any of the taxi drivers, even though almost all had confessed to the FBI. Still, the incident seemed a milestone in the history of racial lawlessness. The FBI and South Carolina police had taken the affair seriously, carrying out a credible investigation. Major newspapers had sent their own reporters to cover the trial, rather than simply passing over the affair in a paragraph or two, as had been common only a few years before. The law had not been vindicated, but it had been a near thing. For lawyers like Shores, and many other observers as well, it seemed as though America was making progress, moving toward law and away from lawlessness.

Shores had such confidence in law and the Constitution that, even when faced with Ku Klux Klan threats, he refused to back down and continued with a suit he had filed on behalf of Samuel Matthews. Matthews had actually built his house thinking he was in an area zoned for blacks, discovering his mistake only when Birmingham building inspectors told him he had built just inside the white area and denied him an occupancy permit. On August 4, Mullins ordered building inspectors to grant Matthews the permit. Shores knew the Supreme Court had already ruled against segregated zoning. He was not surprised when the district court ruled against Birmingham; the decision was not even a close call. Nonetheless, it shocked whites. Stripped of their legal protections, whites turned anew to the Ku Klux Klan.

The collapse of white confidence in using the law and legal institutions to defend segregation became apparent on August 18, 1947, when the Klan's bombing campaign in defense of Birmingham's segregated housing began. Bombers wrecked Matthews's home. Even in the face of such violence, an African American homeowner named Mary Means Monk demanded that blacks be allowed to settle in neighborhoods whites had abandoned. Whites would not even allow that, and Monk filed suit, with Shores as her lawyer. When a circuit judge rejected Shores's petition, he filed a class-action suit in federal court. In 1948, before Shores's case could go to trial, the Supreme Court struck another blow against whites' hopes that they could use the law to keep their neighborhoods segregated. The Court ruled racial covenants unconstitutional. When Southern cities still tried to enforce segregation, district courts declared their ordinances unconstitutional. Such rulings convinced some whites that violence was the only way to protect their all-white neighborhoods. In Birmingham, the city spurned Supreme Court rulings and failed to arrest the bombers of new black homeowners, an approach that helped convince many ordinary whites that they could resist black "aggression" by flouting the law.

In December 1949, the Monk case went to trial. After hearing the evidence, the judge issued a ruling from the bench, once again disallowing the segregation. For whites, this meant the bombing campaign had to continue. In 1949, bombers destroyed three unoccupied houses on Birmingham's Eleventh Avenue. A few months later, bombers targeted two black ministers. In 1950, bombers dynamited the partly constructed home of a black dentist and the home of Benjamin Wells Henderson, located near a white neighborhood. In December, bombers blasted Mary Means Monk's home. Shores commented to an interviewer years later that he had never seen a building so thoroughly wrecked by dynamite.

Blacks had no more confidence in local government than whites and accused the Birmingham police of assisting the bombers, a not implausible theory. After the Eleventh Avenue bombings in 1949, some in Birmingham said that a marked Birmingham Police Department cruiser had been sitting in a nearby intersection, acting as a lookout or guard for the bombers. Such rumors seemed credible largely because Eugene Connor (1897–1973) was police commissioner. Connor had gained power by promising to defend segregation, and he did so, flamboyantly. He once had his officers invade a convention attended by Eleanor Roosevelt to force delegates to separate by race. Connor instituted the practice of placing boards in city buses, demarcating white and black seating.

Ku Klux Klan bombers struck Arthur Shores's own home. Courtesy of the Library of Congress.

Some whites used blacks' accusations of a conspiracy between the Klan and the police as an opportunity to test their theory that anyone believing in natural law rights must be a communist. The Birmingham Police Department reacted to rumors they conspired with the Ku Klux Klan to maintain residential segregation by tracking down the rumor to a black high school teacher named Augustus A. Ward. They reported that Ward's wife was a dues-paying member of a communist front organization. This confirmed what many whites "knew"—that communists instituted black "invasions" of white neighborhoods. Based on criticism of the police department, and his own investigations, a police detective concluded that the Eleventh Avenue bombings were actually part of a well-planned and cleverly executed program by the Communist Party, hoping to stir up bloodshed and violence. The blacks moving into the housing, the police believed, were only communist pawns.

Faced with a completely hostile local government and no concrete assistance from federal government, black Birminghamians began seeking protection for themselves outside the law. By the summer of 1949, they had organized a neighborhood watch to substitute for the protection Birmingham's police refused to provide. The blacks hired a white private detective to infiltrate the Klan, and the detective learned when and where the Klan planned its next bombing. When bombers rolled by the home of the two black ministers, tossing their bombs as they passed, armed blacks guarding the houses answered with gunfire. One African American, Benjamin Wells Henderson, sat in his car on the darkened street and trailed the bombers' car. Resenting the blacks' self-defense efforts, the police harassed and arrested Henderson and not the bombers. Police released him only after a rigorous interview followed by a lie detector test.

Throughout 1949 and 1950, the police pursued an increasingly lawless course of their own. Birmingham Police "investigated" the bombings by arresting the black victims rather than finding the white bombers. In their 1950 investigation, although it was clear that the bombing was the work of white racists, the police nonetheless picked up a black construction worker with dynamite in his truck. The detective acknowledged later that the black man had no connection with the crime but said he "fooled" with him anyway and then jailed him for vagrancy. By "fooled" the policeman meant that he hassled him with questions and abuse.[1] By the time Connor left office in 1953, his police department had a well-earned reputation for corruption. (He was reelected in 1956.)

As Southern police increasingly substituted their own violence for that of the lynch mob, black intellectuals rallied around the teachings of Mahatma Gandhi (1869–1948), seeking a way outside the law to protect their rights. Gandhi's struggle against British colonialism, first in South Africa and then in India, in the 1910s, 1920s, and 1930s, attracted the attention of blacks at Howard University and elsewhere as a method of fighting racial oppression outside institutions. Indians faced discrimination from the British similar to that suffered by African Americans: segregation, denial of the vote, and violence. Gandhi organized poor farmers and laborers against the British in a nonviolent campaign that did not depend on the law of constitutional principle and nonetheless proved spectacularly successful. In 1917, the African American orator and philosopher Hubert Henry Harrison had urged black Americans to follow Gandhian principles. Disenchantment with World War I accelerated interest in Gandhi's pacifist teachings. Two years after Harrison's call, W. E. B. Du Bois had written that black Americans should identify with India's struggle against England. "We are all one—we the Despised and the Oppressed, the 'niggers' of England and America."[2] African American intellectuals made personal contact with Gandhi. Howard Thurman, a professor in Howard University's School of Religion, traveled to India in 1935, meeting Gandhi. Three years later the civil rights leader James Farmer went to Howard University where his mentor, Thurman, introduced him to Gandhi's ideas.

Gandhi taught satyagraha, an aggressive form of active pacifism that focused on natural rights rather than statutory or constitutional rights. Satyagraha encouraged direct action and asked the people to take the law in their own hands. It promoted both a turning inward to an intense self-discipline and belief in universal values. Disciplined nonviolent protesters voluntarily and patiently accepting suffering in the name of their cause could soften the oppressor's heart, promoting a feeling of kinship with the sufferer. Nonviolent protest is supposed to suggest human unity at a level above the state and law. Law relies on compulsion, intimidation, and violence; satyagraha relies on love. Satyagraha was a program as well as a methodology, a long campaign of carefully planned steps including demonstrations, picketing, and sit-down strikes structured to challenge the government with the power of the people.

Martin Luther King Jr. discovered Gandhi through Mordecai Johnson, president of Howard University. By 1951, Gandhi's message had spread so far beyond Howard that Andrew Young, a middle-class African American youth living in New Orleans, encountered them at a church camp in rural Indiana. Reading a book on Gandhi by Jawaharlal Nehru, Young became increasingly excited, realizing that his methods could work in the American South. He called his encounter with Gandhi a life-changing experience. At the same time black leaders discovered Gandhi, black churches in every Southern city were gathering strength. Black migration from rural areas to the cities enlarged their congregations. Urban churches developed powerful financial resources, allowing them to offer better salaries to their ministers, converting them into full-time pastors. The most successful ministers learned the value of performance and charisma and built their organizational skills. Churches began offering more programs and activities, opportunities for fellowship and community awareness, and networking. Independent of white economic power, black churches in Birmingham and elsewhere emerged as powerfully autonomous organizations dedicated to human rights.

The demand for rights that simmered in church basements and sanctuaries followed a different road than the law-based strategy the NAACP favored. Some NAACP leaders, though, could be every bit as politically aggressive and assertive as their rivals. In Florida, NAACP leader Harry T. Moore represented a new generation of leadership, one committed to voter registration and political activism over lawyerly courtroom appeals. For that reason, Moore frequently quarreled with the NAACP leadership in New York, still dedicated to law. Moore attracted white hatred just as much as Shores because he effectively rallied black political power. In January 1950, he vowed to register 250,000 blacks to vote in Florida. He never met that goal, but in five months he had 31 percent of eligible black voters registered to vote, a better percentage than any other Southern state. By November, 51 percent of eligible black voters had registered in Brevard County, where Moore supported a challenger to the political boss. When the challenger won, the county leaders blamed Moore and black activism for their defeat. Moore also upset whites by agitating on behalf of the "Groveland boys," three young men convicted of raping a white woman. Moore protested that the young men had not received a fair trial, and the U.S. Supreme Court agreed, reversing two of the convictions and ordering new trials. However, the sheriff shot the two young men while transporting them to their new trial, claiming they tried to escape, although chained together. One man died, and from his hospital bed the survivor told reporters there had been no escape attempt. Moore demanded an investigation and called for the sheriff's ouster.

Whites reacted to Moore's political approach much as they had to Shores's lawyering. What led white racists to the bomb rather than the rope in Florida can best be explained by an increasing tendency toward bombing in the Sunshine State. The first Florida bombings began in March 1951, when bombers attacked two schools and a hotel, violence that seemed unconnected with Moore's civil rights work. In June, bombers targeted the Northside Jewish Center. The state fire marshal blamed the bombings on a gang of youths. By the end of 1951, the bombers switched their focus to African Americans. Since the bombers struck Jewish and black targets, Jews and blacks forged an alliance to fight the violence.

As in Birmingham, black demands for additional housing, threatening all-white neighborhoods, sparked the violence. In Miami, the "Negro district" lay in the northwest part of the city, a 284-acre tract packed with sixty thousand residents. Every effort to expand this tract to relieve the crowding met violent resistance from whites. African Americans finally got their opportunity to break out in 1951, when James A. Bonvier Jr. and Malcolm Wisehart opened Carver Village, a rental housing development, to black tenants. Located north of Sixty-seventh Street and extending from Seventh Avenue to Twelfth Avenue, Carver Village comprised fifty acres, previously a white slum area. Property south of Carver Village had been settled by white residents, property on the west side occupied by black residents. A large federal housing project intended for black occupation had been developed to the southwest of Twelfth Avenue in the immediate vicinity. Property on the north side remained partly undeveloped and partly developed by whites. Whites organized as the Edison Center Civil Association strenuously objected to Carver Village. Some whites began a bombing campaign there.

African Americans living in Carver Village were not yet ready to protest openly; most likely, they calculated that such an approach would be suicidal. Desperately needing help, they looked to the federal government, which meant convincing authorities that local whites had attacked their rights under the U.S. Constitution. The FBI had long been reluctant to intervene in civil rights matters. The NAACP had often asked the bureau to direct its considerable resources against lynching. As the FBI considered how to respond to this new request, the bombings seemed to stop. In this initial quiet, FBI Director J. Edgar Hoover eagerly concluded that, because there had been no serious trouble, local police protection had been adequate. The quiet did not fool Wisehart and Bonvier, who had more to lose than Hoover, and, still worried that the white protest would become more militant, they asked the FBI to intervene. Already, blacks had received threats that they would lose their jobs if they did not give up their rentals. The FBI wanted no part of the trouble. Its agents explained that the federal government had no jurisdiction so long as officers of the state played no direct role in the violence.

Local government had no more enthusiasm for arresting the bombers than the FBI. Miami's white elite tried to evade the problem. First, on September 19, 1951, Miami's city commission voted four to one to acquire Carver Village for municipal purposes and convert the property to nonresidential uses. The city commissioners' "solution" did not satisfy the racists. Three days later, at 2:15 a.m., two bombs exploded on the west side of the building located at the corner of Northwest Tenth Court and Sixty-ninth Street. Residents found a third bomb consisting of eighty sticks of 40 percent dynamite unexploded at a third spot, on the same side of the building. Police estimated the damage at two hundred thousand dollars, but the bombers had been careful to strike at an unoccupied building, and no injuries occurred. The Miami city government proposed to avoid trouble by forcibly evacuating black residents from Carver Village. Miami's city attorney asked the federal government if it would object to the evacuation, pleading that the bombings had created an emergency situation. The Department of Justice advised that the black tenants had a constitutional right under federal law to live in the apartments if they wanted to do so. Such rights under the Constitution cannot be abrogated by any kind of emergency, the department advised Miami's attorney.

While the Department of Justice issued pronouncements that Miami could not force blacks from their homes, it nonetheless rejected calls from people in Miami that it actively protect African Americans' constitutional rights. More bombings led the nervous owners of Carver Village, Bonvier and Wisehart, to renew their calls for federal intervention. Trying a new tactic, the two landlords urged that, since a federal agency, the Federal Housing Administration, had acquired title to the first mortgage on the property, the federal government might take jurisdiction to protect its financial interests. The Department of Justice easily brushed aside that claim. Pushing the right buttons, Miami Chief of Police Walter Headley blamed the explosions on a communist plot to incite racial hatred. Federal officers understood full well that white Southerners reflexively blamed black protest on the Communist Party, but the FBI had almost a hypersensitivity to the communist conspiracy and saw fighting communism as its job. The FBI did not expect or want the Miami Police Department to combat the worldwide communist conspiracy on its own. Nonetheless, while it took the communism angle more seriously than the effort by Bonvier and Wisehart to invoke the Federal Housing Administration, the FBI rebuffed this gambit as well. The bureau's confidential informants inside the Communist Party revealed that the party had become too disorganized in Florida to pull off anything like what the local police alleged.

Despite press reports in Miami's leading white newspapers of an all-out drive to smash local terrorism, blacks' hopes for federal action initially achieved only slight results. Once his superiors in the Department of Justice ordered him to investigate, Hoover reacted with characteristic speed, but his initial response consisted primarily of revising previous memoranda to add some new detail to them. Pointedly, Hoover asked the attorney general if anyone had complained that local law enforcement conspired with the bombers. Hoover understood fully that any justification for a federal investigation would have to be based on the Fourteenth Amendment, which forbade biased state action, not misconduct by individuals like youth gangs or the Ku Klux Klan. By asking if there had been a complaint that state officers had conspired in the bombings, he implicitly reminded his superiors of this point and suggested the FBI might not have any jurisdiction.

The FBI's attitude changed on Christmas night in 1951, when a bomb outside Mims, Florida, blasted Harry T. Moore and his wife through their bedroom ceiling. Members of the Ku Klux Klan had crawled under Moore's house and put their explosive charge directly under his bed. Both Moore and his wife ultimately died of their injuries. To this day, no one knows which Klansman set the bombs, but the Klan clearly responded to Moore's civil rights activities. In an earlier day, a mob would have hanged Moore from a tree, but in 1951 Moore threatened white power at a time when white racists had made bombing the new lynching, especially in and around Miami. By making himself the symbol of black resistance, Moore became a target, but because he did his work in 1950 and 1951, Moore became one more casualty of the bombers.

While bombing unoccupied buildings in Carver Village left Hoover uncertain about federal jurisdiction against the Florida bombers, the sensational dynamite lynching of Moore resolved all doubts. The FBI launched a massive, all-out effort to capture the killers. One sign of the government's seriousness came in March 1952, when the FBI received permission to carry out "technical surveillance" against Florida Klansmen, tapping their telephones. The bureau recruited confidential informants and interviewed anyone with knowledge of Moore's floorplan. The best clue in the case seemed to be that the bombers had known exactly where to place the bomb so that it would be right under Moore's bed.

Black efforts to stir the FBI into action took greater effect in September, when the FBI recruited a confidential informant claiming to know the names of the Ku Klux Klansmen responsible for the Carver Village bombings. Lawyers in the Department of Justice decided to focus on Klansmen who had filled out applications for government employment. Several of the Klansmen worked for the post office and other government agencies and, when applying for their jobs, had lied on their application forms. The applications asked, "Are you now or have you ever been a member of any organization which appears on the Attorney General's subversive list?" and "Are you now or have you ever been a member of any organization which advocates and practices the suppression of the rights of others by force and violence?" It is possible that the Klansmen did not know the Ku Klux Klan was on the attorney general's list of subversive organizations. It is also possible, unlikely but at least possible, that some members of the Ku Klux Klan saw themselves as protecting their own rights, not taking away the rights of others. Empathy was not strong in the Klan. Nevertheless, lawyers in the Department of Justice believed the statements the Klansmen made on these forms would allow prosecution in federal court.

On October 6, 1952, Florida blacks watched as a federal grand jury convened to investigate the bombings. By going to a grand jury, Department of Justice lawyers hoped to shake loose evidence the FBI had not yet been able to uncover. The proceedings may also have been a "perjury trap," designed to tempt members of the Ku Klux Klan into lying. If that was the plan, it worked. On May 28, 1953, the grand jury indicted William Orwick, Harvey De Rosier, William Bogar, Harvey Reisner, T. J. McMennany, Robert Judah, Emmet M. Hart, Helen Russell, and Arthur Udgreen for giving false testimony concerning their knowledge and participation in various acts of violence in central Florida. In October, the government took De Rosier to trial.

He was convicted in part due to the testimony of an undercover agent working for the FBI. The district judge sentenced De Rosier to a ninety-day prison term, and he subsequently lost again on appeal. After its success prosecuting De Rosier, the Department of Justice hoped to proceed against the remaining defendants, but the U.S. district judge dismissed the indictments. The judge offered almost no explanation for his action, and the department considered an appeal but finally decided to let the cases go. Ultimately, the question would come down to whether the prosecution of the Klansmen represented an unwarranted intrusion into matters of purely state concern. The Department of Justice hesitated to get into a fight over that question before the Fifth Circuit, a court that often seemed biased in favor of states' rights.

As the federal prosecutions stalled and then failed in a Florida courtroom, an effort to use Gandhi-style extralegal tactics took shape in Louisiana and across the South. In June 1953, Baton Rouge, Louisiana, black church leaders organized a mass protest against segregated bus transportation. Boycott leaders compromised with whites but emerged from the protest claiming at least a limited victory. Such successes, however limited, alarmed white Southerners and encouraged black organizing. In Mississippi, Aaron Henry established the Clarksdale NAACP branch the same year as the Baton Rouge boycott. Elsewhere in the state, Amzie Moore organized the Cleveland branch, and Clinton C. Battle formed a chapter in Indianola. A year later, Medgar Evers became the NAACP's Mississippi field secretary.

In 1954, the most famous attempt to protect rights through law reached its climax at the U.S. Supreme Court with the great case of *Brown v. Board of Education*. Led by Thurgood Marshall, the NAACP won its case, prompting the Supreme Court to denounce the segregation whites once expected government to protect. The NAACP's success against segregated schools set off a wave of violence. Recent scholarship has suggested that *Brown* did more to unleash racist violence than to desegregate the schools. In August 1955, after *Brown*, Eldon Edwards launched the U.S. Klans, Knights of the Ku Klux Klan, Inc. From the first of January 1955 to the first of January 1959, the eleven states of the old Confederacy experienced 210 recorded acts of racial violence. This included six murders and twenty-nine assaults. Bombs exploded in six schools, seven churches, seven Jewish temples, a YWCA, and an auditorium.

The most notorious act of racial violence in the aftermath of *Brown v. Board of Education* came in Mississippi. Emmett Louis Till was born near Chicago in 1941, four years before his father died in World War II. In 1924, Emmett Till's mother, Mamie Till, had come to Chicago from Tallahatchie County, Mississippi, part of the great stream of Mississippi blacks who migrated North. In the summer of 1955, Mamie sent her son back to Talla-hatchie County to spend time with his cousins and his uncle, Moses Wright. On the evening of August 24, Emmett Till and his cousins drove to Money, a tiny cluster of stores in Leflore County, where a white World War II veteran named Roy Bryant operated a small business. His young wife Carolyn man-aged the store when her husband was away. On August 24, Roy Bryant was hauling shrimp to Texas.

A risk taker who loved to be at the center of attention, Emmett Till en-tered the Bryants' store to buy two cents' worth of bubble gum. Some wit-nesses said that Till wolf-whistled Carolyn as he left the store or that he just said "Bye baby." Almost every narrative of the Till affair omits Carolyn Bryant's version of her confrontation with Till, but she did testify in court about what happened. She said she had held her hand out to take Till's money for his purchase but that, instead of giving her the money, he had grabbed and squeezed her hand and said, "How about a date, baby?" When she recoiled, Till blocked her path and held her waist, saying, "Don't be afraid of me, baby. I ain't gonna hurt you. I been with white girls before." Bryant said in court that Till had badly frightened her but that she knew what to do in the face of such insolence. She went to her car to get her gun. Outside the store, she saw Till again. This time he whistled at her. Till's mother was not present during her son's encounter with Bryant, but she ques-tioned family members who were present. One of Emmett Till's cousins told her that her son made the whistling noise only because of a speech impedi-ment. "Emmett made that whistling sound when he got stuck on a word." Another cousin said he did whistle at Bryant but did so only as a joke, "to be playful." They did agree with Bryant on one point. They saw her go get her gun. That was when they ran away.[3]

At first nothing happened. Carolyn Bryant confided in her friend Juanita Milam, and the two women decided to keep the incident to themselves. Among African Americans, the incident became a matter of gossip and con-versation. Roy Bryant learned of the exchange between his wife and Emmett Till from local blacks. Bryant was a marginal character in Leflore County, barely one step removed from poverty. For blacks to gossip about a black youth getting away with taking a liberty with his wife was intolerable. Not only his pride but also his standing among his fellow whites, and blacks, was at stake. On August 27, Bryant joined his half-brother, Juanita's husband, John W. Milam. "Big" Milam was also a combat veteran of World War II, one who prided himself on his ability to control blacks. He had a .45 pistol.

According to their own confession to a journalist after they had been ac-quitted, the two men went to Moses Wright's house after dark, where they knew Emmett Till was sleeping with his cousins. Milam and Bryant may have been accompanied by Carolyn Bryant, and by black men acting as helpers, or perhaps other white men. By their own account, the two white men kidnapped Till from Wright's home, pistol-whipped him, and threatened to throw him off a cliff. As Milam and Bryant told the story later, Till would not back down and instead spoke insultingly to them. Milam shot him, and the pair dumped his body in the Tallahatchie River, tied to an old cotton-gin fan.

The two lynchers, for the nation immediately identified them as such over the protests of many Mississippi whites, including the state's governor, did not conceal their identity when they went to Moses Wright's home. Authorities arrested the pair and put them on trial for murder. News media from across the nation descended on the Mississippi courthouse in Sumner. For many Northerners, the trial of Milam and Bryant exposed the underside of Mississippi racism. Northern journalists encountered tobacco-chewing bigots in a segregated courtroom. For many, the scene looked like an artifact from a bygone era. The incident, though little different from thousands of similar incidents that received little attention, came to symbolize racial violence and lynching. Very likely, had the Supreme Court not drawn attention to the issue of white racism with its *Brown v. Board of Education* decision, the Emmett Till killing would have disappeared from view, one more underground lynching overlooked by the press. The black press covered the trial in detail, photographing the proceedings and sending investigative reporters into the countryside looking for secret witnesses. African American magazines published a photograph of Emmett Till's horribly disfigured and decomposed head, the stuff of nightmares for many readers. At trial, uncooperative local officials refused to confirm that the body recovered from the Tallahatchie River really was that of Emmett Till, but Mamie Till insisted it was, and Moses Wright courageously pointed out the two men who had kidnapped his nephew, Milam and Bryant. Nonetheless, jurors acquitted the two men.

After their acquittal, Milam and Bryant confessed their crime to a national news magazine and tried to justify themselves by saying they acted to resist agitation for civil rights. Speculation has swirled around the details of this case for over fifty years. In 2004, after a filmmaker produced a documentary on the Till killing, the Department of Justice investigated the murder of Till for the first time, collecting evidence that Henry Lee Loggins, a black farmhand, and Carolyn Bryant were present when Milam and Bryant abducted Till. In 2007, a Mississippi grand jury refused to indict anyone for the crime, saying the FBI failed to provide conclusive evidence of Carolyn Bryant's guilt. Milam died in 1981; Bryant in 1994. Neither spent even one night in jail for the crime.

In the face of such violent opposition to civil rights, NAACP worker Amzie Moore went from church to church, recruiting people for a grassroots effort against white racism and segregation. He had an advantage over other organizers. He could use his position in several gospel-singing groups to gain entrée. Moore sang and then made his NAACP speech. He then led groups down to the courthouse to register or to vote. Medgar Evers, an NAACP officer in Mississippi, investigated racial violence, publicizing his findings. He had no shortage of cases to investigate. Between 1956 and 1959, whites killed at least ten black men, crimes the state authorities could not seem to solve. Local black organizers faced death threats and brutal violence. In 1955, assassins in Mississippi blasted Rev. George W. Lee in the face with a shotgun after he urged blacks to register to vote. Law enforcement, local, state, and federal, all failed to seriously investigate Lee's death. Thus encouraged, white racists next gunned down Gus Courts, who had also urged black voting. Unlike Lee, Courts survived but left the state. Another advocate of black voting, Lamar Smith, went down to whites' gunfire that same year. NAACP leader Robert Smith simply disappeared.

Amzie Moore and Medgar Evers organized local networks, fighting white supremacy with grassroots politicking rather than appeals to the Constitution, but Supreme Court decisions still had an impact. The pastor at Birmingham's Bethel Baptist Church, Fred Shuttlesworth, had a combative style inspired, in part at least, by the Supreme Court's *Brown* decision. Shuttlesworth later told his biographer he had been "electrified" by the Supreme Court's decision. He felt born again. "I had felt like a man when I passed the newspaper stand and saw the Supreme Court outlawed segregation. I felt second only to when I was converted. Second greatest feeling in my life. I felt like a man. The Supreme Court decision made me personally feel as if I was a man. I had the same rights, my kids had the same rights as other folks."[4]

Despite the inspiration he drew from the Supreme Court, Shuttlesworth was a transitional figure, one who moved away from relying on the Constitution. The crucial moment may have come in 1956, when the Ku Klux Klan tried to lynch him with dynamite. In that year, Alabama whites, faced with the Montgomery bus boycott, successfully used their courts to put the NAACP out of business in Alabama. In June, a circuit judge issued a temporary injunction forbidding the organization from operating in Alabama. Arthur Shores seemed to reveal the limits of legal action when he told the NAACP's Birmingham branch it could do nothing without risking a contempt citation.

Shuttlesworth, unknown just a year before, had an alternative approach. He now stepped forward to found a new organization, the Christian Movement.

He quickly developed a reputation for advocating strong, in-your-face street protest against white racism. On December 20, he delivered an ultimatum to Birmingham's city commission: desegregate city buses by December 26 or face black protest. On Christmas Day, a bomb exploded next to his bedroom. The blast devastated his home, but he escaped serious injury. Not only did the bomb fail to deter Shuttlesworth, but his survival seemed miraculous, evidence that God had taken sides in the struggle. A police officer surveyed the ruins and said, "Reverend, if I were you, I'd get out of town as fast as I could." Shuttlesworth responded, "Officer, you're not me. You go back and tell your Klan brethren if God could keep me through this then I'm here for the duration."[5] The next day, Shuttlesworth led his followers onto the white sections of city buses.

The Shuttlesworth bombing came amidst a new bombing campaign. Bombers blasted Martin Luther King's house twice. After the Supreme Court declared Montgomery's segregation ordinance unconstitutional, so much violence had erupted that city officials shut down bus service. Bombers attacked schools in Tennessee, Florida, North Carolina, Louisiana, and Virginia. In a few instances, Southern state courts convicted and imprisoned the bombers. In Charlotte, North Carolina, a jury convicted the bombers of a black elementary school. But a Georgia jury acquitted the bomber of a Jewish synagogue in Atlanta. Montgomery jurors freed two men accused of dynamiting churches and homes, even though one had signed a confession. Some saw the widespread nature of the bombings as evidence of an interstate conspiracy. Newspaper columnists Drew Pearson and Pat Watters blamed a single gang for the troubles, and Congressman Kenneth Keating (R-NY) agreed. Congress considered a bill making it a federal crime to transport or possess dynamite intended for use against education or religious buildings. Sam Ervin, a segregationist senator from North Carolina proud of his expertise on the Constitution, supported the proposed bill, which Congress finally passed in 1960. Thus, Congress finally passed an antilynching law.

But this law neither reinvigorated the law-based approach Arthur Shores promoted nor derailed Shuttlesworth's extralegal tactics. Blacks found they could expect little relief from the new law. By the time Congress passed it, the FBI had long since adopted a deep hostility to investigating lynchings, abandoning the credible work it had done in the 1940s. The law led to few FBI bombing investigations. On June 10, 1963, the FBI's office in Atlanta prepared a listing of forty Georgia bombings between 1959 and 1963. One racially motivated explosion in Ringgold, Georgia, killed a woman, and several blasts sent victims to a hospital. Most of the explosions tied to racial

strife involved homes located in fringe areas between black and white residential areas. Local police cleared, or solved, three of the forty incidents. Few
obviously involved interstate gangs of the sort targeted by the legislation. As
a historical source, the FBI's catalog of bombings is, to say the least, prob-
lematic. As it included explosions from gas leaks, labor strife, and childish
pranks like firecrackers in mailboxes, the FBI was able to report that only half
the bombings obviously resulted from racial hate.

The FBI's catalog of bombing horrors recorded the relentless hate beneath
the big newspaper stories, the violence that filled the function of lynching
outside the ritual of lynching. The FBI reports documented the odor of dynamite, the shattered windows, the ammonium nitrate residue, and the
craters: "Police found a hole in the lawn approximately 14 inches in diame-
ter and 6 inches deep"; "It caused a hole in the ground approximately ten
inches deep and about the size of an automobile wheel in circumference";
"The explosion left a hole approximately twenty-four inches by twelve
inches by twenty-four inches deep in the ground." In 1961, Atlanta hosted
an integrated revival service, where whites sat next to blacks. Almost inevitably, this attracted the bombers, and the police probably just guessed at
the dimensions of the resulting crater: "approximately twelve inches by
twelve inches by eight inches deep." In this chronicle of hate, one could almost picture the South as a kind of lunar landscape with crater following
crater. And at the bottom of every page summarizing a bombing, measuring
the crater, the FBI agent relentlessly typed, "No FBI investigation was requested and none was conducted."[6] Seemingly, the new law against bombing
changed FBI procedures very little.

During the same time period covered by the FBI's list of possible Georgia
bombings, one "traditional" lynching occurred in the entire United States.
In 1959, a white mob entered a jail and abducted Mack Charles Parker,
charged with rape of a white woman. Parker's abductors killed him, dumping
his body in the Pearl River. Although the Parker lynching came the closest
to resembling the kind of ritualized killing most often associated with lynching, some whites thought it insufficiently ritualistic to meet the definition of
a true lynching. C. L. Wilson of Ocean Springs, Mississippi, wrote Mississippi
Governor J. P. Coleman to complain that Parker's death had "no symptom of
a white lynching." Wilson continued, knowingly, "I am an old man and I
have seen a few Lynchings in Mississippi," and whites never carried out
lynchings with just eight or ten people under cover of darkness. When white
people lynch, Wilson insisted, "it was from 100 to 5000 with no masks and
after the victim was dead he was taken to some PUBLIC place and hung

where all could see him." Wilson thought the secrecy proved that blacks must have killed Parker. "I just wonder if it wouldn't be a good idea to make a secret inquiry among the Negroes and find if any strange negroes were in the vicinity."[7]

By the time lynchers killed Parker, most if not all Southern governors wanted to shed the South's lynching image. Mississippi's J. P. Coleman had made it his goal to get through his term as governor (1956–1960) without a single lynching, a goal ruined by the Parker incident. Later, Coleman said he had wanted to clean up Mississippi's image as a state poisoned with widespread lynching violence, to attract industry. To do so, he needed to convince investors that the state had genuinely turned away from its violent past. Those same economic concerns spread across the South. Birmingham's business community shared Coleman's worries. They wanted to attract industry to their city and understood that a reputation for violence and racism deterred those efforts. In 1960, Harrison Salisbury of the *New York Times* horrified Birmingham's Chamber of Commerce when he wrote two lengthy articles criticizing Birmingham for its racial hate and violence. Salisbury accurately reported that violence had infested not just the city but also its police force and even state government.

In 1963, Martin Luther King Jr. led street demonstrations in Birmingham, demanding that downtown stores hire black clerks and desegregate their facilities, including fitting rooms, restrooms, and water fountains. In July, the U.S. Fifth Circuit Court of Appeals ordered Birmingham's public schools to desegregate. To prevent implementation of the decision, Governor George Wallace stationed state police around the schools slated for desegregation. Wallace had narrowly escaped a federal contempt citation years before and desperately wanted to avoid another confrontation with the federal judiciary. So, while he obviously defied a federal court order, he insisted he did so only to prevent disorder. To make sure there really was disorder for him to prevent, Wallace secretly communicated with the Ku Klux Klan. This, at least, is the story Mills Thornton tells in his important book on the Birmingham crisis. His evidence is a tape-recorded conversation between Klansmen and neo-Nazis telling each other they had consulted Governor Wallace. As Alabama schools inched toward desegregation and as Wallace insisted on barring any progress whatsoever, the Alabama Ku Klux Klan made an egregious miscalculation.

Southern whites had traditionally used lynching to overawe blacks into submission. The nature of the violence had changed, with dynamite replacing the traditional hangman's noose or the funeral pyre, but some whites remained confident that a shocking act of violence—a spectacle—would derail desegregation in Birmingham. It did not. The impact of the bombing at least matched that of the street demonstrations.

Many historians have argued it was the demonstrations that convinced President John F. Kennedy to intervene. Birmingham Public Safety Commissioner Eugene "Bull" Connor's use of powerful fire hoses and dogs against the demonstrators, including small children, certainly shocked Kennedy, prompting him to rethink the timid civil rights program he had proposed in February. Also in Birmingham, Kennedy saw that King could barely contain a rising tide of black anger. King preached nonviolence, but some Birmingham blacks armed themselves with rocks and bottles, threatening to attack the white policemen they saw attacking King's peaceful protesters. King's aides scrambled to maintain a nonviolent posture, pleading with angry young men to go home, but found it tough going. Kennedy could see the situation getting frighteningly out of hand, but his reading of Reconstruction history taught him that federal efforts to intervene in Southern society in the 1860s and 1870s had been misguided. Based on the—now discredited—history he had learned at Harvard, Kennedy took office with no appetite to try again what he thought had failed one hundred years before. He therefore sought to mediate, conciliate, and compromise but not to intervene. After the Birmingham demonstrations Kennedy went to work trying to build a consensus behind a stronger civil rights law. In June, he made a moving speech to the nation on behalf of civil rights and proposed a comprehensive law against discrimination. None of this would have happened without the Birmingham violence. On June 22, when Kennedy met with civil rights leaders, including Fred Shuttlesworth, the president said he was meeting with the leaders only because of the violence in Birmingham. Yet, the riots had worked no magic on the U.S. Senate. On June 27, one of the president's men calculated that a strong civil rights law would attract only forty-seven votes in the Senate. Real change came after Kennedy's assassination and when the Klan bombed the Sixteenth Street Baptist Church. When members of the Ku Klux Klan killed four little girls with their dynamite, the spectacle effectively put an end to protests against school desegregation in Birmingham. Glen Eskew has written that the bombing showed how little Birmingham had been changed by the street protests. Howell Raines, a white native of Birmingham and later a *New York Times* writer, took a more positive view, explaining that Martin Luther King's street demonstrations convinced many whites that continued segregation was impractical. The bombing convinced them that segregation was immoral.

Notes

1. J. W. Henson to C. L. Pierce, captain of detectives, April 13, 1950, 1125.3.7, surveillance files, Birmingham Police Department, Birmingham Public Library; J. R. Davis and J. W. Henson, to C. L. Pierce, captain of detectives, April 13, 1950, 1125.3.7, surveillance files, Birmingham Police Department, Birmingham Public Library.

2. Sudarshan Kapur, *Raising Up a Prophet: The African-American Encounter with Gandhi* (Boston: Beacon Press, 1992), 10–23; Leilah C. Danielson, "'In My Extremity I Turned to Gandhi': American Pacifists, Christianity, and Gandhian Nonviolence, 1915–1941," *Church History* 72 (June 2003): 361–89; Howard Thurman, *With Head and Heart: The Autobiography of Howard Thurman* (New York: Harcourt Brace, 1979), 103–36; Martin Luther King Jr., *Stride toward Freedom: The Montgomery Story* (New York: Harper and Row, 1958), 96–97; Andrew Young, *An Easy Burden: The Civil Rights Movement and the Transformation of America* (New York: HarperCollins, 1996), 57; John Lewis with Michael D'Orso, *Walking with the Wind: A Memoir of the Movement* (New York: Simon and Schuster, 1998), 84–93.

3. Carolyn Bryant's testimony appeared in the *Jackson Daily News*, September 23, 1955, and is reprinted in Christopher Metress, ed., *The Lynching of Emmett Till: A Documentary Narrative* (Charlottesville: University of Virginia Press, 2002), 93–95. For Mamie Till-Mobley's version of events, see Mamie Till-Mobley and Christopher Benson, *Death of Innocence: The Story of the Hate Crime that Changed America* (New York: Random House, 2003), 122.

4. Andrew M. Manis, *A Fire You Can't Put Out: The Civil Rights Life of Birmingham's Reverend Fred Shuttlesworth* (Tuscaloosa: University of Alabama Press, 1999), 79.

5. Glenn T. Eskew, *But for Birmingham: The Local and National Movements in the Civil Rights Struggle* (Chapel Hill: University of North Carolina Press, 1997), 132; Manis, *A Fire You Can't Put Out*, 108–9; J. Mills Thornton III, *Dividing Lines: Municipal Politics and the Struggle for Civil Rights in Montgomery, Birmingham, and Selma* (Tuscaloosa: University of Alabama Press, 2002), 197–99.

6. "Alleged Bombings, 1959–1963, Territory Covered by the Atlanta Division of the FBI," section 17, file 144-012, Classified Subject Files, Civil Rights Division, DOJ, RG 60, National Archives.

7. C. L. Wilson to governor, n.d., folder 16, box 19, J. P. Coleman Papers, Mississippi Department of Archives and History, Jackson.

CHAPTER SIX

~

Hate Crimes

The path to the next strategy of resistance against racial violence began most improbably in 1964 at the Republican National Convention in San Francisco, where the Republicans had gathered to nominate a conservative Arizona senator named Barry Goldwater for president. Goldwater's nomination in 1964 marked a turning point for the Republican party: the ascent to power by the party's conservative wing, long frustrated by decades of moderate control. Conservatives did not like civil rights legislation; Goldwater, in fact, voted against the Civil Rights Act of 1964. It is an irony, then, that conservatives' determination to turn crime and the victims of crime into a winning issue led directly to the campaign to pass laws against hate crimes. African Americans' final strategy, so far, against lynching involved forming new alliances in a new political environment, one that focused the public's attention on crime victims.

In his acceptance speech, Goldwater presented himself as an honest man opposed to communism, and while he offered fairly conventional rhetoric championing freedom, he also warned that liberty without order licensed "the mob and the jungle." He went on to criticize violence in American streets and called for security from domestic violence. When Goldwater said he wanted to take American streets back from marauding bullies he touched a nerve among middle-class Americans. By accusing Democrats of permitting and even encouraging street violence, Goldwater invoked law and order as a campaign issue. His vice presidential running mate made law and order a recurrent theme in his speeches. Goldwater's campaign ultimately went down to a humiliating landslide defeat that year, but Goldwater had successfully identified what would one day be a winning issue for Republicans and taken a first step toward guiding Americans away from their confidence in government programs, including Social Security and Medicare, that the Democrats had been cultivating since 1933.[1]

White, working-class Americans resented the Supreme Court's defense of criminals' rights, and they bristled at the antiestablishment, countercultural nature of the civil rights movement. Liberals dismissed such fears as bigotry and saw the specter of racism and prejudice thinly hidden beneath the veneer of Goldwater's rhetoric. By the time Goldwater gave his speech, George Wallace, an Alabama politician and a notorious white supremacist, had already tested attacks on the federal judiciary as a campaign issue. Civil rights, Wallace said, moved America toward the kind of centralized power characteristic of Nazi Germany or Communist Russia and away from the free-market capitalism most Americans saw as the hallmark of their society and nation. Federal judges, Wallace said, used dictatorial tactics akin to Hitler's Germany.

In the summer of 1964, newspaper reporting of spectacular crimes seemed to both confirm liberals' indictment of Wallace and inflame the fears he exploited. Americans learned that Mississippi Ku Klux Klansmen had murdered three civil rights workers in Neshoba County. Just a week before Goldwater gave his speech attacking crime in the streets—meaning urban crime committed by blacks—the FBI recovered the bodies of Andrew Goodman, Michael Schwerner, and James Chaney. While the murders of three civil rights workers confirmed the continuing danger posed by such racist groups as the Klan, black discontent erupted in Northern cities, discomforting middle-class whites. Goldwater gave his speech even before the riots erupted, breaking out in Harlem, Rochester, Jersey City, and Philadelphia. The *New York Times* thought so much black rioting represented something new in American history, since previous race riots pitted whites against blacks. There had been black riots before, the paper conceded, but this was epidemic. Though African Americans most often attacked their own neighborhoods, they thoroughly frightened whites by attacking them in their cars, throwing rocks, looting stores, and invading their homes. These black people scared whites so much that Democrats began calling the riots "Goldwater rallies." Polls began showing that many white voters thought the civil rights movement had gone too far, with whites complaining that blacks received "everything on a silver platter."[2] Even as racial crime by whites against blacks continued, black crime began to emerge as a winning issue for conservatives, one that implied liberal Democrats cared more for black rights than for their white victims. Although the resentment simmered and poll-sters detected the potential for backlash, in the fall of 1964 few whites indi-cated they would change their vote or party affiliation based on black vio-lence. That would come later.

Rioting in 1964 led journalists to coin the term "long, hot summer" to de-scribe the tension and violence. Americans went into the summer of 1965 wary of another "long, hot summer." Journalists speculated in their columns and on televised news broadcasts about the prospect for renewed violence. Some warned that the urban poverty that fostered uprisings in 1964 remained. Any hope that passions might have cooled vanished in August when extensive riot-ing erupted in Los Angeles, in Watts. A year after the Watts violence, rioting broke out in Chicago and Atlanta. Newark, Detroit, Milwaukee, and Harlem ri-oted in 1967. The summer rioting for 1968 began in April, when uprisings swept Chicago, Washington, Pittsburgh, and Baltimore. The New York Times warned that the seemingly endless aggression, summer after summer, undermined sup-port for civil rights, encouraging apathy or hostility among whites[3]—Martin Luther King shared the same concerns, as did Lyndon Johnson.

At the same time American cities rioted, Huey P. Newton and Bobby Seale organized the Black Panther Party for Self-Defense. Dressed in black clothing and openly carrying shotguns and other weapons, the Black Pan-thers organized to protect themselves from white police officers, they ex-plained. Newton told journalists that his organization would seize political power through armed force. In 1967, thirty armed Black Panthers strode into California's general assembly chamber, startling and alarming lawmakers be-fore confronting state police officers. The Black Panthers, headquartered in Oakland, California, drew inspiration from Robert F. Williams, the Lowndes County Freedom Organization in Alabama, and the Revolutionary Action Movement, a proposed underground army for black people. H. Rap Brown explained the need for the Black Panthers by saying that white Americans intended to kill all black Americans. The Black Panthers described police of-ficers as an occupying army and sometimes shadowed police cars patrolling through urban black neighborhoods. The execution of a police officer, they said, would be like the killing of a German soldier by the French resistance in World War II. The Black Panthers were a small group, numbering between seventy-five and two hundred in 1967, according to the New York Times. But in their clashes with police, with killings on both sides, they attracted atten-tion from newspapers and television networks. For many whites, the Black Panthers symbolized black urban youth, frightening and threatening.

By 1968, Republicans had honed their thinking, and party leaders laid plans to take back power by organizing a backlash on behalf of crime victims.

Republicans consciously stoked the tide of resentment. At the Republican National Convention, Richard Nixon declared freedom from violent crime the first civil right of every American. Nixon's language, race neutral on its surface, implied that he would protect the white victims of crime perpetrated by black criminals coddled by the Democrats over the previous eight years. Nixon urged his fellow Republicans to do a better job at marshalling public opinion against disorder, implicitly recognizing that Democrats had rallied public opinion to their side by calling for sympathy for the victims of discrimination, poverty, and racism. No longer should poverty or past wrongs, Nixon said, be allowed to excuse crimes. California Governor Ronald Reagan also spoke to the Republicans that year, agreeing with Nixon and making points that would later be the hallmarks of his presidency. Criminals rampaged through the streets, Reagan said, and he criticized the courts for supposedly approving, and even underwriting, such conduct. He eschewed the idea that society's shortcomings led to crime; individual criminals had to shoulder the responsibility for their own shortcomings and misconduct. For Reagan, it was time to restore the idea that each individual must be held accountable for his actions. He also insisted that race had little to do with crime. Asserting that criminals acted without racial prejudice, Reagan insisted color had nothing to do with their misconduct—they just wanted the money. A major part of the Republicans' war on crime involved guarding the rights of victims.

Reagan believed American constitutionalism had gone off track, and he planned to wrestle it back onto its proper course. Conservatives like Reagan believed liberals had hijacked the courts, turning them from their proper role as neutral arbiters into the political engines of the Left's reform agenda. Reagan's solicitor general later opined that the Left had an exaggerated faith in government and bureaucracy and such a deep skepticism of anything outside government regulation that it even doubted the legitimacy of punishing individual criminals. He said that liberals believed society created criminality and had only itself to blame for crime. Reagan wanted to overturn this liberal orthodoxy, first as governor of California and then as president. Claiming that low crime rates in the Great Depression proved that criminality could not be traced to poverty, Reagan denounced those who attributed crime to criminals' hardships or poverty or social inequities. He saw the antidiscrimination regulations Democrats enacted in the 1960s and 1970s as placing an undue burden on business. Reagan's strident attacks on affirmative action benefited him politically, but his defenders insisted he had no manipulative or cynical agenda. He just genuinely doubted government could really engineer a better society.

In fact, Reagan had used the crime issue politically. Shortly after his election as California governor in 1966, he had begun to focus public attention on crime as the number one problem. In 1967, saying he wanted to make the public more aware of crime, he tried to recruit mass media outlets to his cause. This effort quickly achieved success, especially given the media coverage of the Black Panther Party's activities that year. Recognizing that he had an issue that attracted public support, Reagan called on the public to sympathize with the victims of crime, rather than the offenders. He pushed for new laws that enhanced the penalties for certain kinds of crime, those where the criminal used a gun, for example. In 1971 Reagan most dramatically politicized crime control, by charging that violent protesters had, without success, made an ideological effort to capture and subvert society along racial and class lines. Revolutionary crime tied to social protest and aimed at American values, he announced, had tried but failed to divide society. He warned that while some still turned to violence to reform America, it was up to the citizens to resist violence. Moreover, Reagan said that law-abiding citizens should feel no obligation to appease criminals by spending money to improve the economic or social conditions that Democrats said produced crime. His message that social conditions did not produce crime took hold in the public's mind. For many, the idea that crime came from the character flaws of individual criminals seemed increasingly appealing, especially during the economic recession of the 1970s.

Reagan's appeals reached into the Democrats' core constituency, rank-and-file unionized labor. Such conservative rhetoric, repudiating violent protest and championing individual rights, proved devastatingly successful for Republicans and catastrophic for Democrats. When Nixon in 1968 and then Reagan in 1980 won landslide victories in their presidential bids, carrying districts long thought safe for Democrats, liberals scrambled to figure out what had hit them. Under Republican attack, Democrats hastily declared their own opposition to crime and wasted no time in polishing their own crime-fighting credentials. Within the Democratic Party, strategies to exploit the new political reality soon percolated up from the grass roots.

In 1976, Leon Ralph, an African American Democratic lawmaker from Watts, wrote a California state law aimed at protecting people from violence based on their race, color, religion, ancestry, national origin, political affiliation, sex, or position in a labor dispute. California's Ralph Act attempted to position blacks as the victims of crime rather than as criminals. Some have called the Ralph Act a "precursor" and a "foundation" for the hate crime laws that came later. Any political advantage for the Democrats in the Ralph Act, though, came very slowly. In 1976, few in California noticed Ralph's law, with the state's leading newspapers ignoring its passage. Ralph did not call his act a law against "hate crime"; that term did not yet exist, and journalists dismissed it as a boringly technical liability law.

In 1977, Frank Collin made ethnic intimidation a national topic by announcing he wanted to demonstrate for his rights in the Chicago suburb of Skokie, Illinois. Collin was a neo-Nazi; he and his followers donned uniforms featuring brown shirts and swastikas similar to those worn by Hitler's World War II Nazis. Collin and his Nazis wanted to claim constitutional rights for white people and reverse a generation of judicial concern with the rights of minority groups and criminal defendants. While the American Civil Liberties Union defended Collin's free speech rights, others on the Left doubted a group of Nazis really should be allowed to exercise their freedom to speak in Skokie, which had a large Jewish population, including seven thousand aging Holocaust survivors. Skokie's city government fought the planned demonstration, getting an injunction and passing city ordinances aimed at the neo-Nazis. Collin sued. Though Collin's Nazis never marched in Skokie, they did win their battle in court for the right to do so. Many thought that Collin and his Nazis, without meaning to, had made a good argument that government had to act to protect minorities from offensive prejudice.

Jarred by the Skokie controversy, the Anti-Defamation League of B'nai B'rith (ADL) began tracking anti-Semitic incidents. After three years, the ADL reached an alarming conclusion: between 1978 and 1981, such prejudice had increased dramatically, from 49 anti-Semitic incidents to 974. The ADL's counting recalled the National Association for the Advancement of Colored People's tabulation of lynchings earlier in the century, and, just as the NAACP lobbied for a law against lynching based on its statistics, the ADL began pressing for laws against "ethnic intimidation." In 1981, the ADL drafted a model statute that defined ethnic intimidation as a crime where the perpetrator chose his or her victim because of the victim's group. Just as Reagan had once called for enhanced penalties for particular kinds of crime, the ADL model called for tougher punishments in the kinds of crime it most feared, and also urged governmental monitoring of hate crimes. The ADL model proved influential. In 1981, the states of Washington and Oregon passed laws similar to the ADL proposal. Washington made malicious harassment motivated by race, color, religion, ancestry, or national origin a crime. Oregon made it a crime to intimidate by reason of race, color, religion, or national origin. Other states passed similar laws.

Journalists paid scant attention to the Washington and Oregon laws. No legislator in either state used the term "hate crime," and leading newspapers in both states thought their readers were more interested in tax hikes and capping teacher pay increases than what seemed to be nothing more than a technical criminal statute against a kind of crime lawmakers described as "malicious harassment." Pressure to pass such laws nonetheless increased, in part because other organizations joined the ADL effort. The National Gay and Lesbian Task Force; the Center for Democratic Renewal, originally known at the National Anti-Klan Network; the Southern Poverty Law Center, which started its Klanwatch Project in 1980; and the National Institute against Prejudice and Violence all became pressure groups, lobbying Congress and the states to pass laws designed to protect their particular group from violence. Some scholars have argued that the formation of so many important lobbying groups helps explain why most states, and ultimately Congress, passed laws against what would be called "hate crimes."

A more decisive impetus for such laws came from a dramatic shift in American politics. In 1980, Reagan and the Republicans stunned Democrats by winning the presidency and taking control of the U.S. Senate. The 1980 election seemed to repudiate the Democrats' commitment to policies based on human rights in favor of the Republicans' hard-boiled "realism." Jimmy Carter, the incumbent Democrat Reagan defeated, claimed human rights represented the principles of the nation, but Reagan seemingly cared little for such principles and won the election.

The first laws against hate received bipartisan support in state legislatures. Washington had passed its intimidation law with a Republican governor, a solid Republican majority in its state House of Representatives, and only one vote short of a Republican majority in the state senate. Oregon passed its law through a state legislature completely dominated by Democrats. Neither party made an issue of those states' intimidation laws.

Nonetheless, Democrats soon recognized an opportunity to take back the crime issue from Republicans, and the issue became more political. Through the 1980s, Democrats increasingly saw laws designed to protect minorities as a political opportunity to show voters that government could effectively respond to a serious social ill. They wanted to challenge Reagan's claim that bias had nothing to do with crime, although the earliest efforts had little to do with race. In 1981, New York Congressman Mario Biaggi introduced legislation to make it a federal crime to vandalize religious properties. In New York City, Democratic Mayor Ed Koch and other leaders organized Victims Rights Week and called for increased funding for programs designed to help crime victims. In 1982, in a three-day conference where Democrats debated how best to respond to the Republicans' anticrime initiatives, the party tried to present itself as more committed to victims' rights than the Republicans. Nixon, Democrats decided, had been right in 1968—freedom from crime was the new civil right. In 1983, the effort received another boost when the U.S. Civil Rights Commission issued a report entitled *Intimidation and Violence: Racial and Religious Bigotry in America*, urging better tracking of crime inspired by religious, racial, or ethnic prejudice. A year later, Connecticut Congress-woman Barbara B. Kennelly, alarmed by a series of synagogue arsons in her congressional district, introduced a bill to require the FBI to include such criminality in its Uniform Crime Reports. Kennelly explained that such crimes threatened America's basic precepts, and reliable statistical data would measure the extent to which Americans did or did not live up to their fundamental ideals.

Just as Republicans had claimed that street crime posed a national crisis, an epidemic when their rivals held power, Democrats now pictured hate crime as on the rise and a national emergency. When the Washington state legislature debated its malicious harassment law in 1981, it did so amid re-ports in the *Seattle Post-Intelligencer* and other papers that a wave of violence terrorized Asian refugees. Democrats in the Oregon legislature declared a state of emergency existed when it passed its intimidation statute in 1981. Testifying before Congress in 1988, the veteran civil rights leader Rev. C. T. Vivian, born in 1928, said that he had never seen so many groups involved in racist violence as in the 1980s, calling the crisis in racial violence the worst since 1900. Even some Republicans found Vivian persuasive. Con-gressman George Gekas of Pennsylvania, who worked to make sure violence aimed at homosexuals was not included in the bill, agreed that a rising tide of biased violence had made the problem in the 1980s worse than any other period in U.S. history.[4]

Although Ronald Reagan had been elected president in 1980 partly on a platform of sympathy for crime victims, his administration opposed passing laws aimed at protecting minority victims of crime. Reagan's opposition to hate crime laws touched the fundamental difference between Republicans and Democrats. While Reagan stressed individual responsibility, Democrats really believed government could, in the words of one Lyndon Johnson aide, accomplish great things. In Johnson's time, this meant ending the poverty that fostered crime. After Reagan and the conservatives seized power in 1980, Democrats had less room to maneuver. Through the 1980s, conserva-tives pressed the doctrine of individual responsibility with considerable suc-cess. In response, liberals began to argue that violent racists should take in-dividual responsibility too.

In 1985, Reagan administration officials tried to prevent Congress from passing its first hate crime law, a statute requiring the FBI to tally hate crimes. Members of the Department of Justice testified before a House committee chaired by Democrat John Conyers. A member of the Black Caucus, Conyers made a name for himself as a prominent congressional liberal, so much so that President Richard Nixon put his name on his infamous "Enemies List," a roster of prominent people Nixon disliked so much he targeted them for harassment by various governmental agencies.

The FBI officials told Conyers that requiring the FBI to include hate crimes in its annual tally of crime would force the government to read the minds of criminals, requiring guesswork to determine if an attack across racial lines resulted from hate or more ordinary criminal motivations. A white thief might rob a black victim for reasons having nothing to do with race, for example. Conyers answered such concerns with the realities of raw political power, "If I can get 218 Congressmen and 51 Senators, we are going to make it a law." When FBI officials suggested tracking hate crimes through newspaper clippings, the basic technique for studying lynchings for nearly one hundred years and still used by some scholars, Conyers impatiently dismissed the notion as entirely inadequate.[5]

Conyers eventually got his votes, and the Hate Crime Statistics Act became law in 1990. Some commentators warned against the "folly" of such legislation, doubting such laws could really change social realities. Critics charged that hate crime laws really attacked free speech, since convicted persons received stiffer penalties based on what they said. Some argued that the United States did not face an epidemic or crisis, or a rising tide of hate crime. James Jacobs, a law professor, and Kimberly Potter, an attorney in private practice, argued that Conyers and his allies had coined the term "hate crime" for political reasons. Hate crime laws, they said, were political efforts by groups to win special privileges for themselves based on their ethnic identity.

Despite such criticism through the 1980s, and continuing today, state legislatures rushed to pass laws against crimes motivated by prejudice. These new laws took five forms. First, some states have defined new crimes such as "ethnic intimidation" to enable them to punish biased individuals. Other states have enacted enhanced penalties for hate criminals. States with penalty enhancement statutes require judges to impose stiffer penalties to persons convicted of assault, murder, robbery, or some other already existing crime, when prosecutors can show that the convicted person acted on the basis of prejudice. States have also passed laws requiring that state governments collect data on hate crimes, along the lines of the first federal hate crime laws. Some states have also created special enforcement units to police hate crimes. Finally, several states passed laws similar to California's Ralph Act, permitting hate crime victims to sue their attackers.

Press reporting of sensational incidents seemed to confirm that a hate epidemic plagued the nation and encouraged passage of hate crime laws. In 1986, a group of white teenagers attacked three black men in a Queens, New York, pizzeria. The black men's car had broken down, leaving them stranded in Howard Beach. The white teenagers forced the black men out of the restaurant and chased one man, Michael Griffith, onto a freeway, where he was struck and killed. At first, government prosecutors seemed unable, or unwilling, to build a court case against any of the whites involved in Griffith's death. Some black New Yorkers took this as evidence of continuing white racism and toleration of lynching, an impression confirmed when 1,200 protesting African Americans marched into Howard Beach and white residents greeted them with racist taunts. Ultimately, New York Governor Mario Cuomo appointed a special prosecutor, who persuaded a jury to convict four whites of manslaughter.

In 1989, a gang of whites gunned down sixteen-year-old Yusuf Hawkins. On the night of August 23, Hawkins and three black friends had entered the predominantly white Bensonhurst section of Brooklyn, looking for a used car. Believing one of the blacks planned to visit one of their former girlfriends, as many as thirty white youths armed themselves with baseball bats. At least one also had a gun and shot Hawkins twice in the chest. Eight members of the mob went on trial for murder and other offenses. Prosecutors had trouble finding sufficient evidence that the mob was, in fact, a mob. The government's lawyers depended on confessions made by members of the mob, evidence that could not be used in court against other defendants. As a result, the government had trouble proving the obvious, that the mob was a lynch mob, acting in concert and not as individuals. In the end, the jury convicted only Joseph Fama, the man who actually shot Hawkins.

Two years later, a Los Angeles resident videotaped a police mob beating Rodney King after officers caught him speeding. King led pursuing officers on a high-speed chase before stopping. The police kicked him, shocked him with a stun gun, and clubbed him fifty-six times, breaking his leg and bones in his face. Although the police arrested King, they soon released him, declining to press charges. On March 15, 1991, a Los Angeles grand jury indicted four white police officers for the beating. A judge moved the trial of the four officers to Simi Valley, an area that was 90 percent white. No blacks served on the jury, which acquitted all four officers of every charge but one, use of excessive force. The incident sparked a massive riot in Los Angeles. A federal jury later convicted two officers of violating King's civil rights and sent the two whites to prison.

Five months after the Rodney King beating, a Jewish man drove his car onto a sidewalk in Crown Heights, New York, killing a black pedestrian and injuring his seven-year-old cousin. A rabbi announced that the Jewish community would not apologize for the accident, while African Americans demanded that police arrest the driver. Rev. Al Sharpton led protest marches through Crown Heights. When a grand jury refused to indict the driver, rioting erupted that left a Jewish rabbinical student dead, apparently killed by a black youth. Police officers testified that Lemerick Nelson Jr. had admitted joining a mob of youths that surrounded and hit Yankel Rosenbaum and then stabbed him. Nonetheless, a jury acquitted Nelson in 1992. Jurors said later that they considered police testimony unreliable.

In 1997, New York City police brutalized and sodomized Abner Louima, an immigrant from Haiti. Police had arrested Louima outside a nightclub in a street brawl, then took him to their station's bathroom, where they tortured the man with a stick. White officers later testified that they disliked Louima's defiant attitude; Louima, they said, had cursed the officers and punched one on the street. A Brooklyn jury convicted one police officer, and another pled guilty and received a sentence of thirty years in prison. Louima sued New York City for damages, settling for a $7.125 million award, the largest amount of money the city of New York ever paid in a police brutality case.

The next year, three white Texans encountered James Byrd Jr., an African American man, walking along an isolated Texas road in Jasper County, one hundred miles northeast of Houston. The three men picked up Byrd, chained him to the back of their truck, and dragged him to death. Some journalists thought the killing resembled a classic lynching, but unlike earlier lynchings, authorities in Jasper County prosecuted and convicted all three killers. The hatred that drove lynchers did not disappear from the American scene with the so-called demise of lynching.

Such incidents served at once as evidence of a new wave of biased violence and proof that racist violence remained a fixture on the national landscape. When Congress and the states passed hate crime laws, they claimed to be enforcing fundamental values enshrined in the Declaration of Independence and the Constitution. Opponents argued that hate crime laws violated those fundamental values, breeching First Amendment protections of free speech and, more fundamentally, individual accountability.

Hate crime laws punished people for what they did and for what they said about what they did. Hate criminals served extra time in prison for making racist statements. Lawyers for persons convicted of hate crimes complained that the law violated their clients' free speech rights. In 1983, the Supreme Court rejected such arguments when it ruled that a judge could consider a defendant's membership in the Black Liberation Army and his speech calling for a race war when deciding on a sentence. The First Amendment did not protect belonging to an organization that promoted violence and making specific statements threatening violence, the Court decided. On the other hand, the Court also ruled that judges could not consider a defendant's abstract beliefs, when those beliefs could not be connected to any specific crime but seemed far removed for actual violence. Those two precedents sensibly separated the potential for concrete action from abstract thinking.

The Court considered this distinction when it struck down a city hate crime law in *RAV v. City of St. Paul*, a case where a white youth had put a flaming cross on a black family's lawn. The Court began by stating the basic principle that governs free speech. The government is not allowed to prohibit speech because it disapproves of the ideas expressed. Some kinds of speech can be punished: obscenity, defamation, and words that provoke violence. The Court applied this principle and found that St. Paul had written its law so loosely that it would, for example, allow the city to prosecute speakers for criticizing the government. St. Paul wanted to practice "viewpoint discrimination," punishing racial epithets but not words that provoked violence without invoking race. The rule is that any words that provoke violence can be punished. The government is not allowed to single out particular ideas for punishment. Justice Antonin Scalia wrote the opinion of the Court, saying, "Let there be no mistake about our belief that burning a cross in someone's front yard is reprehensible." He continued, "But St. Paul has sufficient means at its disposal to prevent such behavior without adding the First Amendment to the fire."[6]

One day later, the Wisconsin Supreme Court followed suit, striking down that state's hate crime law, a penalty enhancement statute, as a violation of free speech. Ironically, in the Wisconsin case the hate criminals were black and the victim white. The case began when Todd Mitchell and other black youths attacked a white victim. Mitchell had asked his fellows, "Do you all feel hyped up to move on some white people?" The group had then viciously assaulted a white victim chosen at random, leaving the man in a coma. Guilty of assault, normally a crime that carried a maximum sentence of two years, Mitchell got a seven-year sentence under Wisconsin's hate crime law. Had he kept quiet, his sentence would have been only two years. The Wisconsin Supreme Court accused the state legislature of creating a "thought crime," punishing people for their thoughts rather than just for their actions.[7]

In 1993, the Supreme Court reversed the Wisconsin Supreme Court's decision. In upholding the Wisconsin law, Chief Justice William Rehnquist pointed out that for centuries judges had considered defendants' motives when determining punishment. Traditionally, courts punished persons with motives especially repugnant to society more harshly. Rehnquist agreed the state had a legitimate right to use the law to remedy racism. He did not accept the notion that Mitchell's free speech rights had been violated. Rehnquist and his fellow justices thought it unlikely that hate crime laws would have a chilling effect on free speech and pointed out that defendants' declarations had been used in courts for generations.

Increasing political pressure to pass more legislation on behalf of hate crime victims encouraged Congress to pass a new hate crime law, one that directly attacked the problem rather than merely tallying the number of incidents. The 1994 Violent Crime Control and Law Enforcement Act required the U.S. Sentencing Commission to enhance sentences for those convicted in federal court of hate crimes and brought federal courts in line with laws passed by most states. Before 1994, federal prosecutors could not go after racially violent offenders unless they willfully deprived their victims of a federally protected civil right. The Violent Crime Control and Law Enforcement Act shifted the focus from protecting rights to singling out hate criminals for extra punishment.

Some authors have begun to claim that hate crime laws reflect continuity with past laws, that the movement to criminalize violent hate began not in the 1980s but actually in the 1860s. Clear differences distinguish the Reconstruction-era civil rights laws and the hate crime legislation passed after 1980. Reconstruction laws promised to protect "any person within the jurisdiction of the United States," while hate crime laws single out particular groups for protection. The 1871 Ku Klux Klan Act targeted individuals acting "under color of any law, statute, ordinance, regulation, custom, or usage of any State." The authors of the Ku Klux Klan Act feared—and sought to control through punishment—haters sanctioned by the dominant white group. In other words, in the so-called age of lynching groups threatened individuals. By the end of the twentieth century, this perception had reversed. Hate crime laws target individuals acting against groups. Americans have largely decided to solve the problem of racial violence by going after individual misconduct, not the ills of society. Reagan's administration could not prevent Congress from enacting hate crime laws, but his determination to hold individuals and not society accountable clearly shaped the new legislation.

Hate crime laws define lynching in a new way, twisting the old hatreds into new shapes, making the violence into the work of individuals rather than society itself. In fact, several of the most brutal hate crimes actually did involve small mobs. After all, Emmett Till had been "lynched" by just two men. Journalists who first traveled to Jasper, Texas, for example, thought the dragging of James Byrd by three men qualified as a lynching. But ultimately they decided Byrd's murder was not a lynching and wrote stories concentrating on the three killers' individual failings, their time in prison, and their racist tattoos. The town of Jasper and society in Texas were not to blame.

In the new age of individual responsibility, blame could be reassigned for some old crimes once considered the fault of groups or communities or neighborhoods. When Byron de la Beckwith shot Medgar Evers in 1963, he acted alone but clearly understood himself as representing all white people against a black interloper. In that sense, Beckwith had lynched Evers. Two trials in 1964 failed to convict Beckwith, ending in mistrials when the juries could not agree on a verdict. In 1994, though, Mississippi authorities put Beckwith on trial for the third time. Beckwith once again faced a Mississippi jury, but times had changed. National values had finally replaced local standards, much as T. Thomas Fortune had envisioned one hundred years before. In 1963 and 1964, Beckwith's actions had seemed all too understandable and even acceptable to Mississippi whites. In 1994, the young Mississippi prosecutor found Beckwith almost beyond understanding, crazy. Jurors eyed Beckwith as some distasteful object left over from a different era. In 1964, no Mississippi jury would convict Beckwith; in 1994, perhaps no jury would have failed to convict. Beckwith had evolved from lyncher to hate criminal, the representative of society to the enemy of society, all in the space of one old man's lifetime.[8]

What strategies of resistance did black Americans employ against the implacable evil of white violence? The short answer is that African Americans did everything they could to survive in a sea of evil. Some, like Henry Adams, fled, or tried to flee the South for some safer locale, in Kansas or Liberia. Some accommodated whites. Many others, like Thomas Fortune and John Mitchell, spoke out, and did so boldly. Ida B. Wells and Monroe Work reshaped the knowledge that determined Americans' understanding of lynching, making national lists of lynchings that could challenge claims made by the neighborhoods that sponsored lynchings. Wells and Work challenged the structure of power in America by changing the information Americans had about lynching. They helped make it legitimate for a national audience to scrutinize and criticize the actions of villages and communities even when those local people claimed special insider knowledge. Wells and Work had special knowledge, too, drawn from many communities all over the United States. They drew conclusions based on national data, scientifically collected. They facilitated the work of Walter White, Charles Hamilton Houston, Thurgood Marshall, and Arthur Shores as they argued that black people deserved constitutional protection in federal court. Building on their successes, but also frustrated by the lack of real progress, blacks moved into the streets to confront whites directly. Gandhi legitimized turning away from the Constitution and law.

And yet, the hunger for constitutional protection persisted through all this. After whites changed the landscape of racial violence with dynamite, and after white conservatives reshaped the context of American political life in the 1960s and later, black Americans still sought solace in law. John Conyers called violent acts based on prejudice "constitutional violations." And in the end, that is what it came to. Violence based on hate offended the ideal of due process and order promised in the U.S. Constitution.

Notes

1. Barry Goldwater with Jack Casserly, *Goldwater* (New York: Doubleday, 1988), 185–86; Charles Mohr, "Goldwater's Votes Estimated at 600," *New York Times*, June 5, 1964; Tom Wicker, "Convention Ends," *New York Times* July 17, 1964.

2. M. S. Handler, "66 Cities Called Racially Restive," *New York Times*, August 5, 1964; "300 Negroes Riot in Philadelphia," *New York Times*, August 29, 1964; "Miller Pledges Era of Respect for Law," *New York Times*, August 30, 1964; Joseph Lelyveld, "Riots Viewed Against History of Clashes Almost as Old as U. S.," *New York Times*, September 11, 1964; Fred Powledge, "Poll Shows Whites in City Resent Civil Rights Drive," *New York Times*, September 21, 1964; Michael W. Flamm, *Law and Order: Street Crime, Civil Unrest, and the Crisis of Liberalism in the 1960s* (New York: Columbia University Press, 2005), 13–31; Dan T. Carter, *The Politics of Rage: George Wallace, the Origins of the New Conservatism, and the Transformation of American Politics* (Baton Rouge: Louisiana State University Press, 1995), 156–60, 195–225.

3. Gene Roberts, "Civil Rights: A Turning Point," *New York Times*, September 19, 1966.

4. *State v. David Talley*, 122 WN 2d 192 (1993); Congress, House, Mario Biaggi on Legislation to Curb Antireligious Violence, 97th Cong., 1st sess., *Congressional Record* (February 25, 1981), vol. 127, pt. 3, 3123; Congress, House, Subcommittee on Criminal Justice of the Committee on the Judiciary, *Hate Crime Statistics Act*, 99th Cong., 1st sess., March 21, 1985, 2l; Congress, House, Subcommittee on Criminal Justice of the Committee on the Judiciary, *Racially Motivated Violence*, 100th Cong., 2d sess., May 11 and July 12, 1988, 14; Congress, House, George Gekas, 100th Cong., 2d sess., *Congressional Record* (May 18, 1988), vol. 134, pt. 8, 11394.

5. Congress, House, Subcommittee on Criminal Justice of the Committee on the Judiciary, *Hate Crime Statistics Act*, 99th Cong., 1st sess., March 21, 1985, 55.

6. *RAV v. City of St. Paul*, 505 U.S. 377 (1992).

7. *State v. Mitchell*, 169 Wis. 2d 153 (1992).

8. Christopher Waldrep, *The Many Faces of Judge Lynch: Extralegal Violence and Punishment in America* (New York: Palgrave Macmillan, 2002), 188.

~

Documents

Henry Adams Describes Racial Violence

Born in Georgia, Henry Adams came to Louisiana as a child, where he remained a slave until emancipation. After the Civil War, he learned to read and write while serving in the army and began recording the horrifying violence so characteristic of the American South. This document is something very rare, an examination of nineteenth-century racial violence written by an African American. Adams recorded his personal encounters with white racism and his efforts to help his fellow blacks escape white violence. Notice that even after the fall of slavery, and after ratification of the Thirteenth Amendment constitutionally ending slavery, whites still thought blacks like Adams should have a master. The violence Adams recorded seems a constant in his life; he lived in a truly brutal environment. There is no reason to believe his experience differed greatly from other black Americans living in the South immediately after the Civil War.

Statement of Affairs and Outrages in the South, 1866
[Compiled by Henry Adams]

In the year 1866, in the parish of Caddo, State of Louisiana, I seen hanging to a limb of an oak tree about six miles south from Shreveport, the body of a colored man—he was dead when I seen him. About six miles north from Keachie I saw a wagon belonging to a colored man burning with all his things; even his mules were burned to death. While on my way to Sunny Grove, I seen the head of a colored man lying side the road. Whilst traveling on my way to

De Soto Parish a large body of armed white men met me and asked me who I belonged to. I answered them and told them that I belonged to God, but not to any man. They then asked me where was my master? I told them the one I used to have was dead, and I have not had none since 1858; worked for those who would hire me and pay the largest price, as I was still a slave, and during the time I was passing through this parish a black man was not allowed to preach the Gospel any wheres, any more than he was before, in 1865. As he was, he daren't to preach such doctrines as was suitable to the congregation, and a truth from the Holy Bible, but he had to preach just what they (the white men) wanted, and what they told him to preach. My father was a preacher, and he is even until this day, and they all, or least the most of them says they cannot preach the gospel as they wish, for the white people did not nor do not allow them to do it. For the white men says the preachers make meaner niggers, and that they cannot rule the nigger. I have heard them tell the colored men to not preach such doctrines as that to the nigger, because the nigger will get above himself and above their business; and if you do, you are in danger of losing your own life. Such is the language they used to the colored preacher, for they said they will not stand such to be preached. They told me that I must give up all that I got to them, because they had the law in their hands to take all of what a nigger had. So they said to me give us your money and your whisky, your horse, and then you can live; but if you don't, you have got to die right here; so I had to give it up to them to save my life, and I then reported to the courts, but the law would not do anything about it.

So the next incident what I saw was when I was passing a place—I saw white men whipping colored men just the same as they did before the war, or before freedom in this State. I saw white men take a colored man because he had been a United States soldier; they beat him all but to death; that was between Shreveport and Logansport, in the parish of De Soto. I did not know his name, but I heard him cry, saying that I will not ever soldier again no more if you will not kilt me, and they made him swear and curse all of the soldiers in the United States Army, and the officers of the Army also.

Manuel Adams, my cousin, and myself was on our way to Logansport, De Soto Parish, and about one mile from that place we were surrounded by six armed white men, who taken us and then demanded us to give up our watches. Manuel having his watch in sight, they took the watch from him, but they did not see any watch on me. They turned our pockets and searched us for money, but we did not have any, so they told us if we ever told any one about it that they would kill us on the first sight, and asked us if we had rather die than to keep that to ourselves? We told them that we had rather give them all we had in the world than to die and go to hell. They said that we were right to keep it to ourselves.

The next incident of importance that came beneath my observation was the finding of ten or fifteen colored men floating in Red River; this was in the year 1866; some of them was tied by the sides of logs, some with ropes round their necks; some of them was shot, and some had their throat cut; this was between a plantation called Gold Point and Shreveport, on the parish line of Caddo and Bossier. . . .

And in 1868 the same thing was still going on between New Orleans and Fort Jackson. I landed at a plantation below New Orleans called the Magnolia plantation; the boat laid up there all night; I heard a gun fire twice and then saw two colored men running. I hailed them and asked them what was the matter. They said they had been working there two or three months, and they had not been paid in full since they had been there and they had asked the boss for their pay as he had threatened to whip them that day; so again that night they asked him to pay them what he owed them, and he told them all right, then he took his gun and shot at them, and did not pay them a cent.

Adams served in the army from 1866 to 1869.
Discharged, he returned to Shreveport.
I landed in Shreveport, Caddo Parish, La., September the 25th, 1869, and went about trying to rent a house, but it was rumored all over town that a boat load of discharged Union soldiers had come, and the whites would not rent us their houses. Finally we came up with a Baptist preacher, and he let us have his house.

After we had been there a few months the white people began saying they were going to kill us; to kill all the discharged negro soldiers; that these discharged men were going to spoil all the other negroes, so that the whites could do nothing with them; for the colored people would get these discharged soldiers to look over their contracts and agreements they had made with the white people who they were working for. I would tell them to go and have a settlement of accounts, and get what was due them, and pay what they owed. I figured up accounts for them, and of ten seen where the whites had cheated the colored people who had made contracts with them out of more than two-thirds of their just rights, according to their contracts. I told a great many of them to take their contracts to lawyers and get them to force the parties to a settlement; but they told me they were afraid they would be killed.

Some few reported to the court, but told me afterwards that it did not do. Some even were whipped when they went home. These white men told them if they would take a whipping they might go, but if they did not take the whipping they would have them put in jail, as it was a general rule they had of going to the colored people and telling them they had a warrant for their arrest, or, in order to seize what they had, and they would seize all the colored people had.

I saw two colored men come out of the woods, and they told me that they had not been out of the woods for seven years. They came out in 1869; one was named John Dunlow and the other Billy Scrapp. They said they had seen crowds of white men kill more than two hundred colored men while they were in the woods. That is why they thought they were not free. From the latter part of 1867 till 1869 I done much traveling along the roads west of Shreveport—on the road called Jefferson Road. I saw stuck on an old stump the head of a colored man; I inquired of some colored people why and who put it there? They said that some white men brought from Shreveport a colored man who they killed and put his head on the stump. Thousands of colored persons told me they were driven from home and their crops and all they possessed taken away from them, and that exists even now.

I was at an election in 1870, in November, in the city of Shreveport, and I heard white men tell colored men that if they voted the Republican tickets that they would not let them have any more credit, nor would they bond them out of the jail; that they would have to go to the d——n Yankees or carpet-baggers to take them out, and the colored men told them that they were afraid to vote the Democratic ticket because they might make them slaves again. Many of them asked me what did I think was best? I told them I was nothing but a rail-splitter and wood-chopper, and did not know anything about politics; had never seen a poll for an election before, but thought if we voted the Democratic ticket we would have to carry passes from one parish to another and from one State to the other. I told them as to our freedom, our rights, and our votes that no Southern man was our friend; only the Northern men, Army officers, and United States troops were our friends; that the Southern people would always be arrayed against us as long as we lived because we were free.

In Shreveport large bodies of armed white men would go to break up our churches, during the same year, and on Sunday night before the election, and Monday also, a large body of armed men [white] went out and about to scare colored men from coming to the polls to vote the next day. So the colored people met them and told them to go back, for if they interfered with the churches that we, the colored men, would burn the city; but they did not go back, and it frustrated the colored people so they got scared and the churches were broken up. Tuesday, the day of the election, one colored man named

Squire Norman was killed by a Jew for distributing tickets (Republican) to the colored people.

I was told by several white persons on that day that they had me spotted; said I was spoiling the other negroes so they could not do anything with them, just because I told them to let my race vote the Republican ticket; let us Republicans advise Republicans, and the Democrats advise Democrats. They told me all such negroes as me had to be killed; I told them if they did kill me only give me my rights while I am living. . . .

During the year about twenty-five colored persons showed me their contracts and their account sales of their cotton; and their accounts due their employees and merchants, after balancing all, I found they had been swindled out of about seventeen hundred and ninety dollars. Some went to law to recover it, but it did no good; the courts were against the colored man; those that did not go to law were better off, for those that went to law some of them were killed, some whipped, and some ran away.

Many that did not even go to law were whipped also; I seen three white men go into a colored man's grocery in Shreveport and run him out, his mother, wife, and all his family, and took charge of the grocery themselves, and invited other white men to come in and drink. The colored man who owned the grocery was named A. Leroy. . . .

In February, 1871, a crowd of white men approached the house where I lived and sent me word by one of their number to leave home; they had made threats the day before that they intended to kill me and also all the discharged colored soldiers in and around Shreveport, Louisiana. But I did not leave my house; I staid there; I had made up my mind to face the battle. They told me their reason for wanting to kill me and all discharged colored soldiers was because they were ruining the other negroes. They had already jumped on several of the discharged colored soldiers, but they got as good as they sent. These colored men were then arrested and put in jail, and charges made against them; but the case was so plain they came out clear. While those men were in jail, then they approached my house; they were about fifty strong, yet they did not attack us. Then crossing Red River on my way to Homer I saw a white man on the ferry beat a colored man badly, giving him about twenty lashes as hard as he could put them on, and the man was afraid to raise up his head. . . .

In the year 1873 I served on the grand jury in Shreveport in the parish of Caddo; and there were ten colored men on the jury and six white. The colored prisoners told me that they did not get half enough to eat; some of them told me they were beat and whipped in jail by the jailer; a white man and the white men on the grand jury tried to find a true bill against every colored man that was indicted by a white man. I saw little colored boys in there for stealing one can of oysters. I seen little girls in there for stealing such things as thimbles, scissors, &c.; and was several colored men in prison and only two white men were put in jail for crimes they had committed; and most all the colored people whose cases came before us were indicted by white men. There was several colored ladies. There was no affidavit made against any white lady. The judge, lawyers, district attorney, and foreman of the grand jury and clerk all favored the rich man [white]. That is my opinion, however preposterous it may seem. All the cases that were fixed and came up during that sitting of the court there was but one white man tried, and it was for killing a colored man in cold blood, and he was cleared; but his trial was, and had been, standing for more than a year. The prisoners had not near enough blankets to keep them from catching severe cold and suffering untold misery.

During the year 1873 I saw many colored people swindled out of their crops. I led them into the light how it was done, but they were afraid to make affidavits against them. It is generally in this way that the white people rob the colored people out of two-thirds of what they make; for instance, the contract for one-third or one-quarter of the crop that is made as the case may be. They take it in every bale, and will not divide it at the gins, but ship it to the city; then when the cotton is sold they figure and figure until there is but little left to the colored man; then they do not settle, but wait until the next crop is pitched, say in February, and sometimes even in June, before they will say the cotton is sold. Generally about March they commence settling with the colored people. Some divides the cotton at the gin, but very few of them does, and it is in this way in which they plunder the poor colored men in this State. In the year 1874 in the month of January, I was in the parish of East Baton Rouge and St. Helena; also during the month of February and also in the parish of Lexington I seen colored men cheated out of their crops. I saw a white man from the town of Baton Rouge go to Strong Point, or North of Strong Point, La., and take a poor colored woman's bale of cotton and had it taken to Baton Rouge and sold it for a debt that a colored man owed him. A woman named Rachel Hopkins and her children made the cotton; I seen a colored man that lived in the same parish shot. His name was Shoemaker. He said that the white man shot him because he could not make him stop hunting with his own gun in the woods. . . .

I have seen along the banks of the Red River colored people who were afraid to talk with me at landings; some would ask me if the times would never get better. . . . They told me . . . we have been working hard ever since the surrender, and have not got anything that we can carry off the places if we attempt to go. Such is the case all along the Red River. A few of us can ran away at night, but a very few. In some instances old missus tells old massa we have or he has been a good nigger and worked so hard, let him have that old horse and wagon, that cow and hog, and some of that corn, and one bale of cotton. Only a very few even gets this much, although they have worked on that place for three or four years since the surrender. He says to me, look at aunt Nancy, she has to wait on old missus for four or five years for nothing; that is the way nearly all the whites do us on Red River, and when we go to vote they ask us what sort of a ticket we are going to vote. We tell them a Radical ticket; they tell us to vote their ticket (Democratic). We tell him we cannot vote that ticket; then he tell us if we do not vote their (Democratic) ticket we have to get off that place and leave just as you came, and carry, nothing away; you all brought nothing, and you shall carry nothing off; and that is the way the whites do us about voting; and if we dont do like they say they will kill some of us; run some of us off, and make us leave our crops; beat some of us nearly to death.

In Shreveport, Caddo Parish, La., in April and May, I could see every day colored people (women & men) and they told me they were coming from the country because the whites were running them away from their place, shooting some, killing some, and beating others, on account of their crops and the contracts; when they would ask them to pay to them their part of the crop according to the contracts the whites would then bring in old bills and say to the colored people, you owe me this, and I want it paid; the whites would then take all the colored people had, horses, mules, hogs, cows, chickens, beds and bedding, and then run them off the place or kill or shoot them. The white men killed during them two months eight men and boys (colored). The bad men (white) in this part of the State have organized themselves into bands, called White League, and white man's party, and they ride through all the parishes of the State, and threaten [that] any white man or black man that gets the nomination on the Republican ticket shall be killed.

The parish of Caddo was infested with such men and talk, and even the Democratic newspapers spoke it plainly. And if any colored man voted the Republican ticket he should not have any work. All this was done and said before the election came off.

Source: U.S. Congress, Senate, Select Committee, *The Removal of the Negroes from the Southern States to the Northern States*, 46th Cong., 2d sess., 1880, part II: 101–214.

*   *   *

Testimony of Ku Klux Klan Victim William Coleman

In 1866, a small number of former Confederate soldiers organized the Ku Klux Klan in the Tennessee town of Pulaski. A terrorist organization, the Ku Klux Klan did not become popular until Congress took control of Reconstruction, in 1867, mandating that former slaves be allowed to vote in state elections. This electrified white Southerners, and the Ku Klux Klan, along with similar vigilante groups under other names, spread across the South like wildfire. In 1871, Congress initiated a massive investigation into the Klan violence, calling hundreds of witnesses and creating a verbatim record of their testimony. Congress then published a thirteen-volume record of its investigation, the best record available of the Ku Klux Klan in Reconstruction.

Testimony of William Coleman before the Joint Select Committee to Inquire into the Condition of Affairs in the Late Insurrectionary States, 1871

William Coleman (colored) sworn and examined.
Macon, Mississippi, November 6, 1871.

Question: Where do you live?

Answer: I live in Macon.

Question: How long have you lived here?

Answer: I came here about the last of April.

Question: Where did you come from?

Answer: I came from Winston County.

Question: What occasioned your coming here?

Answer: I got run by the Ku-Klux. . . .

Question: Tell how it occurred. . . .

Answer: Well, I don't know anything that I had said or done that injured any one. Further than being a radical in that part of the land, as for interrupting any one, I didn't. . . .

Question: Did the Ku-Klux come to your house? . . .

Answer: They came about a half hour or more before day, as nigh as I can recollect by my brains, being frightened at their coming up in this kind of way. They were shooting and going on at me through the house, and when they busted the door open, coming in and shooting, I was frightened, and I can only tell you as nigh as my recollection will afford at this time that it was about a half hour to day.

Question: What did they do to you?

Answer: None of the shot hit me, but they aimed to hit me; but I had one door just like that at the side of the house and the other at this side, and there was the chimney, and there was my bed in that corner opposite, and they came to that door first, [illustrating,] and hollered, "Hallo"; bum, bum, bum, on the lock. I jumped up and said "Hallo." Then one at the door said, "Raise a light in there." "What for; who is you?" I said. He says, "Raise a light in there, God damn you; I'll come in there and smoke my pipe in your ear." He said that just so. I said, "Is that you, uncle Davy?" Says he, "No, God damn you, it ain't uncle Dave; open this door." Says I, "I am not going to open my door to turn nobody on me that won't tell me who they are before I do it. Who are you?" He says, "God damn you, we didn't come to tell you who we are." I was peeping through a little crack in the door. . . .

I saw men out there standing with horns and faces on all of them, and they all had great, long, white cow-tails way down the breast. I said it was a cow-tail; it was hair, and it was right white. They told me they rode from Shiloh in two hours and came to kill me. They shot right smart in that house before they got in, but how many times I don't know, they shot so fast outside; but when they come in, they didn't have but three loads to shoot. I know by the way they tangled about in the house they would have put it in me if they had had it. They only shot three times in the house. The men behind me had busted in through the door; both doors were busted open. By the time the fellows at the back door got in the door, these fellows at the front door busted in, and they all met in the middle of the floor, and I didn't have a thing to fight with, only a little piece of ax-handle; and when I started from the first door to the second, pieces of the door flew and met me. I jumped for a piece of ax-handle and fought them squandering about, and they were knocking me with guns, and firing balls that cut several holes in my head. The notches is in my head now. I dashed about among them, but they knocked me down several times. Every time I would get up, they would knock me down again. I saw they were going to kill me, and I turned in and laid there after they knocked me down so many times. The last time they knocked me down I laid there a good while before I moved, and when I had strength I jumped to split through a man's legs that was standing over me, and, as I jumped, they struck at me jumping between his legs, and they struck him and, he hollered, "Don't hit me, God damn you," but they done knocked him down then, but they hadn't knocked him so he couldn't talk. I jumped through and got past him. They didn't hit him a fair lick, because he was going toward them, and it struck past his head on his shoulder. If it had struck his head, it would have busted it open. I didn't catch that lick. I got up then; they had shot their loads. I grabbed my ax-handle, and commenced fighting, and then they just took and cut me with knives. They surrounded me in the floor and tore my shirt off. They got me out on the floor; some had me by the legs and some by the arms and the neck and anywhere, just like dogs string out a coon, and they took me out to the big road before my gate and whipped me until I couldn't move or holler or do nothing, but just lay there like a log, and every lick they hit me I grunted just like a mule when he is stalled fast and shipped; that was all. They left me there for dead, and what it was done for was because I was a radical, and I didn't deny my profession any-where and I never will. I never will vote that conservative ticket if I die.

Question: Did they tell you they whipped you because you were a radical?

Answer: They told me, "God damn you, when you meet a white man in the road [lift] your hat; I'll learn you, God damn you, that you are a nigger, and not to be going about like you thought yourself a white man; you calls yourself like a white man, God damn you."

Source: Testimony Taken by the Joint Select Committee to Inquire into the Condition of Affairs in the Late Insurrectionary States, Mississippi, 42d Cong., 2d sess., House of Representatives Report No. 22, part 11 (USGPO, 1872), 482–83.

*   *   *

African Americans Protest White Violence to the President

White violence prompted black Americans to write their president. Ulysses S. Grant, commander of Union armies in the Civil War, became president in 1869 and was reelected in 1871. A Republican, Grant represented the same party that had produced the Emancipation Proclamation. The letters he received from African Americans painted a horrifying picture of anarchic violence as insurgent whites bru-talized blacks in a bid to regain power.

A. Freeny and Seven Others, La Grange, Ga., Letter to U. S. Grant, September 2, 1874

Dear Sir, the republican party Troup County requested of me and the County Executive committee to write you in refference to our next elec-tion as we hasve been so badly oppressed at the polls heretofore & was not allow a Citizen chance to vote. We therefore thought it proper to ask you what steps would be best to pursue in the next Campaign. We was oppressed at the last Governor & President's Election so that there was not more than half of us could or did vote. They dealt with us in such a man-ner that one half of us could not get to the polls until in the later part of the Evening. When they saw that they had scattered the crowd, they al-low the remainder to come up and vote. Is that right? They had a whole lot of names on a piece of paper of which they said had not paid their tax of which cause lots that had paid to not vote. What shall we do with such? Sir in every Condition we are opprassed. Where as our election will come off next fall for Congressmen & Legislatur men, and we perceive that their will be riots and bloodshed at the polls without some protection from the higher authorites & whereas their has been already 300 Three hundred Guns laid up for shooting purpous by the Dimocratic party. These Guns they intended to use the Day of our nomination but as God was merciful to us, we escaped without any [fight] at all.

In short they are allow to takeout Grant's Military arms; we have non. They have a little County Court here of which is [ruining] the colored people henceforth and forever, it ough to be done away with. I Sir I am requested to ask you what must we do next fall? Be shot down at the polls or be driven from the polls like Dogs? I am a Candidate for the next Legislatur, but Sir I am expecting nothing more nor less than a riot. Will you therefore send the Garrison down here for pace & for nothing but pace? I mean on the Day of our Election of which will come off next some time in next month. Dear Sir aint their no possible way, whereby that Taxs may be sot a side until after the Election if theris any possible way please let us know immediately. The Election is drawing near and We want to get every thing in shape to meet it. Please let us have and answer from you soon as this reach you. I will close by asking you to Write soon . . . dont send any answer to the ordinary for he is a full Dimocrat and will not let us know what you said.

Source: Letters Received by the Department of Justice from Georgia, 1871–1884, General Records of the Department of Justice, Roll 2, M996, RG 60, National Archives microfilm.

President Grant, this Letter is Swore by 20 Black men of Tipton. We dont sign no names to it because the White men Mighty Catch up with us; we hafter slip our Letters to you if We can. So We says to you the White men is fixing for War evry day & he tells us to Lookout for ourselves for he Exspects to Kill us all out & We thought We mus fix for them & We went to town to buy amination & he wont sell it to us & that is the case in evry Little town. We send & therefore We Called Our Collar togather & Write to you to send us men to stand Untill we gets Redy thats all we ask them. Let us get Reddy for war before he starts on us & if you pleas send us men to Stand untill We is Reddy for them & then you maie turn them aloose. There air 300 men in Covington Reddy for Drilling & We here with our hands Empty. Sen us Rainforcement if you pleas. We dont want them to fight. We Wants them to keep peace untill We Gets Reddy. We knows whats the matter with them; this Civil right Bill is the cause of it & We demand it passage.

Source: Letters Received by the Department of Justice from Georgia, 1871–1884, General Records of the Department of Justice, Roll 2, M996, RG 60, National Archives microfilm.

*   *   *

Home Rule, 1879

After the Civil War, white Southerners feared the national government would make the wartime expansion of its powers permanent. This threat seemed especially worrisome when federal judges allowed African Americans to serve as jurors. Since grand juries investigate crimes, and have the power to put lynchers on trial as criminal defendants, biracial juries threatened the mob violence that defended the heart of white privilege. Whites fought back by claiming home rule as a constitutional privilege, a creation of the framers of the Constitution. This document, an editorial protesting federal "interference" in local affairs, comes from the Danville (Virginia) Daily News.

The Conflict of Judicial Authority

No subject of graver importance or more far reaching in its relations can engage public attention than that which has been thrust forward by the United States court for the western district of Virginia at its term in Danville just closed. We are no alarmist and abhor mere AGITATION, but we cannot close our eyes to the fact that the course of the federal judge for this district has precipitated a contest in which every vestige of the sovereignty of the commonwealth of Virginia—and indeed of every one of the commonwealths composing the Federal Union—is involved. The good people of Virginia have need to be aroused to a due sense of the importance of the issue presented, because upon its solution depends the very fabric of the government which was founded by the fathers of the Republic. If the pretensions of absolutism of the federal administration now set up [shall] be enforced everything like State autonomy, community independence, or "home rule" (as the modern phrase is)—principles dearest of all to the heart of the American citizen—might as well be surrendered as among the things of the happy past, and only thought of as we regard the parchment of an Egyptian mummy.

Source: editorial, *Danville (Virginia) Daily News,* March 5, 1879.

*   *   *

T. Thomas Fortune Demands Equal Rights

By 1884 the journalist T. Thomas Fortune offered a different view of the Constitution than that advanced by the Danville Daily News in 1879. Fortune had become one of the leading black orators in the nation. In 1884, he spoke at a banquet honoring the great Massachusetts senator Charles Sumner. Fortune gave a fiery speech, insisting that the Constitution guaranteed black rights against white aggres-

sions. Fortune made a constitutional argument, quoting the Fourteenth Amendment. He called for blacks to "agitate! Agitate! AGITATE!*" for their rights in the face of white violence.*

T. Thomas Fortune Speech, 1884

The black men of this republic have a herculean labor to perform. They need not look to others, to men and to parties, to perform it for them. The South had already wrenched from us the freedom and power of the ballot, and the doors of courts of law have been slammed in our faces. Star chamber justice has been instituted throughout the South, and mob and ruffianly outlaws execute the decrees of the star chamber. The criminal is denied the protection of the law; the innocent have no immunity from violent taking off; the laborer is defrauded of his honest wage; and our women are reduced to indignities which would arouse the vengeance of a savage. The South is now under the influence of a reign of terror. The usual processes of the law are suspended and individual license and hatred are the standards by which black men must measure the volume of their security of life and property. It is a sad picture that we are called upon to contemplate, not without parallel, indeed, in the history of mankind, but utterly without parallel in the history of our country. . . .

Unless I have watched the signs of the times erroneously, unless I have read history as I would read a romance, there will be a reaction in the South. Oppression forces the fetters of its own enslavement, lawlessness breeds its own deadly antidote. Oppression breeds rebellion and rebellion produces revolution. "Large oaks from little acorns grow."

The State denies us protection, and the National government says it has no jurisdiction, so that the black citizens of the South are absolutely without the pale of the law. What shall they do? Where shall they turn for succor or protection? What champion have they on the wave of politics . . . to present their grievances and urge with matchless zeal and eloquence that impartial justice shall be done? . . .

I have the courage here to-night . . . to declare the Supreme Court to be at fault, and to appeal from its arbiter dictum, . . . I care not to what that appeal leads. If it leads to another such conflict as the one which gibbetted treason at Appomattox, let it come. Better that tons of treasure and millions of lives were sacrificed on the field of battle than that the infamous principle should be established that there was one citizen of this grand republic who had not equal and inalienable rights with each and every one of his fellow-citizens. That the just laws incorporated in the Constitution of our country shall have full and ample vindication; that lawlessness may be throttled at

Danville, Virginia, and in Copiah county Mississippi, I appeal to the honest sentiment of the country; I appeal to the courage and manhood and intelligence of the race, and I trust that I shall not appeal in vain. We ask for no special favor; we ask for no law reared upon subterfuge or chicanery; we ask for no particular immunity on account of race, we ask simply for justice; we demand justice, pure and simple, and though it be delayed a quarter of a century, *justice we will have*! Let our pulpits thunder against oppression; let our newspaper be as diligent in defense of the people as the newspapers of the enemy, and let us by individual effort and in convention keep alive these questions until within our ample domains there shall not remain one citizen who cannot flee, with assurance of absolute protection, the feet of the Goddess of Liberty, the beautiful embodiment of our greatness, our [magnanimity] and our justice. Let us agitate! *Agitate!* AGITATE! Until the protest shall awake the nation from its indifference, and pave the way to the grand sentiment evolved out of the fires of the French revolution: "Liberty! Fraternity! Equality!"

Source: "Charles Sumner," *New York Globe*, January 19, 1884.

*   *   *

Frederick Douglass on Lynching

Born a slave in Maryland, Frederick Douglass escaped to the North, where he became the leading African American abolitionist and champion of freedom until his death in 1894. After the fall of slavery, Douglass challenged lynch law as the great evil black Americans faced. Like Fortune and so many black writers at this time, he also warned whites that they could not expect endless patience from the victims of their violence. When Douglass speaks of "the peculiar crime so often imputed" to African Americans, he means rape.

Lynch Law in the South, 1892

When men sow the wind it is rational to expect that they will reap the whirlwind. It is evident to my mind that the negro will not always rest a passive subject to the violence and bloodshed by which he is now pursued. If neither law nor public sentiment shall come to his relief, he will devise methods of his own. It should be remembered that the negro is a man, and that in point of intelligence he is not what he was a hundred years ago. Whatever may be said of his failure to acquire wealth, it cannot be denied that he has made decided progress in the acquisition of knowledge; and he is a poor student of the natural history of civilization who does not see that the mental energies of this race, newly awakened and set in motion, must continue to advance. Character, with its moral influence; knowledge, with its power; and wealth, with its respectability, are possible to it as well as to other races of men. In arguing upon what will be the action of the negro in case he continues to be the victim of lynch law I accept the statement often made in his disparagement, that lie is an imitative being; that he will do what he sees other men do. He has already shown this facility, and he illustrates it all the way from the prize ring to the pulpit; from the plow to the professor's chair. The voice of nature, not less than the Book of books, teaches us that oppression can make even a wise man mad, and in such case the responsibility for madness will not rest upon the [male] but upon the oppression to which he is subjected.

How can the South hope to teach the negro the sacredness of human life while it cheapens it and profanes it by the atrocities of mob law? The stream cannot rise higher than its source. The morality of the negro will reach no higher point than the morality and religion that surround him. He reads of what is being done in the world in resentment of oppression and needs no teacher to make him understand what he reads. In warning the South that it may place too much reliance upon the cowardice of the negro I am not advocating violence by the negro, but point out the dangerous tendency of his constant persecution. The negro was not a coward at Bunker Hill; he was not a coward in Haiti; he was not a coward in the late war for the Union; he was not a coward at Harper's Ferry, with John Brown; and care should be taken against goading him to acts of desperation by continuing to punish him for heinous crimes of which he is not legally convicted.

I do not deny that the negro may, in some instances, be guilty of the peculiar crime so often imputed to him. There are bad men among them, as there are bad men among all other varieties of the human family, but I contend that there is a good reason to question these lynch-law reports on this point. The crime imputed to the negro is one most easily imputed and most difficult to disprove, and yet it is one that the negro is least likely to commit. It is a crime for the commission of which opportunity required, and no more convenient one was ever offered to any class of persons than was possessed by the negroes of the South during the War of the Rebellion.

There were then left in their custody and in their power wives and the daughters, the mothers and the sisters of the rebels, and during all that period no instance can be cited of an outrage committed by a negro upon the person of any white woman. The crime is a new one for the negro, so new that a doubt may be reasonably entertained that he has learned it to any such extent as his accusers would have us believe. A nation is not born in a day.

It is said that the leopard cannot change his spots nor the Ethiopian his skin, and it may be as truly said that the character of a people established by long years of consistent life and testimony, cannot be very suddenly reversed. It is improbable that this peaceful and inoffensive class has suddenly and all at once become changed into a class of the most daring and repulsive criminals.

Now, where rests the responsibility for the lynch law prevalent in the South? It is evident that it is not entirely with the ignorant mob. The men who break open jails and with bloody hands destroy human life are not alone responsible. These are not the men who make public sentiment. They are simply the hangmen, not the court, judge, or jury. They simply obey the public sentiment of the South, the sentiment created by wealth and respectability, by the press and the pulpit. A change in public sentiment can be easily effected by these forces whenever they shall elect to make the effort. Let the press and the pulpit of the South unite their power against the cruelty, disgrace and shame that is settling like a mantle of fire upon these lynch-law States, and lynch law itself will soon cease to exist.

Nor is the South alone responsible for this burning shame and menace to our free institutions. Wherever contempt of race prevails, whether against African, Indian, or Mongolian, countenance and support are given to the present peculiar treatment of the negro in the South. The finger of scorn at the North is correllated to the dagger of the assassin at the South. The sin against the negro is both sectional and national, and until the voice of the North shall be heard in emphatic condemnation and withering reproach against these continued ruthless mob-law murders, it will remain equally involved with the South in this common crime.

Source: Frederick Douglass, "Lynch Law in the South," *North American Review* 155 (July 1892): 22–24.

*　　*　　*

Letters to the Editor of the *Indianapolis Freeman*

Edward E. Cooper urged blacks to improve themselves, much like Booker T. Washington would two years after this letter. But he published in his newspapers letters from readers that led him to despair. This letter says that black Americans were in hell, lynched, abused, and ridiculed. Its author complained that blacks had helped build America and yet were confronted with cruel and brutal racism. He concluded by saying that blacks must do something to save themselves.

Letter to the Indianapolis Freeman, August 19, 1893

When I survey the Southern States of America and view the surroundings of the Negro, comparing his advantages with the disadvantages. I ask myself the question, are not the Negroes in hell? Hell is only a place of horror and punishment. How much more horror can hell have for its victims, than the Southern States has for the Negroes? We are falsely accused, ridiculed, imprisoned for trifles, lynched on false accusations, and robbed of the rights of citizenship. This is hell in the first degree. Let us see if we are such hell deserving creatures. Have we not always been loyal? When the war of secession was in full blast. General Hunter stationed at Port Royal S.C., received ordered to enlist all loyal people; he enlisted Negroes, and when called to account for it, he stated that Negroes were the only loyal people in that locality. All through this war the Negro showed manhood, and while the white men who were forced into service from the South, was from home, the Negroes worked and supported their families and improved their farms. Now they pay us for it by every tyrannical deed they can perpetrate. We have done more by physical strokes, to build up these United States than any race mentionable. When we are reined up before the courts, we appear before jurors of the white race, and they are stuffed with Negro hatred. In the rural districts they seem to pick most of them that are totally illiterate, some of them to my knowing could not understand their own name printed in letters as large as a house. Still they must say wither the Negro must be punished. They say every time, if the Negro is prosecuted by a white man, "A way with the Negro! Sink him to degradation!!" And it is done. That is hell. The whites of every class will not allow the Negro to converse with the females of their race; but on the other hand they will slip around and bribe and intermingle with the fairest of our race Negroes. Take the whites for example, protect your females at the peril of your lives. Do to them as they would do to you in such a case in these Southern States, where the laws forbid intermarriages, we much forbid intermingling. We must stand up for our rights, though we die. Have race pride, respect ourselves and make others respect us. We hope that the leading Negroes will meet at some designated place and take steps to perfect some measure to the betterment of our condition, as mentioned by Bishop Turner in one of his latest articles. We must do something.

Perkins
Pensacola, Florida

Source: Perkins, editorial, *Indianapolis Freeman*, August 19, 1893.

*　　*　　*

Paul Laurence Dunbar on the Constitution Trampled Underfoot

In 1903, still five years before the Springfield violence, the African American poet and writer Paul Laurence Dunbar (1872–1906) published a bitter satire on Independence Day that captured what many blacks saw as the true situation. He recited the names of Northern cities recently disgraced with racial violence: Belleville, Wilmington, and Evansville. Every news dispatch, and not just from the South, reported some new outrage. He also cited the massacre of Jews in Kishinev, Russia. American newspapers reported that, in April, priests led bloodthirsty mobs against Jewish men, women, and children. American blacks fared no better than Russian Jews, Dunbar suggested. Blacks, he complained, watched the destruction of every principle the Declaration of Independence and the Constitution stood for and yet still celebrated the Fourth of July. In his poem, Dunbar described blacks as beaten and abused, bloody from torture, and yet still singing patriotic hymns. At the end of his text, he beseeched God, asking how long the suffering would continue.

Born in Dayton, Ohio, Dunbar made his name documenting the effects of racism. He expressed his dismay that racial violence seemed to have poisoned the entire nation, moving beyond the South. Dunbar published four novels and six volumes of poetry and was the first native-born black writer to win international praise for his writing.

Paul Laurence Dunbar on the Fourth of July, 1903

Belleville, Wilmington, Evansville. The Fourth of July, and Kishineff, a curious combination and yet one replete with a ghastly humor. Sitting with closed lips over our own bloody deeds we accomplish the fine irony of a protest to Russia. Contemplating with placid eyes the destruction of all the Declaration of Independence and the Constitution stood for, we celebrate the thing which our own action proclaims we do not believe in.

But it is over and done. The Fourth is come and gone. The din has ceased and the smoke has cleared away. Nothing remains but the litter of all and a few reflections. The skyrocket has ascended, the firecrackers have burst, the roman candles have sputtered, the "nigger chasers"—a pertinent American name—have run their course, and we have celebrated the Nation's birthday. Yes, and we black folks have celebrated.

Dearborn Street and Armour Avenue have been all life and light. Not even the Jew and the Chinaman have been able to outdo us in the display of loyalty. And we have done it all because we have not stopped to think just how little it means to us.

The papers are full of the reports of peonage in Alabama. A new and more dastardly slavery there has arisen to replace the old. For the sake of reenslaving the negro, the Constitution has been trampled under foot, the rights of man have been laughed out of court, and the justice of God has been made a jest and we celebrate.

Every wire, no longer in the South alone, brings us news of a new hanging or a new burning, some recent outrage against a helpless people, some fresh degradation of an already degraded race. One man sins and a whole nation suffers, and we celebrate.

Like a dark cloud, pregnant with terror and destruction, disfranchisement has spread its wings over our brethren of the South. Like the same dark cloud, industrial prejudice glooms above us in the North. We may not work save when the newcome foreigner refuses to, and then they, high prized above our sacrificial lives, may shoot us down with impunity. And yet we celebrate.

With Citizenship discredited and scored, with violated homes and long unheeded prayers, with bleeding hands uplifted, still sore and smarting from long beating at the door of opportunity, we raise our voices and sing, "My Country 'Tis of Thee"; we shout and sing while from the four points of the compass comes our brothers' unavailing cry, and so we celebrate.

With a preacher, one who a few centuries ago would have sold indulgences to the murderers on St. Bartholomew's Day, with such a preacher in a Chicago pulpit, jingling his thirty pieces of silver, distorting the number and nature of our crimes, excusing anarchy, apologizing for murder, and tearing to tatters the teachings of Jesus Christ while he cries, "Release unto us Barabbas,"* we celebrate.

But there are some who sit silent within their closed rooms and hear as from afar the din of joy come muffled to their ears as on some later day their children and their children's sons shall hear a nation's cry for succor in her need. Aye, there be some who on this festal day kneel in their private closets and with hands upraised and bleeding hearts cry out to God, if there still lives a God, "How long, O God. How long."

Source: "The Fourth of July and Race Outrages," New York Times, July 10, 1903.

*   *   *

George P. Upton on the Facts about Lynching

In 1875, the Chicago Tribune announced that changes in business required a new and more scientific writing style based on facts, numbers, and tables. It began keeping

---

* According to Passover custom, Pilate could commute one death sentence by popular outcry. The mob cried for Barabbas and not Jesus. Matthew 27:16; Mark 15:7; Luke 23:18–19; John 18:40

statistics on lynching in 1881, and George P. Upton, an associate editor at the Tribune, ran the lynching statistics project. He gathered his data from other newspapers and did not consider what kind of definition of lynching his fellow editors might be using when they called some killings lynchings but not others. Because Americans do not have a common definition of lynching, all statistical counts of lynching are false, almost always greatly underestimating the extent of the actual violence whites perpetrated against blacks. Upton's statistics are nonetheless quite significant for presenting a supposedly objective and scientific picture of lynching across the entire nation. The Tribune statistics showed that rape did not often motivate lynchers and that whites killed blacks for many reasons, ranging from the "serious" to the "grotesque" according to Upton. Notice that the legitimacy of lynching was so well established that Upton could not say all lynching was unjustified. Instead, he could only find "most of them unjustifiable."

George P. Upton, "The Facts about Lynching," 1904

There has never been a time when the lynching evil has so largely occupied public attention as now, or when it has been discussed more seriously and thoughtfully. It has been forced upon the national consideration not so much by the prevalence of the evil or its alarming increase as by the occasional manifestations of savagery in Northern communities, which previously had maintained apparently agreeable relations with the colored race. It seems, therefore, an opportune time to present some facts concerning this dangerous form of mob violence which may give those who are studying the subject ample material for consideration and perhaps some fresh suggestions as to causes and remedies.

What are the facts in the case?

There have been 2,875 lynchings since 1885 is as follows:

1885....................210
1886....................162
1887....................125
1888....................144
1889....................175
1890....................128
1891....................193
1892....................236
1893....................200
1894....................189
1895....................166
1896....................131
1897....................166
1898....................127
1899....................107

1900	115
1901	101
1902	96
1903	104
Total	2,875

The record of lynchings by States and Territories since 1885 is as follows:

North.

Indiana	38
Kansas	38
California	33
Nebraska	33
Wyoming	33
Colorado	31
Montana	29
Idaho	21
Illinois	19
Washington	16
Ohio	13
Iowa	12
South Dakota	11
Oregon	10
Michigan	6
North Dakota	5
Nevada	5
Minnesota	4
Wisconsin	4
Alaska	4
Maine	3
Pennsylvania	3
New York	2
New Jersey	1
Connecticut	1
Delaware	1
Total	376

South.

Mississippi	298
Texas	272
Louisiana	261
Georgia	253
Alabama	232
Arkansas	207
Tennessee	191
Kentucky	148
Florida	128
South Carolina	100

Virginia..............................84
Missouri 79
North Carolina 58
Indian Territory.................54
West Virginia.....................43
Oklahoma 38
Maryland...........................20
Arizona 18
New Mexico 15

Total 2,499

Massachusetts, New Hampshire, Vermont, Rhode Island, and Utah are the only States where lynchings have not occurred, tho Connecticut, Delaware and New Jersey have but one to their discredit. This speaks well for four of the New England States and our new Mormon State. Is this immunity, however, due to a greater respect for law than the other States have shown, or is it due the comparatively few negroes in their population? Analyzing the results by geographical divisions, lynchings have taken place as follows: South, 2,499; West, 302; Pacific slope, 63; East, 11.

It will be seen by these figures that notwithstanding the South has more than six times as many lynchings as the rest of the country, the evil is not local or sectional. The mania for mob murder has manifested itself in every State save five, and in Indiana, Kansas, Illinois and Delaware mobs have been as cruel and savage as their methods of punishment and their lust for torture as in the most remote and ignorant sections of the South. The cross roads and back settlements of Mississippi and Georgia have witnessed no worse barbarity than was inflicted upon victims by mobs at Pittsburg, Kans.; at Belleville and Danville, Ill.; or at Wilmington, Del. To this extent lynching is not merely the disgrace of the South. It is a blot upon American civilization—a national, not a sectional, evil.

What are the causes of lynching?

That it has been an easy matter to find pretexts for lynching is shown by the fact that these 2,875 persons have been sacrificed to the cruelty and fury of the mob for seventy-three different reasons, many of them serious, most of them unjustifiable, some of them grotesque. Whenever a negro is lynched for criminal assault the Southern newspaper, and sometimes the Northern, will headline its "story" or its editorial comment, "Lynched for the usual cause." This glaring misstatement is unjust to the negro race. Criminal assault is not the "usual cause." Persons lynched for this crime since 1885 numbered 564, while 1,099 have been lynched for murder. Adding to the former those lynched for attempted, alleged and suspected criminal assault, for complicity

in the crime and for the double crime of criminal assault and murder, the total is 702, as compared with 1,277 cases in which murder was directly or indirectly charged against the victims. About one-third of the blacks and one-
sixth of the whites were lynched for criminal assault. Of course, white men
are more liable to [be] hanged or sent to the penitentiary for the crime. It was
stated recently, in a letter to the New York *Evening Post,* that "in Sing Sing
prison to-day, out of the 1,032 whites, 65 are there for rape. Of the 143 blacks
only 2 are there for the same crime." The claim, therefore, that lynching is
the summary punishment for a single crime is not only misleading, but dis-
honest. If any crime can be called "usual," it is murder. Startling as it may
seem, statistics will show that murder is the national crime.

Besides the 1,979 cases already mentioned, 896 others have been lynched
for no less than 56 different causes, prominent among which are 106 for arson, 326 for theft, burglary and robbery; 94 on account of race prejudice, and
134 unknown persons lynched for unknown reasons. Negroes to the number
of 53 have been lynched for simple assaults, 18 for insulting whites and 16
for making threats—offenses which would hardly have been noticed had the
offenders been white. Seventeen persons have been lynched merely because
they were unpopular in their neighborhoods. Ten were found to be innocent
when it was too late. The remaining causes present a heterogeneous array,
not one in the 1st offering the slightest justification for mob murder. Con-
cisely stated, they are slander, miscegenation, informing, drunkenness, fraud,
voodooism, violation of contract, resisting arrest, elopement, train-wreck-
ing, poisoning stock, refusing to give evidence, political animosity, disobedi-
ence of quarantine regulation, passing counterfeit money, introducing small-
pox, concealing criminals, cutting levees, kidnapping, gambling, riots,
testifying against whites, seduction, incest, and forcing a child to steal. One
young fellow was actually lynched for jilting a girl, who subsequently and
quite promptly consoled herself by marrying another. A reformer was
lynched for advocating colonization, a colored man for enticing a servant
away from her mistress, and a mountaineer for "moonshining." In the beginning of the lynching period under consideration murder and criminal assault were the "usual causes," for at that time other offenses were taken into
court. The variety of causes since that time, however, shows how insidiously
the evil has progressed. Blacks and whites are now lynched for offenses
which have no relation to criminal assault, and many, if not most, of which
in a well regulated and law abiding community would be disposed of in the
lower courts. How insidious this evil is, how rapidly, when not opposed, it
tends to barbarize, is also shown by the exceptionally cruel lynchings which
have occurred in Northern communities during the last two years. This

shows, as Bishop Candler, of Georgia, recently declared, that "lynching is due to race hatred and not to any horror over any particular crime," and that unless it is checked it may involve anarchy; "for men will go from lynching persons on account of their color to lynching other persons on account of their religion, or their politics, or their business relations." The record already begins to show cases of this kind.

These are gruesome facts and figures, but one who has watched them year after year, who has studied the circumstances of each case of lynching, who has kept track of the increase of repressive legislation and observed its effects, cannot help but note a more encouraging trend of public sentiment. There is a brighter side to the picture. It is impossible not to believe that the lynching evil is on the decrease. It never may be possible entirely to prevent crime. It never may be possible in a country as large as this and with such a heterogeneous population completely to prevent lynching, but it is possible to make it an exceptional crime. There is every reason to believe that things are working to such an accomplishment. The number of lynchings is decreasing. It is encouraging that the number is fast decreasing in those States which formerly were the worst offenders. Both the Governors of Alabama and Mississippi in their messages to the Legislature last year boasted of their immunity from lynching as compared with previous years, and have called attention to the more resolute action of sheriffs and to the excellent working of recent anti-lynching legislation. There is hardly a Southern State which has not adopted repressive measures of some kind and given new powers to Governors and county authorities. It is evident that there is a strong revulsion of feeling in the South and that law-abiding and law-respecting men are doing everything in their power to vindicate justice and restore the authority of the courts. Public prosecutors also are performing their duties more efficiently. Grand juries are growing more courageous. Mob murderers no longer boast of their cruel work, but seek to conceal their share in it. The general agitation of the question which was aroused, as already said, not because of an increase of lynchings in the South, for they are on the decrease, but because of the needless barbarity which recently has characterized lynchings in the North, has been healthy. It has incited the best citizens, North and South, to fresh efforts for the restriction and, if possible, the suppression of the evil. It has come to be recognized, as Justice Brewer said, that lynching is murder, and, as Justice Love said, that in the end it means anarchy, that it is an evil dangerous to civilization, and that if it is not checked it inevitably will increase rapidly under the joint influence of mob cruelty and race hatred.

Another citation from these statistics—and a significant one—indicates there is [a] brighter side to the picture. While there is a decrease in lynchings there is an increase in legal executions, and this increase is specially notice-able in those States where lynching has been most common. There have been 123 persons legally hanged this year, seventy-eight of them in the South. Five years ago nearly every one of these seventy-eight would have been lynched. Wherever the law works promptly and the authorities are en-ergetic and resolute in its enforcement lynchings decrease and legal execu-tions increase. There is no reason to be discouraged. The outlook is hopeful.

Source: George P. Upton, "The Facts about Lynching," Independent 57 (Sep-tember 29, 1904): 719–21.

*   *   *

Senator Ben Tillman Defends Lynching

Before becoming a senator, Ben Tillman served as governor of South Carolina from 1890 to 1894, denouncing lynching and dispatching the national guard against lynch mobs, though his opposition to lynching weakened when he thought the lynch-ers went after rapists. In 1892, he told a crowd he opposed lynching but would "willingly lead a mob in lynching a negro who had committed an assault upon a white woman." Tillman represented South Carolina in the U.S. Senate from 1895 until his death in 1918. In 1907 Tillman defended lynching on the floor of the Sen-ate, linking whites' sexual fears with their supposed need to commit acts of racial violence. Of course, the Chicago Tribune data in the previous document, based on local newspapers reporting the lynchers' own claims, showed that violent white racists did not even pretend that their victims had raped anyone most of the time—in those events the newspapers chose to call lynchings.

Congressional Record—Senate, 1907

SENATOR TILLMAN: Now let us suppose a case. Let us take any Senator on this floor. I will not particularize—take him from some great and well ordered State in the North, where there are possibly twenty thousand negroes, as there are in Wisconsin, with over two million whites. Let us carry this Sena-tor to the backwoods in South Carolina, put him on a farm miles from a town or railroad, and environed with negroes. We will suppose he has a fair young daughter just budding into womanhood; and recollect this, the white women of the South are in a state of siege; the greatest care is exercised that they shall at all times where it is possible not be left alone or unprotected, but that can not always and in every instance be the case. That Senator's daughter undertakes to visit a neighbor or is left home alone for a brief while. Some lurking demon who has watched for the opportunity seizes her; she is choked or beaten into insensibility and ravished, her body prostituted, her purity destroyed, her chastity taken from her, and a memory branded on her brain as with a red hot iron to haunt her night and day as long as she lives. . . .

In other words, a death in life. This young girl thus blighted and brutalized drags herself to her father and tells him what has happened. Is there a man here with red blood in his veins who doubts what impulses the father would feel? Is it any wonder that the whole countryside rises as one man and with set, stern faces seek the brute who has wrought this infamy? Brute, did I say? Why, Mr. President, this crime is a slander on the brutes. No beast of the field forces his female. He waits invitation. It has been left for something in the shape of a man to do this terrible thing. And shall such a creature, because he has the semblance of a man, appeal to the law? Shall men coldbloodedly stand up and demand for him the right to have a fair trial and be punished in the regular course of justice? So far as I am concerned he has put himself outside the pale of the law, human and divine. He has sinned against the Holy Ghost. He has invaded the body of hollies. He has struck civilization a blow, the most deadly and cruel that the imagination can conceive. It is idle to reason about it; it is idle to preach about it. Our brains reel under the staggering blow and hot blood surges to the heart. Civilization peels off us, and all of us who are men, and we revert to the original savage type whose impulses under any and all such circumstances has always been to "kill! kill! kill!"

Source: Congressional Record, 59th Cong., 2d sess., January 12, 1907, 1441.

*   *   *

The NAACP Confronts Lynching

First organized in 1909, the National Association for the Advancement of Colored People (NAACP) fought lynching for most of the twentieth century. In May 1918, after the murder of a white farmer, whites rampaged across southern Georgia through one bloody, horrific weekend. On Friday, May 17, lynchers killed two black men, Will Head and Will Thompson. Thereafter, the mob killed Hayes Turner and his wife, Mary, after she protested the death of her husband. Mary Turner was pregnant, and the mob used her condition to torture her, tying her upside down and burning her. The lynchers cut Mary Turner open and ripped out her fetus and crushed it underfoot. Georgia newspapers seemed a bit defensive about killing a woman, indicating that she had made "unwise remarks" and that she had had a gold watch belonging to the murdered man.

It is not known who at the NAACP wrote this memorandum. Clearly, the brutal murder of Mary Turner prompted the organization to try to understand how white Georgians could be so brutal. Georgia, the author of this memorandum wrote, had a long history of racial violence. In the end, the memorandum asks why the self-respecting people of Georgia do not do something themselves to end the barbarism. There is no answer.

Anonymous Memorandum, NAACP Papers, [1918]

While within the past thirty years, few states have been wholly free from the lawless pastime of lynching, Georgia has engaged in this bloody industry with so vigorous an application as to have attained over her nearest competitors in this sanguinary business an evil pre-eminence.

The press of the country is ever and anon hailing the state of Georgia before the bar of public opinion as the crowning disgrace of a lynch-crazed section. And even as the elevation of mob violence over the orderly processes of law is confined almost entirely to the Southern group of states, so in that state the most crushed and broken beneath the tyrant heel of a criminal frenzy, one section thereof is more completely enslaved, more tightly chained by this mastering brutality than any other.

Though the conquest of Georgia by the mob has been accomplished with a fair degree of thoroughness throughout the state, the law-abiding elements are in general restive, and at times able to prevail even against the might of the hated oppressor. But in South Georgia the grip of the mob is secure, the sentiment is firm; and the law writhes in agony as it is torn to shreds by the all powerful lyncher. The 1918 atrocities in Brooks and Lowndes Counties but serve to accentuate the awful blood-lust to which the neighboring counties are subject. The territory running from the Atlantic Ocean to the Chattahoochee and bounded on the South by Florida and on the North by the counties of Stewart, Webster, Sumter, Dooly, and Wilcox, and the Ockumlgee and Attamaha Rivers, reeks with the disgrace of a dreadful barbarity. There it is that over thirty percent of the Georgia lynchings have been placed with certainty and there is a large probability that goodly number of the twenty-six lynchings in a locality undetermined but known to have occurred within the borders of that state, took place in Georgia.

The number of persons lynched in Georgia from 1889 to 1918 inclusive is three hundred and eighty-six. Of that number, one hundred and nineteen have been lynched in South Georgia, two hundred and forty-one in other parts of the state, and twenty-six at a place unknown. Of the forty-eight counties in Georgia, thirty-nine, so far as can be definitely ascertained, have had no lynchings within one thirty-year period. Of these thirty-nine, six, namely Appling, Miller, Terrell, Charlion, Camden, and Glynn are in South Georgia, the other twenty-eight counties in that section being credited with all its lynchings. Counting the twenty-six lynchings in an undetermined locality as among those happening in some part of Georgia other than the Southern and we yet have 119 persons lynched in 28 counties of South Georgia as against 267 persons in 115 counties scattered over the rest of the state, or an average of 4¼ persons a county in South Georgia as against an average of approximately 2⅓ persons a county in the rest of the state. The percent of the number of persons lynched in South Georgia out of the whole number lynched in the entire state is 30.8. The county having the largest number of persons lynched is Lowndes in South Georgia, with its total of 15 lynchings, giving a percent of 3.9. The county with the next highest number is Early in South Georgia, with a total of 10 persons lynched, the percent being 2.6. No other counties in the state have had more than 9 lynchings, and of three counties possessing [that] number, two, Brooks and Decatur, [are in] South Georgia. Wayne County has had eight lynchings, Ware seven. Mitchell six; while Worth, Lee and Randolph Counties have each had five.

The block of counties beginning with Brooks and ending with Wayne, extending diagonally from the Florida line to the 'tamaha River, has had 42 lynchings, or 35.3 percent of the total number in South Georgia, and 10.8 of the total for the entire state, an average for the seven counties under consideration (Brooks, Lowndes, Echols, Clinch, Ware, Pierce, and Wayne) of 6 persons lynched per county. If, as is probable, a majority of the twenty-six lynchings happening in a locality not known with a definite exactness actually occurred in South Georgia, the disgrace cast on the rest of the commonwealth by that barbarous section becomes even more pronounced.

And nowhere have lynchings been accompanied by more gruesome features and horrible cruelties than in South Georgia. Then, as to exemplified in the lynching of Mary Turner at Valdosta in May 1918, the mob delights in the infliction of the most unheard of torments, and, in ghoulish glee, continues its savage enjoyment after the death of its victim in the mutilation of the body and the erection over the grave of a scurrilous headstone.

Is it any wonder that salesmen refuse to do other than a cash business in South Georgia, that they openly condemn the people of that section as untrustworthy, as lacking in every instinct of business honesty? Is it not likely that a community the chief pastime of which is the doing to death of human beings by the most awful barbarities imaginable, can spare sufficient time from its periodic auto-da-fes to attend to a mere matter of business. And certainly the people of such a community can have no sense of economic values. In the thrill of the man hunt, they forget the value of the man; as long as it is a pleasure to kill Negroes, they toss carelessly aside any stray thoughts concerning the necessity of Negro labor, and watch contentedly, with a selfish disregard of the good of their section and of their state, which hundreds upon hundreds of Negroes flee terror-stricken before their murderous fury.

It is in the light of these facts that we gently query—why do not the self respecting people of Georgia do something to suppress these disgraceful conditions, and especially to rid their state of that criminal element which, by inhuman practices, rules with such destructive sway, so fine a section of a mighty commonwealth as South Georgia?

Source: Memorandum, I-C-353, Series A, Part 7, NAACP Papers, Manuscript Division, Library of Congress, Washington, D.C. (microfilm, reel 10). [filed with Mary Turner]

*　　*　　*

The Burning of Jim McIlherron

Two weeks after he joined the NAACP staff, in February 1918, Walter White left for Estill Springs, Tennessee, where a mob of one thousand white people had chained Jim McIlherron to a tree, tortured him with hot irons, cut his body horribly, and then burned him alive. White passed as a white man to gain the confidence of the white people living in and around Estill Springs, a geographically isolated hamlet of about two hundred people strongly committed to religious fundamentalism. His interviews revealed that whites resented McIlherron for his economic success and refusal to accept racial conventions. McIlherron had lived in the North for a while, and local white people thought that experience had ruined him for living in Tennessee. When two whites harassed him, throwing rocks, McIlherron shot and killed them. Even some of the white people White interviewed conceded that McIlherron had acted in self-defense. But that did not matter. In the minds of many whites, no black man could kill or assault any white person for any reason.

The Burning of Jim McIlherron: An NAACP Investigation, 1918

The Town

Estill Springs, the scene of the third within nine months of Tennessee's burnings at the stake, is situated about seventy-four miles from Chattanooga, being midway between that city and Nashville. The town itself has only two hundred inhabitants; with the territory within the radius of a half-mile, about three hundred. Franklin County, in which Estill Springs is located, had a white population of 17,365 and 3,126 colored inhabitants in 1910, according to the census. Estill Springs is not incorporated and, therefore, has no mayor or village officials. It is a small settlement located midway between the larger and more progressive villages of Decherd and Tullahoma, each having about 2,000 inhabitants. Winchester, fifteen miles from Estill Springs, is the county seat.

Estill Springs is made up of a small group of houses and stores gathered about the railway station. The main street is only three blocks long. Its few business establishments are located on one side of this street. There is one bank, the Bank of Estill Springs, purely local in nature; a barber shop, a drug store and five general merchandise stores of the type indigenous to small rural communities of the South. The settlement's sole butcher left on the day that the investigator reached there, to work in a nitrate factory in a nearby town as the butcher trade of the community was not sufficient to support his shop. Simply stated, Estill Springs is one of the thousands of small settlements of its type, poorly located from a geographic and economic standpoint and with little prospect of future growth. Its static condition, naturally, tends to make the minds of its inhabitants narrow and provincial. The people of the surrounding country are farmers and because of the failure of the cotton crop last fall, occasioned by an early frost, corn was the only crop on which they made money. Such of the people as were interviewed were leisurely of manner and slow of speech and comprehension.

Paradoxical as it may seem, in the light of the event which has put Estill Springs on the map in a kind of infamy of fame, the settlement seems to have a strong religious undercurrent. Small as the community is, it has four white churches, two Baptist, one Methodist and one Campbellite. In addition, there are two colored churches, one a Baptist and the other a Methodist, of which latter the Rev. G. W. Lych was pastor. There is a local Red Cross unit among the white women which was planning to inaugurate meetings to knit for the soldiers. In the windows of a number of homes, the emblem of the National Food Conservation Commission was displayed. The son of the proprietor of the only hotel is local agent for the sale of Thrift Stamps. The town purchased its allotment of both the first and second liberty loans.

The Cause of the Trouble

About one mile from the railway station of Estill Springs, there lived a Negro by the name of Jim McIlherron. He resided with his mother, several brothers and father, who bears the reputation of being wealthy, "for a Negro," as he owns his own land and is prosperous in a small way. The McIlherrons do not appear to have been popular with the white community. They were known as a family which resented "slights" and "insults" and which did not willingly allow its members to be imposed upon by unfriendly whites. However, there appears to have been no serious trouble between them and their white neighbors up to the time of the street fight which resulted in the shooting for which Jim McIlherron was later burned at the stake. One white woman expressed in a local phrase the opinion of the family when she said that the McIlherron family were "big-buggy niggers," meaning that they were prosperous enough to have a few articles other than bare necessities, among these being a larger buggy than was common in the section. Most of the whites in the locality, it must be explained, were of the poorer country folk.

Jim McIlherron bore the reputation in Estill Springs of being a "bad sort." It was gathered from remarks made that this implied that he shared the family characteristic already alluded to of resenting "slights" and "insults." In other words, he was not what is termed "a good nigger," which in certain portions of the South means a colored man or woman who is humble and submissive in the presence of white "superiors."

McIlherron was known to be a fighter and the possessor of an automatic revolver. (Laws against "gun-toting" are observed in the breach, apparently, in this region.) He was, therefore, classed as a dangerous man to bother with. A little over a year before the lynching, he became involved in a fight with his own brother in which the latter was cut with a knife wielded by the former. For this he was arrested by Sheriff John Rose, the sheriff of Franklin County. At the time of this affair, McIlherron threatened to "get" the sheriff if he was ever arrested again by that officer. It is an admitted fact in the community that the sheriff was afraid of McIlherron. Soon after the trouble with his brother, McIlherron went to Indianapolis where he worked in an industrial plant, proceeding later to Detroit. In Detroit he had an attack of rheumatism and was forced to return to his home shortly before the shooting. His having lived in the North tended to increase his disfavor with the white people of the community, as he was credited with having absorbed during his residence there certain ideas of "independence" which were not acceptable to the white citizens of this small rural community.

Sharing popular disfavor with McIlherron was the pastor of the Methodist church in Estill Springs, the Rev. G. W. Lych. He had repeatedly advised the colored people to assert their right to be free from the petty tyranny alleged to have been imposed upon them by the white people, assuring them that they were made of the same clay and were as good as anybody else.

The Shooting
On the afternoon of Friday, February 8, Jim McIlherron went into a store in the town and purchased fifteen cents' worth of candy. In Estill Springs it had

been a habit of an element of young white men to "rock" Negroes in the community—i.e., throwing rocks or other missiles at them to make them run. This had occasioned frequent tilts between the races, none of which, however, had previously been serious. McIlherron had been the victim of one of these "rockings" and had declared that if ever they got after him again, somebody was going to get hurt. When the trouble started on February 8, it was about five o'clock in the afternoon, in the gloom of early nightfall. It is probable that the Negro believed that they were after him again. He walked down the street eating this candy, going past Tate & Dickens' store in front of which he encountered three white men, Pierce Rogers, Frank Tigert, and Jesse Tigert by name. As McIlherron passed them a remark was made by one of the young men about his eating the candy. The others laughed and several more remarks were made. At this the Negro turned and asked if they were talking about him. Words followed, becoming more and more heated, until threats began to be passed between them. One of the young men started into the store whereupon McIlherron, apparently believing, as one of our white informants said, that they were preparing to . . . start a fight, pulled out his gun and started shooting. Six shots were fired, two taking effect in each man. Rogers died in his tracks, Jesse Tigert died about twenty minutes later and Frank Tigert was carried to the office of Dr. O. L. Walker, Estill Springs' only physician, where he received medical aid. The latter will recover, as his wounds are not serious.

The Man Hunt

Immediately after the shooting, McIlherron, in the attendant excitement, ran down the road leading toward his home. There was no immediate pursuit by the whites. Although everybody knew that he had gone to his home, the white people waited and sent all the way to Winchester, the county seat, some fifteen miles distant, at a cost of sixty dollars, to secure blood-hounds. When these arrived, they succeeded in tracking him only as far as his home, where the scent was lost.

Intense excitement prevailed in the town as news of the shooting spread. In this chaotic state of affairs, no one seemed to know what to do and threats of lynching began to be made. A few of the cooler heads pleaded that the crowd allow the sheriff to handle the entire affair. Knowing of the sheriff's fear of the Negro, the crowd greeted this suggestion with a derisive shout, and cries of "Lynch the nigger" answered this plea. Plans were laid to form posses to catch McIlherron. Word was sent to Sheriff Rose at Winchester, upon receiving which he immediately left for Estill Springs.

Shouts of "Electrocution is too good for the damned nigger." "Let's burn the black ——" and others of the sort rose thick and fast. Led by its more radical members, the mob soon worked itself into a frenzy; a posse was formed and set out on the manhunt.

Meanwhile, McIlherron had gone to his home, gathered his few clothes and proceeded to the home of Lych, who aided him in his flight. On two mules they set out in the direction of McMinnville, in an attempt to reach the Tennessee Central Railroad where McIlherron could get a train that would take him to safety. The preacher went a part of the way with McIlherron and then returned to his home in Prairie Springs, a small settlement about twelve miles from Estill Springs. The news soon spread that Rev. Lych had aided McIlherron in his flight and a part of the mob went to Prairie Springs to "get" him for this. Two members came upon him near his home. One of them pointed his gun at the preacher and pulled the trigger. The gun did not go off, and before he could fire again, Lych snatched the gun from his assailant's hands, broke it and started towards the man with the stock in his hands, when the other man fired a charge into the preacher's breast, killing him instantly.

The hunt for McIlherron continued throughout Friday night, Saturday, Sunday and Monday, large posses of men scouring the surrounding county for him. Monday night he was located in a barn near Lower Collins River, just beyond McMinnville. The barn was surrounded and the posse began firing on it. The Negro answered the fire, this state of affairs continuing throughout Monday night. During this time McIlherron succeeded in holding off the crowd, whose numbers were rapidly augmented, when the news spread that the Negro had been located. In the hundred or more men in the posses were Deputy Sheriff S. J. Byars and Policeman J. M. Bain. In the fusillade of bullets poured into the barn, McIlherron was wounded, one eye being shot out. He also received two body wounds, one in the arm and one in the leg. Finally, McIlherron's ammunition gave out and, weak from the loss of blood, he was forced to surrender when the barn was rushed. When captured, the triumphant members of the mob carried him into McMinnville. The feeling against him was so great that an attempt was made to lynch him in the town of McMinnville, but the citizens of that town refused to allow a lynching in their midst and were able to prevent it from happening. McIlherron was, therefore, placed on Train No. 5, *en route* to Estill Springs, where he arrived at 6:30 P. M. on Tuesday.

The Crowd

In the meantime, news of the capture spread like wild fire and men, women and children started pouring into the town to await the arrival of the victim. They came from a radius of fifty miles, coming from Coalmont, Winchester, Decherd, Tullahoma, McMinnville and from the country districts. In buggies and automobiles, on foot, on mules, they crowded into the little settlement until it was estimated that from 1,500 to 2,000 people were in the town. A high state of excitement prevailed at the time for the arrival of the train drew near. Threats of the torture to be inflicted were made on many sides. Boxes, excelsior and other inflammable materials were gathered in readiness for the event, and iron bars and pokers were obtained. Most of the crowd were grim and silent, but there were some who laughed and joked in anticipation of the coming event.

Finally, the train drew near. McIlherron was so weak upon arrival, from the loss of blood due to three wounds received in the battle with the posse, that he was unable stand and had to be carried to the spot selected for his execution. The leaders of the mob decided that he should be lynched on the exact spot where the shooting occurred. He was, therefore, carried to this place where preparations for the funeral pyre were made. The cries of the crowd grew more and more vengeful as moments passed.

Just as the arrangements had been completed, a few of the braver spirits among the women of the town demanded that the Negro be not burned in the town itself, but be taken out a little way in the country. There were loud objections to this proposal from the now uncontrollable mob. The women insisted, in spite of these objections, and finally it was decided to carry McIlherron across the railroad into a small clump of woods in front of the Campbellite church. This was done and the mob transferred its activities to the new execution ground.

The self-appointed leaders of the mob by this time had great difficulty in restraining the wild fury of the crowd. They were constantly forced to appeal to them not to strike McIlherron or to spit on him . . . to allow the affair to be a "perfectly orderly lynching." The sister of one of the men slain was in the mob and had become frantic in her plea to the men to let her kill the Negro. She demanded that he be killed immediately, not to let him live another moment. It was evident that such a humane thing as instant death would not have appeased the blood-thirst of the mob, in its revengeful mood.

The Torture
On reaching the spot chosen for the burning, McIlherron was chained to a hickory tree. The wood and other inflammable material already collected was saturated with coal oil and piled around his feet. The fire was not lighted at once, as the crowd was determined "to have some fun with the damned nigger" before he died. A fire was built a few feet away and then the fiendish torture began. Bars of iron, about the size of an ordinary poker, were placed in the fire and heated to a red-hot pitch. A member of the mob took one of

these and made as if to burn the Negro in the side. McIlherron seized the bar and as it was jerked from his grasp all the inside of his hand came with it, some of the skin roasting on the hot iron. The awful stench of burning human flesh rose into the air, mingled with the lustful cries of the mob and the curses of the suffering Negro. Cries of "Burn the damned hound," "Poke his eyes out," and others of the kind came in the confusion from the mob. Men, woman and children, who were too far in the rear, surged forward in an attempt to catch sight of and gloat over the suffering of the Negro.

Now that the first iron had been applied, the leaders began eagerly to torture McIlherron. Men struggled with one another, each vying with his fellow, in attempting to force from the lips of the Negro some sign of weakening. A wide iron bar, redhot, was placed on the right side of his neck. When McIlherron drew his head away, another bar was placed on the left side. This appeared to amuse the crowd immensely and approving shouts arose, as the word was passed back to those in the rear of what was going on. Another rod was heated, and, as McIlherron squirmed in agony; thrust through the flesh of his thigh, and a few minutes later another through the calf of his leg. Meanwhile, a larger bar had been heating, and while those of the mob close enough to see shouted in fiendish glee, this was taken and McIlherron was unsexed.

The unspeakable torture had now been going on for about twenty minutes and the Negro was mercifully getting weaker and weaker. The mob seemed to be getting worked up to a higher and higher state of excitement. The leaders racked their brains for newer and more devilish ways of inflicting torture on the helpless victim.

The newspapers stated that McIlherron lost his nerve and cringed before the torture, but the testimony of persons who saw the burning is to the effect that this is untrue. It seems inconceivable that any person could endure the awful torture inflicted, however great his powers of resistance to pain, and not lose his nerve. The statements of onlookers are to the effect that throughout the whole burning Jim McIlherron never cringed and never once begged for mercy. He was evidently able to deny the mob the satisfaction of seeing his nerve broken, although he lived for half an hour after the burning started. Throughout the whole affair he cursed those who tortured him and almost to the last breath derided the attempts of the mob to break his spirit. The only signs of the awful agony that he must have suffered were the involuntary groans that escaped his lips, in spite of his efforts to check them, and the wild look in his eyes as the torture became more and more severe. At one time, he begged his torturers to shoot him, but this request was received with a cry of derision at his vain hope to be put out of his misery. His plea was answered with the remark, "We ain't half through with you yet, nigger."

By this time, however, some of the members of the mob had, apparently, become sickened at the sight and urged that the job be finished. Others in the rear of the crowd, who had not been able to see all that took place, objected and pushed forward to take the places of some of those in front. Having succeeded in this, they began to "do their bit" in the execution. Finally, one man poured coal oil on the Negro's trousers and shoes and lighted the fire around McIlherron's feet. The flames rose rapidly soon enveloping him, and in a few minutes McIlherron was dead.

Source: Walter White, "The Burning of Jim McIlherron," *Crisis* 16 (May 1918): 16–20.

*   *   *

James Weldon Johnson's Outrage over the Lynching of Henry Lowry

In 1920, James Weldon Johnson (1871–1938), a poet, author, and civil rights activist, became the NAACP's first black executive secretary and took charge of the whole organization. He worked vigorously to recruit new members and investigate lynchings. Information about particular lynchings was a powerful tool for both recruiting new members and raising funds for the organization. The brutal lynching of Henry Lowry in Nodena, Arkansas, genuinely outraged Johnson, as did all lynchings, but he also saw it as an opportunity to show the horrors of white racism to a wide audience, attracting new members and contributions.

American Barbarism by James Weldon Johnson, 1921
In the whole history of lynching in the United States, there is not a more revolting chapter than the one written last week in the State of Arkansas.

A colored man by the name of Henry Lowry was accused of murdering two white persons. He made his escape to Texas and was arrested and placed in jail at El Paso. He voluntarily surrendered himself to go back to Arkansas to stand trial, on the understanding that he was to receive protection.

The train on which Lowry was being taken under guard of two Deputy Sheriffs was met at Sardis, Mississippi, at five o'clock in the morning by a heavily armed mob. Lowry was taken off and driven about one hundred miles to the scene of the alleged crime in Arkansas.

The Memphis papers of January 26th carried headlines advertising the fact that the lynching party expected to pass through Memphis on its way to Arkansas. The same papers carried a telegraph statement from the leader of the mob, in which he boasted: "We are going to parade him through the main street when we pass through Memphis; then we are going to take him to Arkansas and that will be the end of him."

Memphis papers of the same date above mentioned carried headlines which read, "May Lynch Three to Six Negroes This Evening." "Lowry Nears Tree on Which It Is Planned to Hang Him." "Taken through Memphis Today."

With all this advertising in the newspapers of what was to take place, nothing was done to uphold the law or to protect the prisoner. The Sheriff offered as an excuse, "Nearly every man, woman, and child in our County wanted the Negro lynched. When public sentiment is that way, there is not much chance left for the officer."

Governor McRay, of Arkansas, according to a report in the Memphis "Press," talked with that newspaper over long distance telephone in the afternoon before Lowry was lynched and said that he had not ordered State Troops to proceed to Nodena, Arkansas, to prevent the lynching threatened to take place that night. He said further, "I can not get in tough with Sheriff Blackwood of that County so I would not know whom to send the Troops to."

On the night of January 26th, Lowery was lynched; no, not lynched, but as one newspaper headline expressed it, "He Was Killed by Inches."

Let Americans who have any pride in their country read a few excerpts from the report of the lynching in the Memphis "Press" by Ralph Roddy, a special writer on that paper:

More than five hundred persons stood by and looked on while the Negro was slowly burned to a crisp. A few women were scattered among the crowd of Arkansas planters, who directed the gruesome work of avenging the death of O. T. Craig and his daughter, Mrs. C. O. Williamson.

Not once did the slayer beg for mercy, despite the fact that he suffered one of the most horrible deaths imaginable. With the Negro chained to a log, members of the mob placed a small pile of leaves around his feet. Gasoline was then poured on the leaves and the carrying out of the death sentence was under way.

Inch by inch the Negro was fairly cooked to death. Every few minutes, fresh leaves were tossed on the funeral pyre until the blaze had passed the Negro's waist. As the flames were eating away his abdomen, a member of the mob stepped forward and saturated his body with gasoline. It was then only a few minutes until the Negro had been reduced to ashes.

Even after the flesh had dropped away from his legs and the flames were leaping toward his face, Lowry retained consciousness. Not once did he whimper or beg for mercy. Once or twice he attempted to pick up the hot ashes in his hands and thrust them in his mouth in order to hasten death. Each time the ashes were kicked out of his reach by a member of the mob.

These excerpts do not refer to the deeds of the so-called savages in the dark places of the earth. They are the deeds of so-called superior white men, and women too, in a so-called Christian and civilized State of the so-called great American Democracy.

The whole thing is sickening. It is maddening. It is sufficient to make Negro citizens of this country hysterical, either with the quakings of fear [or] the desires of vengeance.

There is one thing certain. If this nation does not arise and stamp out the sort of thing which took place last week in Nodena, Arkansas, it had as well be conceded that it is on its way to Hell and Destruction.

Source: James Weldon Johnson, "American Barbarism," *New York Age*, February 5, 1921.

*   *   *

The Department of Justice on the Definition of Lynching

In the early morning hours of January 30, 1943, three white Georgia law enforcement officers, Mack Claude Screws, Frank Edward Jones, and Jim Bob Kelley, arrested Robert Hall, a black man, and beat him to death outside the courthouse in Newton, Georgia. The NAACP investigated, collecting photographs and statements from witnesses. The Department of Justice began its own investigation.

The NAACP first described the killing of Hall as a lynching by the three officers. The Department of Justice asked the NAACP not to use the word lynching in connection with the case. The government sensed they had a real chance to win a conviction of the three killers in federal court, though the jury would be white men from the same area where the killing occurred. To persuade a jury to convict, the government wanted to avoid making the affair into a cause célèbre. The word lynching was so inflammatory that labeling the killing with that term was bound to excite public opinion. By its intervention with the NAACP, the government successfully prevented Hall's death from becoming known as a lynching.

Letter by Wendell Berge, Assistant Attorney General, to the NAACP, February 25, 1943

Gentlemen:

. . . The death of Robert Hall was reported to the Department by T. Hoyt Davis, United States Attorney, Macon, Georgia, by letter dated February

11, 1943. Mr. Davis requested an immediate investigation by the Federal Bureau of Investigation. The Department requested such investigation under date of February 12, 1943.

The information concerning this investigation is given to you under the strict admonition that no publicity should be had with reference thereto. The Department is of the opinion that any publicity of an investigation at this time would be harmful to the success of the investigation.

It is noted that in your letter of February 19, 1943, you referred to Mr. Hall's death as a "lynching." It is believed advisable to have a definite understanding as to the use of this word, and it is suggested that the next time Mr. Walter White or Mr. Thurgood Marshall are in Washington they, or either of them, call upon Mr. Rotnem to discuss this matter.

Source: Wendell Berge to National Association for the Advancement of Colored People, February 25, 1943, A407, NAACP Papers, Manuscript Division, Library of Congress.

*   *   *

The NAACP on the Definition of Lynching

The Robert Hall "lynching" illustrates that the word lynching had value more as a tool to inflame public opinion than as a term susceptible to objective definition. No scholar has ever successfully defined lynching, and in fact, while the word evokes strong images in the minds of ordinary people, Americans have never reached a consensus on what constitutes a lynching. The NAACP, organized to fight lynching, struggled with conflicting meanings of the term, finally deciding that technical definitions served only to restrict the word's use as a political tool. In the two documents that follow, NAACP staffers discussed various competing definitions. Clifford Case, a Republican congressman from New Jersey, and an ally of the NAACP, proposed defining lynching as an act of violence, or an attempted act of violence, based on various kinds of prejudice, against a person or that person's property. Case's first definition did not require any kind of corrective intent. Notice that he thought property could be lynched. Some proposed definitions would have limited lynching to fatal punishments, but others, like the Case bill, did not, and the NAACP decided not to narrow the meaning of lynching in that way. Notice also that none of the definitions debated by the NAACP in 1947 would have included violence carried out by law enforcement personnel or deputized citizens. Today, almost all scholars of lynching agree that posse violence should be included as lynchings along with violence by ordinary citizens.

Memorandum to the Legal Department from
Julia E. Baxter, June 4, 1947

The President's Committee on Civil Rights has asked us to supply them with our NAACP definition of lynching. They have also asked us to distinguish between our definition and that employed by Tuskegee Institute. When I pointed out that our definition was identical with that language employed by the current Case bill, H. R. 3488, the question of whether this definition is consistent with our earlier definition arose.

I should like to bring to your attention the following definitions as embodied in NAACP sponsored anti-lynching legislation:

H.R. 3488 (Introduced in House of Representatives, May 15, 1947 by Clifford P. Case, R., N. J.) *Section 4*:

Any assemblage of two or more persons which shall, without authority of law, (a) commit or attempt to commit violence upon the person or property of any citizen or citizens of the United States because of his or their race, creed, color, national origin, ancestry, language, or religion, or (b) exercise or attempt to exercise, by physical violence against person or property, any power of correction or punishment over any citizen or citizens of the United States or other person or persons in the custody of peace officer or suspected of, charged with, or convicted of the commission of any criminal offense, with the purpose or consequent of preventing the apprehension or trial or punishment by law of such citizen or citizens, person or persons, or of imposing a punishment not authorized by law, shall constitute a lynch mob within the meaning of this Act. Any such violence by a lynch mob shall constitute lynching within the meaning of this Act.

H. R. 1698 (Introduced in House of Representatives, January 23, 1945 by D. Lane Powers, R., N.J.) *Section 2*:

Any assemblage of three or more persons which exercises or attempts to exercise by physical violence and without authority of law any power of correction or punishment over any citizen or citizens or other person or persons in the custody of any peace officer or suspected of, charged with, or convicted of the commission of any offense, with the purpose of consequence of preventing the apprehension or trial or punishment by law of such citizen or citizens, person or persons, shall constitute a "mob" within the meaning of this Act. Any such violence by a mob with results in the death or maiming of the victim or victims thereof shall constitute "lynching" within the meaning of this Act.

Our NAACP Annual Report for 1940, page 14, states that after a conference held with Tuskegee Institute and the Association of Southern Women for the Prevention of Lynching, the NAACP agreed to this definition: "A lynching is regarded as an activity in which persons in defiance of the law administer punishment by death to an individual for an alleged offense to an individual with whom some offense has been associated."

In connection with the distinction made by Tuskegee Institute with regard to a definition of lynching, I should like to call your attention to correspondence between Mr. Ralph N. Davis of Tuskegee and Mr. White. On July 28, 1941 Mr. Davis wrote Mr. White stating that our definition of lynching as printed in our Annual Report of 1940 was erroneous and that at the conference held by the three agencies a definite criteria to be used in classifying lynching was worked out. These included (1) a dead body (corpus delicti) (2) person or persons met death illegally (3) person or persons met death at the hands of a group (4) the group acted under pretext of service to justice, race, or tradition.

You can appreciate the confusion which exists among outside organizations that are ready to accept the NAACP as an authoritative voice on the matter of lynching. Will you please supply me with an official definition for specific use by our department. The President's Committee on Civil Rights is anxious to include our definition in its interim report to be released immediately.

Source: Julia E. Baxter to Legal Department, June 4, 1947, Papers of the NAACP, Manuscript Division, Library of Congress, Washington, D.C.

Memorandum to Mr. White from Marian Lynn Perry, June 11, 1947
We have received a memorandum from Miss Baxter, of our Research Department, requesting us to furnish her with the official definition of a "lynching" as used by the N.A.A.C.P.

To date, the only published definition of a lynching made by the N.A.A.C.P. is that contained in the annual report for 1940 which grew out of the Tuskegee conference, which definition is as follows: "A lynching is regarded as an activity in which persons in defiance of the law administer punishment by death to an individual for an alleged offense or to an individual with whom some offence has been associated."

The Legal Department has never felt that this definition was adequate and in the various drafts of anti-lynching bills which have been submitted to Congress, up until the Case bill, the definition has always included maiming as well as death. Thus, the 1945 bill provided in essence that when three or more persons exercised, by physical violence, without authority of law, this constitutes a mob and that any violence by such a mob which results in death or *maiming* constitutes lynching. The 1947, or Case version of the anti-lynching bill is, as you know, much broader than previous bills in many ways and this bill included, as did the other bills, the commission of violence upon a person under the circumstances similar to those described above whether or not such violence results in death.

Both the earlier versions and the Case version include attempts at lynching as well as lynching itself and it is clear that attempts do not result in death.

It is likewise clear that the difference between our official definition of a lynching for statistical purposes and the definition which we have sponsored in legislation is bound to cause confusion and we recommend that it be immediately resolved by adopting as the definition of lynching that set forth in the Case bill.

Source: Marian Lynn Perry to Walter White, June 11, 1947, Papers of the NAACP, Manuscript Division, Library of Congress, Washington, D.C.

*   *   *

Walter White Calls for a Federal Law against Lynching

Walter White made many trips to Congress, lobbying for a federal law against lynching. In 1948, a subcommittee of the House Judiciary Committee allowed White to speak at length on racial violence. White used the opportunity to go over specific lynchings to show the need for a law. By 1948, the FBI investigated all lynchings, and the Department of Justice relied on civil rights laws originally enacted in 1870 and 1871 to prosecute lynchers. The FBI did a good job gathering evidence, White said, the problem was the weakness of the laws. With a stronger law, the Justice Department would win more convictions.

Statement of Walter White, Executive Secretary, NAACP, 1948

MR. WHITE: Everybody knows about the crime of lynching.

I want to address myself very briefly, therefore, to one or two observations. First I would like to take up the question that has been raised by some critics of anti-lynching legislation who contend that lynching is nothing but murder and should be punished by the States themselves because it is a State responsibility and not a Federal one.

It is our contention that lynching is murder and more than murder; because when a lynching mob goes out to take vengeance on a person of different color, race, creed, or place of birth, he not only takes upon himself vengeance in the way of mob murder but also arrogates to himself the functions of judge, jury, and executioner.

So, in so doing; he lynches the law itself.

Second, there is the contention by some opponents of this legislation that such a law is no longer necessary because of the decrease in the number of lynchings.

I believe that to be very fallacious reasoning. As long as there is a single lynching anywhere in the United States, the whole system of Government on which our whole civilization is based is thereby endangered.

Lynchings have diminished primarily because of the continuing campaign for Federal legislation against the crime, and therefore there is a fear of the Federal Government, which has caused this diminution in the number of lynchings.

It is my measured conviction that if there were not this possible passing of Federal antilynching legislation, we should see immediately an increase in the number of mob murders; particularly if the present spiral of inflation bursts forth into a depression and creates a keen competition for jobs. . . .

There is this statement I should like to make: That the publicity that has been given to the crime of lynching—the growing condemnation of that evil, not only in the North but in the South as well, has resulted in lynchings going on underground.

During 1946, for example, there were numerous cases which are now under investigation—some by the FBI and some by the National Association for the Advancement of Colored People, and some by other organizations—of killing of individuals, particularly in the South where little publicity was given to the murders but where there is considerable reason for belief that they were lynchings which were deliberately kept out of the press so there would be no condemnation of the communities in which they took place.

We also saw immediately after the end of the war a determination on the part of certain people in the South to utilize terrorism of the lynching mob to intimidate Negro veterans returning from overseas, in order to convince them that the fight they had helped make for the democratic process must not under any circumstances be construed as changing their status as inferior persons. . . .

I would like to call attention to the date, August 18, 1946, in Minden, La., concerning John C. Jones, an honorably discharged Negro veteran of the European theater of operations, who had risen to the rank of corporal and returned to his home and family in Minden, La.

There was a dispute between him and a local white man who wanted a war souvenir, which Jones had brought back. This led to feeling in the community and the story began to be spread that Jones was now a difficult and dangerous character because he refused to give up this war souvenir.

Jones and his 17-year-old nephew, who was called Sonny Boy Harris, were charged with having been seen in the late evening in the back yard of a white woman resident of Minden. They were arrested and put into jail.

The white woman in the case refused to place any charges, and said that neither Jones nor his nephew, Sonny Boy Harris, had been seen in the neighborhood, that she had no complaint against them whatsoever.

They were kept in jail for several days and then one night they were told after darkness had fallen that they were now free and could go.

Jones was suspicious at their releasing him at that late hour of the night and refused to leave the jail until the following morning, whereupon certain officers of the law forced him out of the jail into the hands of a lynching mob, which took him and his 17-year-old cousin [or nephew] to an isolated spot, beat Jones so unmercifully that he died and his eyes "popped" from his head. Then they burned his face and hands with a blowtorch to the extent that whereas Jones' skin was light in color, it was jet black, having been charred by the blowtorch.

The 17-year-old boy, Sonny Boy Harris, was left for dead. They thought they had killed him, but fortunately he had survived. He made his way to his father's house, who immediately got him out of the community because he knew the boy would be immediately killed if the mob discovered he was alive.

We were requested by the Federal Bureau of Investigation and the Department of Justice to locate Sonny Boy Harris, which we did. I personally brought this boy down to Washington and turned him over to the Department of Justice.

The Department of Justice did everything within its power to obtain indictments and to secure convictions, but such is the weakness of the present law that despite all of the efforts the Department of Justice and the Federal Bureau of Investigation put forth they were unable to obtain convictions, which is ample proof in my opinion of the necessity of the Federal antilynching law, like H. R. 3488.

MR. CRAVENS: What evidence would they have had if they had the law?

MR. WHITE: They would have had more law from which they could have drawn a jury from a greater area and had the greater authority of the Federal Government as provided in the Case bill.

MR. CRAVENS: Well, you said you had the Federal Bureau of Investigation and the Department of Justice working on it and they were unable to make a case.

MR. WHITE: No, it was not that they were unable to make a case. The Federal Bureau of Investigation got the evidence. Then because of the weakness of the present Federal laws the Department of Justice was unable to obtain convictions.

MR. CRAVENS: You mean if they had this antilynching law they could have secured convictions?

MR. WHITE: They could have, in my opinion.

Another instance similar to this is that of Maceo Snipes, veteran, on July 2[0],1946, who was lynched by a mob because he dared to vote—his constitutional right which he sought to exercise.

Or again the case of George Dorsey, one of the victims of the quadruple lynching, in Walton County, Ga.

MR. CRAVENS: Where was the one you just referred to about the vote?

MR. WHITE: Taylor County, Ga. July 20, 1946.

MR. CRAVENS: And the other was Minden, La.?

MR. WHITE: Yes.

One of the four victims of a quadruple lynching in Walton County, Ga., July 25, 1946, was George Dorsey, also a Negro veteran, who was lynched because he resented the unwelcome attentions paid to his wife by a local white man. In that instance the Federal Bureau of Investigation . . . did a most excellent and thorough job of investigating the lynchings, as well as the NAACP.

The lynchers are known. They are walking free throughout Walton County, Ga., today but because of the weakness of the law they were unable to get indictments of these men and the State courts were unwilling and unable to do what they should have done.

To show you how far a lynching mob would go: A young Negro by the name of Golden Lamar Howard, who was subpoenaed by the Federal grand jury investigating this lynching, answered the subpoena and testified before the grand jury, as he was required to do. Later, he was beaten almost to death by a man because he refused to tell what he had testified before the grand jury.

I cite these as examples of the kind of things that are happening in this country, because always there is this potentiality of mob violence which is used to intimidate citizens from voting, improving their economic status, and obtaining educational advantages which would make them decent and productive American citizens.

I wish to refer very briefly to the charge which is sometimes but fortunately not as is frequently true as the lynch mobs would have you to believe: That those victims have been guilty of sex offenses against white women.

That charge has been repeatedly exploded. Out of more than 5,000 lynchings which have disgraced America since 1889 less than 1 in 6 of the victims have even been charged by the mobs themselves with sex offenses of any character whatsoever.

Yet, as has already been referred to by a previous witness, last night in my native State of Georgia the Ku Klux Klan held a meeting claiming they were coming back into being in order to "protect white womanhood." I believe that white womanhood in the North and the South is in no great danger and wants no violation of the laws of God or man for their protection.

I should also like to refer to the statement that lynching is necessary because the law is too slow. I believe such a contention as that is absurd. Not even the grand dragon of the Ku Klux Klan would have the effrontery to deny that the law is lightning fast when a Negro is charged, accused, or even suspected of a crime against a white person.

There is this over-all consideration of the crime of lynching: Lynchers are cowards and bullies and they use their terrorism created by the lynching mob solely for the purpose of preventing citizens from exercising their constitutional rights.

But I want to point out, as has already been referred to by others, that lynching is just a part of the whole sickness out of which it grows. There is the matter of jobs, the matter of the right to vote. There is the question of obtaining decent educational and health facilities. All of these things are necessary if we are going to wipe out the kind of situation which has existed in America for far too long.

I believe that the President's message to the Congress on last Monday is a courageous and clear blueprint of the kind of course that America must follow if she is going to demonstrate to the world that she means what she says when we claim that we are a democracy.

I had the privilege, during the late war, of traveling in the various parts of the war as a war correspondent, in both the European and Pacific theaters of war.

Wherever I went I was asked these questions by thoughtful people of all races and creeds and colors: "Is it really true that you have lynchings in America? Is it true that people are burned to death by blowtorches? Why do you have a Jim Crow Army—a black army and a white army sent overseas presumably to fight against the Hitler system and his theories of racial superiority?"

I saw pamphlets dropped by Germans from planes to the Arab tribes, in which they used the lynchings and race riots in the United States as an attempted means of proving that the United States was not an honest nation when it said it was fighting for democracy and freedom for all men everywhere.

In the Pacific and other places I saw some of the propaganda of the Japanese, which called the American white man an arrogant, prejudiced, imperialistic individual who should be driven out of the Pacific and out of Asia.

I do not want to see any racial war of any sort, white against black, or black against white. I believe that the form of government we have here in America is the best that mind of man has yet devised, but I do not believe it is going to survive unless we live up to what we say we believe in, namely, justice and freedom for everyone.

Finally, Mr. Chairman, I want to comment on some of the charges of partisanship in connection with this and similar legislation.

I contend that this is not Democratic legislation; that it is not Republican legislation. I contend that it is American legislation. But we have had unhappily in the Congress all too often a conservative coalition of both parties against human rights. I believe in the Eightieth Congress there is enough vision and courage to form an alliance for human rights; and that is why we are particularly delighted to endorse bills H. R. 3488 and H. R. 1352, with the hope that parties, even in an election year, can forget purely political considerations and enact legislation to correct these basic evils here in the United States.

We have a new climate of public opinion. We have the magnificent reaction to the report of the President's Committee on Civil Rights, headed by Charles E. Wilson, of the General Electric Corp., where North, South, East, and West have praised the recommendations of that report.

In the Gallup and other polls we have seen the overwhelming majority of the American people urging the Congress to enact legislation of this sort.

And I believe it is tremendously important that we not wait; that we wipe out all political partisanship as far as is possible, and that we enact this legislation now.

Thank you, Mr. Chairman.

THE CHAIRMAN: Thank you, Mr. White.
Most of us know who you are and what your organization is, and that you are an expert witness.
I wonder, however, if you would state briefly for the record how long you have been connected with this organization and this problem, and [in] general qualify yourself as an expert witness on the facts as well as on the proposed legislation.

MR. WHITE: The length of time you set for me is a little embarrassing. Last Sunday I completed my thirtieth year with the National Association for the Advancement of Colored People.
I would like to add, though, as a matter of self-pride, that I came to the association as a very, very young man.
I happen to possess a skin which—as I sometimes use the phrase—I can use on both sides of the racial fence, and because of that circumstance I have investigated some 41 lynchings and some 12 race riots during the past 30 years. . . .
The National Association for the Advance[ment] of Colored People has 1,627 branches, youth councils and colored chapters and a biracial membership in excess of a half million. Its board of directors consists of distinguished Americans of both races, and it has for 39 years now sought to substitute reason and intelligence for emotion and prejudice in this difficult area of race relations.

Source: U.S. Congress, House of Representatives, Subcommittee No. 4 of the Committee on the Judiciary, *Antilynching,* 80th Cong., 2d sess., February 4, 1948, 48–59.

*   *   *

Ronald Reagan Demands Law and Order

Ronald Reagan complained that liberals had taken over the courts, using them to accomplish their reform agenda. He and his followers scoffed at liberal doubts about punishing individual criminals. He did not agree with liberals that society created criminality and had only itself to blame for crime. Reagan wanted to overturn this liberal orthodoxy, first as governor of California and then as president. Claiming that low crime rates in the Great Depression proved that criminality could not be traced to poverty, in 1968 Reagan, then the governor of California, testified before the Republican platform committee. His statement outlined the major points the Republicans would use to regain power. Democrats had coddled criminals, ignoring crime victims. Reagan did not know it, but his speech began a movement toward greater concern for victims' rights that would lead to legislation against "hate crimes."

Ronald Reagan's Testimony before the
Republican Platform Committee, 1968

Mr. Chairman, members of the Platform Committee.

You have honored me greatly with your invitation. Because you are eminently well-qualified to draft a platform setting forth our Republican philosophy, let me confine my remarks to the broader area of what the president referred to as "the unease pervading our land." . . .

Our nation is agitated by suspicion, hesitant out of fear and aimless from lack of leadership. . . .

Order has broken down in our streets.

Organized rebellion has broken out on our campuses.

The courts approve and often underwrite the very things our individual integrity rejects.

The immorality of it all confounds the mind and exhausts the spirit . . . . and, worst of all, it disenchants our young. . . .

Eight years ago our land was not torn by riots and insurrection. Today it is.

Eight years ago terror did not stalk our streets and parks and schoolyards. Today, it does. . . .

Here at home we must recover the will necessary to make our streets safe, our cities free from violence and our campuses centers for learning rather than for outrage and insurrection. We must reject the permissive attitude which pervades too many homes, too many schools, too many courts.

It is too simple to trace all crime to poverty or color. There is a crime problem in the suburbs as well as in the slums; and, the minority communities are victims of crime out of all proportion to their numbers. Criminals are not bigoted and they are color blind; they . . . rob and maim and murder without reference to race, religion or neighborhood boundaries.

We must reject the idea that every time a law is broken, society is guilty rather than the lawbreaker. It is time to restore the American precept that each individual is accountable for his actions.

Source: "Excerpts of a Speech by Governor Ronald Reagan, Republican National Convention, Platform Committee Meeting, Miami, Florida," July 31, 1968, Ronald Reagan Library, Simi Valley, Calif.

*   *   *

Washington State's Law against Malicious Harassment

In 1977, Frank Collin made violent bigotry a national topic by announcing he wanted to demonstrate for his rights in the Chicago suburb of Skokie, Illinois, which had a large Jewish population, including seven thousand aging Holocaust survivors.

Thereafter, the Anti-Defamation League of B'nai B'rith (ADL) urged states to pass laws against malicious harassment. In 1981, the states of Oregon and Washington became the first states to adopt the ADL's model, passing laws against crimes motivated by hatred. Neither state called its new statute a "hate crime law." The news media hardly noticed what they had done. Nonetheless, these new laws began a wave of lawmaking that swept the nation. Today, hardly any state lacks a law against hate crimes.

Malicious Harassment, 1981

(1) A person is guilty of malicious harassment if he maliciously and with the intent to intimidate or harass another person because of that person's race, color, religion, or national origin:

(a) Causes physical injury to another person; or

(b) By words or conduct places another person in reasonable fear of harm to his person or property or harm to the person [or] property of a third person; or

(c) Causes physical damage to or destruction of the property of another person. . . .

Source: 1981 Wash. Laws 1106.

*   *   *

Congressman John Conyers Confronts the FBI about Counting Hate Crimes

After Americans elected Ronald Reagan as president in 1980, members of Congress began lobbying for federal laws against hate crimes. Although he had pledged himself to oppose criminality, members of the Reagan administration resisted calls for laws against hate crimes. Congressman John Conyers, an African American from Detroit, led the fight to outlaw hate. Notice that he describes racially motivated crimes as "constitutional violations." Targeting someone on the basis of their race, Conyers said, violated their constitutional rights. In his subcommittee, Conyers dueled with Reagan administration officials.

Hearing before the Subcommittee on Criminal Justice of the Committee on the Judiciary House of Representatives, 1985

MR. CONYERS: But these constitutional violations, as troublesome as you may describe them, have got to be caught. These are the things we are more concerned about than car theft, or trespass, or burglary. We are going to the heart of our whole system and way of life. I refuse to be deterred by the fact that it may be a little complicated to classify.

We have these kind of questions of intent coming up in other kinds of crimes that get classified as well. The hypothetical of a rock being thrown through the window eventually gets classified into something. We are not saying that it's permanent for all time, but it gives us an idea of where the problem areas are.

I also think that the fact that we have motivational problems should not prevent us from recording constitutional violations. I think it is very important that we do that.

Your discussion has taken us, in my view, to the tough kinds of questions that occur. But a cross burned on a lawn, or a vandalization of a synagogue, while there may be robbery or some other motive, there's no question—it seems to me that there wouldn't be any reason not to classify some of the obvious cases.

In other words, I am trying to direct your attention to this broad, clear-cut kind of violation, and you are directing mine to the tougher, closer questions.

Now, it seems to me that somewhere, once we all agree that these cases are important enough to be classified and to be recorded, that we can then find a way to do it. And that's what I think the Congress is going to say to you after all these years.

MR. WILLIAM H. BAKER, ASSISTANT DIRECTOR, OFFICE OF CONGRESSIONAL AND PUBLIC AFFAIRS, FEDERAL BUREAU OF INVESTIGATION: Mr. Chairman, I think the message that we try to project to you, both the Department and the FBI speaking collectively, is that we are very concerned about the problem of bigotry and hatred. Certainly, our investigations against the Aryan Nation, the Order, and the three shoot-outs that have involved our agents in as many months just recently, are an indication that when a crime occurs and it is within our jurisdiction, the FBI is out there aggressively.

But here we are trying to protect the integrity of a data collection system, and I don't want to confuse the issue because I know that it is a serious and an emotional issue. But in trying to protect the data, we keep coming back to we depend on over 15,000 submitting agencies, law enforcement officers out at the scene, to give us their response to a crime as they report to the scene.

And what we are asking for here is a motivation determination. And that is where we have the most problem in trying to reach, with you, for an answer and the proper way to gather the data that you are seeking. We believe that in trying to get that officer to determine motivation, we will discredit the integrity of the data collection system.

MR. CONYERS: What about the clear-cut case?

MR. BAKER: There are clear-cut cases, but there are thousands of other cases that are not clear-cut or that do change. I think what I am here to say is that we know that there is a problem. We do not believe that UCR is the apparatus to give you the answer that you want. . . .

MR. STEVEN R. SCHLESINGER, DIRECTOR, BUREAU OF JUSTICE STATISTICS, DEPARTMENT OF JUSTICE: My point is that for those kinds of crimes for which the intention, the motivation, is manifest—and I think you have mentioned a number of them—one could perhaps work through a clipping service, or one could work through a national network of organizations.

MR. CONYERS: We just dismissed that—out of hand. A lynching in the South isn't due to get a lot of public attention—not only in the South. I hasten to add, for the record—we can't depend on the Detroit Free Press to tell the Department of Justice whether there's a basis for a civil rights or a constitutional violation.

I mean, if it were that simple, we would just do that. But what we found out is that many of the incidents do in fact go unreported.

Now, I think if you study this subject, you will find that that's the case. We have been told that constantly in the hearings that we have held on this subject.

MR. SCHLESINGER: Mr. Chairman, perhaps it would be useful if I turn to the other two categories of crime.

MR. CONYERS: Well, you haven't taken care of this one. I mean, the fact of the matter is that in the most obvious kinds of cases and this classification that you have described yourself, you tell me to go to the congressional clipping service, or contract with the local newspapers across America.

Why wouldn't a cop, who has to make these determinations in every other case, why doesn't he understand the meaning of a burning cross on the lawn of a black family that's the first one in the neighborhood—do you think that there would be some misunderstanding? I mean, you are ignoring, sir, the most obvious category of cases of which there shouldn't even be any question about how to classify them, and what the witnesses think and feel, and all of that.

I mean, this is the one kind of case on which I thought we would agree. I thought I had some agreement from the other witness. You can't mistake that, can you?

When someone writes a Jewish denigration across the synagogue wall, do you wonder, was this racially motivated? And if they also steal some silver and [some] other things—do you think we sit around in the real world of police activity and say, well, now, they stole something, they damaged something, they broke and entered, and they also wrote some defamatory ethnic slurs. Now, I wonder how we are going to categorize this?

MR. BAKER: Mr. Chairman, that would be categorized by whichever offense it occurred in under now as it is now and it would be investigated. If it is a burglary along with that, then it would be investigated as a burglary by that department.

MR. CONYERS: That's precisely the point, at mass, the ethnic or racial violations that are going on, and that's why we are trying to create a separate category. Now, if to you it's more important to know the breaking and entering than whether a person's constitutional rights are being violated, we are going to write a law to make it clear. We will send all the computer experts and all the administrative people back to school to figure out a way to come up with a classification.

But may I suggest, for instances where there may be a legitimate difficulty, we could identify a category that is questionable, or for which there may be one or more interpretations, and we would put questionable incidents there. We would then get the picture. But we can't continue into the 21st century in a constitutional democracy and be told by law enforcement officials that the police are not smart enough to determine questions—acts of violation, where there's an intent question involved. There are intent questions involved in other classifications that you are presently making.

A policeman goes out to the scene of a crime and there's a body; he doesn't know if it's murder, suicide, manslaughter, degree, or anything else. And UCR doesn't require that he accurately do that. We have a dead body, we go from there. Sometimes the classification has to be changed. We are not requiring perfection. But we are not going to let technology, or a lack of technology, foil us on this basic question.

These problems are bigger than going to a clipping service. I think that is an absolutely simplistic solution of a problem. I mean, our staff could have figured that out. We wouldn't call you up here to pass a law, and you tell us to clip out of the Washington Post and the Detroit Free Press for a constitutional violation. We are already clipping.

What we find out is that there are many violations that aren't caught. The newspapers don't have any responsibility to report every racial or act of bigotry that comes to them. They say that's the police's job, that's somebody's job—it's not ours.

MR. BAKER: Mr. Chairman, I did not mean to imply a simplistic approach to a very complicated problem. We have given this and your concerns a great deal of insight in preparing our response which we understand is not in line with your desires right now. We have this study that's ongoing. We are expecting the final results of the Abt study, which has been looking into how to better use the data that we collect in UCR, and how to better serve law enforcement. And we intend to take your interests to this group when we meet in April down at Quantico, VA, and to discuss your interests with this group.

MR. CONYERS: Well, that's very encouraging.

MR. BAKER: The other was just something that certainly would have to be considered, but not a simplistic clipping, but a much more serious effort.

MR. CONYERS: Forget the clipping, please; don't take up that suggestion. I have been taking gas on this subject for quite a few years. And if I get 218 Congressmen and 51 Senators, we are to make it a law. So there's two ways we can solve this problem. We pass a law and then force you to add this to the classification—and I don't think this is going to disrupt UCR one bit, just between you and me—or you can come up with some reasonable solution, and it has to be reasonable, it's not just any solution. And please don't ever let anybody tell you to come back and recommend clipping to this subcommittee. That's the one thing I ask you—do not bring it back, because we have been through that already.

Source: Hearing before the Subcommittee on Criminal Justice of the Committee on the Judiciary House of Representatives, 99th Cong., 1st sess., on H.R. 1171 and H.R. 775, *Hate Crimes Statistics Act*, March 21, 1985.

*　　*　　*

The First Federal Hate Crime Law

Congress finally passed the first federal hate crime law in 1990. This very cautious law only required the Department of Justice to collect data on the number of hate crimes committed each year. The law contained provisions that prevented its use to prosecute hate crimes. The names of individuals could not be collected. Notice that section 2 of the law announced that "the American family life is the foundation of American Society." Congress added this "finding" at the insistence of conservative senator Jesse Helms of North Carolina. Helms feared that a law protecting minorities from criminal violence might somehow legitimize homosexuality. To forestall such an eventuality, Helms pressed for the law's second section.

Hate Crime Statistics Act, 1990

(1) . . . the Attorney General shall acquire data, for each calendar year, about crimes that manifest evidence of prejudice based on race, religion, disability, sexual orientation, or ethnicity, including where appropriate the crimes of murder, non-negligent manslaughter; forcible rape; aggravated assault, simple assault, intimidation; arson; and destruction, damage or vandalism of property.

(2) The Attorney General shall establish guidelines for the collection of such data including the necessary evidence and criteria that must be present for a finding of manifest prejudice and procedures for carrying out the purposes of this section.

(3) Nothing in this section creates a cause of action or a right to bring an action, including an action based on discrimination due to sexual orientation. As used in this section, the term "sexual orientation" means consensual homosexuality or heterosexuality. . . .

(4) Data acquired under this section shall be used only for research or statistical purposes and may not contain any information that may reveal the identity of an individual victim of a crime. . . .

Sec. 2. (a) Congress finds that—

(1) the American family life is the foundation of American Society,
(2) Federal policy should encourage the well-being, financial security, and health of the American family,
(3) schools should not de-emphasize the critical value of American family life.

(b) Nothing in this Act shall be construed, nor shall any funds appropriated to carry out the purpose of the Act be used, to promote or encourage homosexuality.

Source: Hate Crime Statistics Act, P.L. 101–275, 104 Stat. 140, April 23, 1990.

*   *   *

Federal Hate Crime Law: Sentencing Enhancement

In 1994, Congress passed a new hate crime law as part of a huge crime control law pushed by the Clinton administration that increased penalties for persons convicted of committing a crime out of prejudice. The law directed the U.S. Sentencing Commission to revise the sentencing guidelines judges use when determining punishments for convicted persons. Under this law, any federal crime can be punished as a hate crime, if the defendant selected his or her victim based on race, color, religion, or five other categories.

Violent Crime Control and Law Enforcement Act of 1994
DIRECTION TO UNITED STATES SENTENCING COMMISSION REGARDING SENTENCING ENHANCEMENTS FOR HATE CRIMES.

(a) Definition.—In this section, "hate crime" means a crime in which the defendant intentionally selects a victim, or in the case of a property crime, the property that is the object of the crime, because of the actual or perceived race, color, religion, national origin, ethnicity, gender, disability, or sexual orientation of any person.

(b) Sentencing Enhancement.—Pursuant to section 994 of title 28, United States Code, the United States Sentencing Commission shall promulgate guidelines or amend existing guidelines to provide sentencing enhancements of not less than 3 offense levels for offenses that the finder of fact at trial determines beyond a reasonable doubt are hate crimes. In carrying out this section, the United States Sentencing Commission shall ensure that there is reasonable consistency with other guidelines, avoid duplicative punishments for substantially the same offense, and take into account any mitigating circumstances that might justify exceptions.

Source: Pub. L. No. 103–322, 108 Stat. 1796, September 13, 1994.

~

Bibliographic Essay

There are several broad surveys of lynching. Christopher Waldrep, ed., *Lynching in America: A History in Documents* (New York: New York University Press, 2006), provides a documentary history, and Christopher Waldrep, *The Many Faces of Judge Lynch: Extralegal Violence and Punishment in America* (New York: Palgrave Macmillan, 2002), offers a narrative of American lynching from its Revolutionary beginnings to the present. Stewart E. Tolnay and E. M. Beck, *A Festival of Violence: An Analysis of Southern Lynchings, 1882–1930* (Urbana: University of Illinois Press, 1995), make a statistical analysis; and Philip Dray, *At the Hands of Persons Unknown: The Lynching of Black America* (New York: Random House, 2002), is anecdotal and journalistic. Other books of interest include Michael J. Pfeifer, *Rough Justice: Lynching and American Society, 1874–1947* (Urbana: University of Illinois Press, 2004); and Margaret Vandiver, *Lethal Punishment: Lynchings and Legal Executions in the South* (New Brunswick, N.J.: Rutgers University Press, 2006). Leon Litwack has a chapter on lynching in *Trouble in Mind: Black Southerners in the Age of Jim Crow* (New York: Knopf, 1998). These surveys follow James Elbert Cutler, *Lynch-Law: An Investigation into the History of Lynching in the United States*, originally published in 1905, the only academic history of lynching from the Revolution to its present other than *The Many Faces of Judge Lynch*. The National Association for the Advancement of Colored People (NAACP) also surveyed lynching: see *Thirty Years of Lynching in the United States, 1889–1918* (New York: NAACP, 1919).

For gender and lynching, see Robyn Wiegman, "The Anatomy of Lynching," *Journal of the History of Sexuality* 3 (January 1993): 456–62; Jacquelyn Dowd Hall, *Revolt against Chivalry: Jessie Daniel Ames and the Women's Campaign against Lynching* (1979; rev. ed., New York: Columbia University Press, 1993); Martha Hodes, *White Women, Black Men: Illicit Sex in the 19th Century South* (New Haven, Conn.: Yale University Press, 1997); and Barbara Holden-Smith, "Lynching, Federalism, and the Intersection of Race and Gender in the Progressive Era," *Yale Journal of Law and Feminism* 8 (1996): 31–78.

Regional and state studies provide an important perspective. See William D. Carrigan, *The Making of a Lynching Culture: Violence and Vigilantism in Central Texas, 1836–1916* (Urbana: University of Illinois Press, 2004); Stephen J. Leonard, *Lynching in Colorado, 1859–1919* (Boulder: University Press of Colorado, 2002); and W. Fitzhugh Brundage, *Lynching in the New South: Georgia and Virginia, 1880–1930* (Urbana: University of Illinois Press, 1993).

Grace Elizabeth Hale, *Making Whiteness: The Culture of Segregation in the South, 1890–1940* (New York: Pantheon, 1998), introduced the concept of "spectacle lynching." James Allen, Hilton Als, John Lewis, and Leon Litwack, *Without Sanctuary: Lynching Photography in America* (Santa Fe, N.Mex.: Twin Palms Publishers, 2000), documented the spectacle, reproducing postcard images of lynchings, along with other photographs. This book dwarfs all the textual surveys in terms of influence and impact on the general public. Dora Apel, *Imagery of Lynching: Black Men, White Women, and the Mob* (New Brunswick, N.J.: Rutgers University Press, 2004), also looks at artistic representations of lynching. Jonathan Markovitz, *Legacies of Lynching: Racial Violence and Memory* (Minneapolis: University of Minnesota Press, 2004), is notable for its look at lynching in cinema. Ken Gonzales-Day, *Lynching in the West, 1850–1935* (Durham, N.C.: Duke University Press, 2006), examines photographic representations of California lynchings.

For connections between the death penalty and lynching, see Charles Ogletree Jr. and Austin Sarat, *From Lynch Mobs to the Killing State: Race and the Death Penalty in America* (New York: New York University Press, 2006); Jesse Jackson, *Legal Lynching: Racism, in Justice and the Death Penalty* (New York: Marlowe, 1996); and John D. Bessler, *Death in the Dark: Midnight Executions in America* (Boston: Northeastern University Press, 1997).

Many books on lynching are case studies of particular incidents: Stephen J. Whitfield, *A Death in the Delta: The Story of Emmett Till* (New York: Free Press, 1988); Christopher Metress, ed., *The Lynching of Emmett Till: A Documentary Narrative* (Charlottesville: University of Virginia Press, 2002);

Mamie Till-Mobley and Christopher Benson, *Death of Innocence: The Story of the Hate Crime that Changed America* (New York: Random House, 2003); Dennis B. Downey and Raymond M. Hyser, *No Crooked Death: Coatesville, Pennsylvania, and the Lynching of Zachariah Walker* (Urbana: University of Illinois Press, 1991); Harry Farrell, *Swift Justice: Murder and Vengeance in a California Town* (New York: St. Martins Press, 1992); Horace Mann Bond and Julian W. Bond, *The Star Creek Papers: Washington Parish and the Lynching of Jerome Wilson*, ed., Adam Fairclough (Athens: University of Georgia Press, 1997); Richard B. McCaslin, *Tainted Breeze: The Great Hanging at Gainesville, Texas, 1862* (Baton Rouge: Louisiana State University Press, 1994); Kenneth C. Barnes, *Who Killed John Clayton? Political Violence and the Emergence of the New South, 1861–1893* (Durham, N.C.: Duke University Press, 1998); Dominic J. Capeci Jr., *The Lynching of Cleo Wright* (Lexington: University Press of Kentucky, 1998); Gail Williams O'Brien, *The Color of the Law: Race, Violence, and Justice in the Post-World War II South* (Chapel Hill: University of North Carolina Press, 1999); Mark Curriden and Leroy Phillips Jr., *Contempt of Court: The Turn of the Century Lynching that Launched a Hundred Years of Federalism* (New York: Anchor, 1999); Ben Green, *Before His Time: The Untold Story of Harry T. Moore, America's First Civil Rights Martyr* (New York: Free Press, 1999); James H. Madison, *A Lynching in the Heartland: Race and Memory in America* (New York: Palgrave, 2001); Laura Wexler, *Fire in the Canebreak: The Last Mass Lynching in America* (New York: Scribner, 2003); Cynthia Carr, *Our Town: A Heartland Lynching, a Haunted Town, and the Hidden History of White America* (New York: Crown, 2006); Steve Oney, *And the Dead Shall Rise: The Murder of Mary Phagan and the Lynching of Leo Frank* (New York: Pantheon, 2003); and Jeffrey Melnick, *Black-Jewish Relations on Trial: Leo Frank and Jim Conley in the New South* (Jackson: University Press of Mississippi, 2000).

These case studies build on the work of recognized classics in the field: Leonard Dinnerstein, *The Leo Frank Case* (New York: Columbia University Press, 1968); James R. McGovern, *Anatomy of a Lynching: The Killing of Claude Neal* (Baton Rouge: Louisiana State University Press, 1982); and Howard Smead, *Blood Justice: The Lynching of Mack Charles Parker* (New York: Oxford University Press, 1986). Dinnerstein, McGovern, and Smead followed pioneering work by several NAACP investigators, most famously, Walter White, *Rope and Faggot: A Biography of Judge Lynch* (New York: Knopf, 1929). Arthur F. Raper also collected a series of case studies in *The Tragedy of Lynching* (Chapel Hill: University of North Carolina Press, 1933). Ultimately, Ida B. Wells stands as the prototypical author of case study collections, published as pamphlets and recounted in her autobiography. Her writings are collected in various places, but see Jacqueline Jones Royster, ed., *Southern Horrors and Other Writings: The Anti-Lynching Campaign of Ida B. Wells, 1892–1900* (Boston: Bedford, 1997). Although Wells died in 1931, her autobiography did not reach print until 1970: Alfred M. Duster, ed., *Crusade for Justice: The Autobiography of Ida B. Wells* (Chicago: University of Chicago Press, 1970). All Ida B. Wells scholarship dates from 1970. Three recent biographies of Wells have appeared: Linda O. McMurry, *To Keep the Waters Troubled: The Life of Ida B. Wells* (New York: Oxford University Press, 1998); Patricia A. Schechter, *Ida B. Wells-Barnett and American Reform, 1880–1930* (Chapel Hill: University of North Carolina Press, 2001); Paula J. Giddings, *Ida, A Sword Among Lions: Ida B. Wells and the Campaign Against Lynching* (New York: Amistad, 2008).

Because this series allows few endnotes, and this book necessarily relies on the work of many historians, it is vital that sources for each chapter be cited so that proper credit can be accorded to the many scholars whose exhaustive work made this synthesis possible.

Introduction. Anne P. Rice, ed., *Witnessing Lynching: American Writers Respond* (New Brunswick, N.J.: Rutgers University Press, 2003), is a useful compendium of many writings, including Angelina Weld Grimke, "Goldie," and Sutton Griggs, "The Blaze." For Oliver Cromwell Cox on lynching, see *Caste, Class, and Race: A Study in Social Dynamics* (New York: Doubleday & Co., 1948). The burning outside Natchez appears fictionally in William Wells Brown, *Clotel* (1853; reprint ed., New York: Arno Press, 1969), 73–78; and in *New York Times*, March 8, 1854; *Mississippi Free Trader*, February 25, 1854; and *New York Tribune*, February 6, 1854. Anne Moody, *Coming of Age in Mississippi* (New York: Dell, 1968), is essential reading. Members of the Supreme Court present the Constitution as a bastion of stability in a troubled world quite often, but I particularly consulted *Vanhorne v. Dorrance*, 28 F. Cas. 1012 (1795), and *Calder et wife v. Bull et wife*, 3 U.S. 386 (1798).

Chapter 1. For popular constitutionalism, see Larry D. Kramer, *The People Themselves: Popular Constitutionalism and Judicial Review* (New York: Oxford University Press, 2004); Sean Wilentz, *The Rise of American Democracy: Jefferson to Lincoln* (New York: Norton, 2005); Gerald Leonard, *The Invention of Party Politics: Federalism, Popular Sovereignty, and Constitutional Development in Jacksonian Illinois* (Chapel Hill: University of North Carolina Press, 2002); Barbara Young Welke, *Recasting American Liberty: Gender, Race, Law, and the Railroad Revolution, 1865–1920* (Cambridge: Cambridge University Press, 2001); and Michael J. Pfeifer, *Rough Justice: Lynching and American Society, 1874–1947* (Urbana: University of Illinois Press, 2004).

Michael W. Fitzgerald, *The Union League Movement in the Deep South: Politics and Agricultural Change during Reconstruction* (Baton Rouge: Louisiana State University Press, 1989), remains invaluable for the Union Leagues. For mob rule, see E. P. Thompson, *The Making of the English Working Class* (New York: Vintage, 1966), 60–65; Robert B. Shoemaker, *The London Mob: Violence and Disorder in Eighteenth-Century England* (London: Hambledon and London, 2004), 27–50, 131; Rachel N. Klein, *Unification of a Slave State: The Rise of the Planter Class in the South Carolina Backcountry, 1760–1808* (Chapel Hill: University of North Carolina Press, 1990). For Dunning's pro-Southern views, consult William Archibald Dunning, *Essays on the Civil War and Reconstruction* (1897; rev. ed., New York: Harper and Row, 1965).

Chapter 2. Emma Lou Thornbrough, *T. Thomas Fortune: Militant Journalist* (Chicago: University of Chicago Press, 1972), is an excellent biography. For the early black journalists, I used Frederick Douglass, *My Bondage and My Freedom* (1855; reprint ed., New York: Dover, 1969), 389; Kenneth D. Nordin, "In Search of Black Unity: An Interpretation of the Content and Function of 'Freedom's Journal,'" *Journalism History* 4 (1977–1978): 123–28; Frankie Hutton, "Social Morality in the Antebellum Black Press," *Journal of Popular Culture* 26 (Fall 1992): 71–84; Lawrence Fortenberry, "Freedom's Journal: The First Black Medium," *Black Scholar* 6 (November 1974): 33–37; Frederick Cooper, "Elevating the Race: The Social Thought of Black Leaders, 1827–50," *American Quarterly* 24 (December 1972): 604–25; and J. William Snorgrass, "The Black Press in the San Francisco Bay Area, 1856–1900," *California History* 60 (Winter 1981/1982): 306–7. For Republican attitudes toward the Constitution in the Civil War, I consulted Michael Caires, "How Adequate Was the Constitution? The Civil War Congress and the Constitution, 1861–1862" (seminar paper, San Francisco State University, 2006). I also used Charles Sumner, *Speech of Hon. Charles Sumner of Massachusetts on his Motion to Repeal the Fugitive Slave Bill* (Boston: Tichner, Reed, and Fields, 1852); David Herbert Donald, *Charles Sumner* (New York: Da Capo, 1996), 1:205–37, 2:72–73; Ronald B. Jager, "Charles Sumner, the Constitution, and the Civil Rights Act of 1875," *New England Quarterly* 42 (September 1969): 350–72; Joel Parker, *The Domestic and Foreign Relations of the United States* (Cambridge, Mass.: Welch, Bigelow & Co., 1862); and William Whiting, *The War Powers of the President and the Legislative Powers of Congress in Relation to the Rebellion, Treason, and Slavery* (Boston: J. L. Shorey, 1863). For Du Bois and Washington, I consulted the standard sources: David Levering Lewis, *W. E. B. Du Bois: Biography of a Race, 1868–1919* (New York: Henry Holt, 1993); and Louis R. Harlan, *Booker T. Washington: The*

Making of a Black Leader, 1856–1901 (New York: Oxford University Press, 1972). Paul Avrich, *The Haymarket Tragedy* (Princeton, N.J.: Princeton University Press, 1984), is useful for the anarchists' dynamite fetish. For John Mitchell, I relied on Ann Field Alexander, *Race Man: The Rise and Fall of the "Fighting Editor," John Mitchell Jr.* (Charlottesville: University of Virginia Press, 2002); and Suzanne Lebsock, *A Murder in Virginia: Southern Justice on Trial* (New York: Norton, 2003). For the Wilmington race riot, see Alfred M. Waddell, "The Story of Wilmington, N.C., Race Riots," *Colliers* 22 (November 26, 1898): 4–5; H. Leon Prather Jr., "We Have Taken a City, a Centennial Essay," in *Democracy Betrayed: The Wilmington Race Riot of 1898 and Its Legacy*, ed. David S. Cecelski and Timothy B. Tyson, 15–39 (Chapel Hill: University of North Carolina Press, 1998). In addition, I used numerous newspapers.

Chapter 3. For Albion Small, I relied primarily on his own writings: Albion W. Small, "Fifty Years of Sociology in the United States (1865–1915)," *American Journal of Sociology* 21 (May 1916): 724–25; and Small, "The Era of Sociology," *American Journal of Sociology* 1 (July 1895): 1–15. Other sources used include James Turner, "The Founding Fathers of American Sociology: An Examination of Their Sociological Theories of Race Relations," *Journal of Black Studies* 9 (September 1978): 3–14; and Elliott Rudwick, "W. E. B. Du Bois as Sociologist," in *Along the Color Line: Explorations in the Black Experience*, by August Meier and Elliott Rudwick, 28–55 (Urbana: University of Illinois Press, 1976). For the *Chicago Tribune* and its "sociology," see *Chicago Tribune*, January 1, 1875, January 1, 1883; and Christopher Waldrep, *The Many Faces of Judge Lynch: Extralegal Violence and Punishment in America* (New York: Palgrave Macmillan, 2002), 112–14. For Sumner, I consulted William Graham Sumner, *Andrew Jackson* (Boston: Houghton Mifflin, 1882), 325; William Graham Sumner, "The Proposed Dual Organization of Mankind," *Appleton's Popular Science Monthly* 49 (August 1896): 433–39; Bruce Curtis, *William Graham Sumner* (Boston: Twayne, 1981), 63; and Robert Green McCloskey, *American Conservatism in the Age of Enterprise: A Study of William Graham Sumner, Stephen J. Field, and Andrew Carnegie* (Cambridge, Mass.: Harvard University Press, 1951), 48, 56, 62, 64. Ida B. Wells remains her own best biographer: Ida B. Wells, *Crusade for Justice: The Autobiography of Ida B. Wells*, ed. Alfreda M. Duster (Chicago: University of Chicago Press, 1970); and Miriam DeCosta-Willis, ed., *The Memphis Diary of Ida B. Wells* (Boston: Beacon Press, 1995). See also Mildred I. Thomson, *Ida B. Wells-Barnett: An Exploratory Study of an American Black Woman, 1893–1930* (Brooklyn, N.Y.: Carlson Press, 1990); Patricia A. Schechter, *Ida B. Wells-Barnett and Ameri-*

can Reform, 1880–1930 (Chapel Hill: University of North Carolina Press, 2001); Linda O. Mcmurry, To Keep the Waters Troubled: The Life of Ida B. Wells (New York: Oxford University Press, 1998); Shirley W. Logan, "Rhetorical Strategies in Ida B. Wells's 'Southern Horrors: Lynch Law in All Its Phases,'" Sage 7 (Summer 1991): 3–9; and Isabelle Fyvie Mayo, Recollections: Of What I Saw, What I Lived Through, and What I Learned, during More than Fifty Years of Social and Literary Experience (London: J. Murray, 1910). For Alice Walker on Wells, see Alice Walker, "Advancing Luna—and Ida B. Wells," in You Can't Keep a Good Woman Down (San Diego: Harcourt Brace Jovanovich, 1981). For railroad segregation, see Joseph H. Cartwright, The Triumph of Jim Crow: Tennessee Race Relations in the 1880s (Knoxville: University of Tennessee Press, 1976); and Barbara Young Welke, Recasting American Liberty: Gender, Race, Law, and the Railroad Revolution, 1865–1920 (Cambridge: Cambridge University Press, 2001). For Wells's suit against the railroad, I primarily relied on the court's file of the case, Ida B. Wells v. Chesapeake, Ohio, and South Western Railroad Co., Tennessee Supreme Court Cases, Tennessee State Library and Archives, Nashville. For Work, the standard source is Linda O. Mcmurry, Recorder of the Black Experience: A Biography of Monroe Nathan Work (Baton Rouge: Louisiana State University Press, 1985), but see also Monroe N. Work, "Crime among the Negroes of Chicago," American Journal of Sociology 6 (September 1900): 204–23. For the Chicago riot of 1919, see William M. Tuttle Jr., Race Riot: Chicago in the Red Summer of 1919 (New York: Atheneum, 1978); for the Elaine riot, see Grif Stockley, Blood in Their Eyes: The Elaine Race Massacres of 1919 (Fayetteville: University of Arkansas Press, 2001); Richard C. Cortner, A Mob Intent on Death: The NAACP and the Arkansas Riot Cases (Middletown, Conn.: Wesleyan University Press, 1988); Walter F. White, "'Massacring Whites' in Arkansas," Nation 109 (December 6, 1919): 715–16; and Todd E. Lewis, "Mob Justice in the 'American Congo': 'Judge Lynch' in Arkansas during the Decade after World War I," Arkansas Historical Quarterly 52 (Summer 1993): 156–84.

Chapter 4. For the NAACP's fight against lynching, the classic work remains Robert L. Zangrando, The NAACP Crusade against Lynching (Philadelphia: Temple University Press, 1980). For the NAACP generally, see especially Charles Flint Kellogg, NAACP: A History of the National Association for the Advancement of Colored People (Baltimore: Johns Hopkins University Press, 1967); and Gilbert Jonas, Freedom's Sword: The NAACP and the Struggle against Racism in America, 1909–1969 (New York: Routledge, 2005). Mark Robert Schneider's "We Return Fighting": The Civil Rights Movement in the

Jazz Age (Boston: Northeastern University Press, 2002) is a history of the NAACP in the 1920s, arguing that the NAACP really was a mass organization and not simply a band of elitists based in New York. Walter White's autobiography, *A Man Called White: The Autobiography of Walter White* (New York: Viking, 1948), is essential, as is Kenneth Robert Janken, *White: The Biography of Walter White, Mr. NAACP* (New York: New Press, 2003). Janken takes a critical look at White, exposing some of his fabrications, as does Schneider in *We Return Fighting*. Mary White Ovington was an important NAACP founder, and she also wrote a brief memoir: *Black and White Sat Down Together: The Reminiscences of an NAACP Founder* (New York: Feminist Press, 1995). See also Carolyn Wedin, *Inheritors of the Spirit: Mary White Ovington and the Founding of the NAACP* (New York: John Wiley & Sons, 1998); and James Weldon Johnson, *Along This Way: The Autobiography of James Weldon Johnson* (New York: Viking, 1933). Roy Wilkins with Tom Mathews, *Standing Fast: The Autobiography of Roy Wilkins* (New York: Penguin, 1982), also covers a vital period in the NAACP's history. See also Susan D. Carle, "Race, Class, and Legal Ethics in the Early NAACP (1910–1920)," *Law and History Review* 20 (Spring 2002): 97–146; Elliott Rudwick and August Meier, "The Rise of the Black Secretariat in the NAACP, 1909–35," in *Along the Color Line: Explorations in the Black Experience*, by August Meier and Elliott Rudwick, 94–106 (Urbana: University of Illinois Press, 1976); Mark Ellis, "Joel Spingarn's 'Constructive Programme' and the Wartime Antilynching Bill of 1918," *Journal of Policy History* 4 (1992): 134–53; and Simon Topping, "'Supporting Our Friends and Defeating Our Enemies': Militancy and Nonpartisanship in the NAACP, 1936–1948," *Journal of African American History* 89 (January 2004): 17–35.

For the Springfield riot, see Roberta Senechal, *The Sociogenesis of a Race Riot: Springfield, Illinois, in 1908* (Urbana: University of Illinois Press, 1990). Every scholar recognizes the important work of William English Walling, and it is important to read Walling's own account of the riot: William English Walling, "The Race War in the North," *Independent* 65 (September 3, 1908): 529–34. Niagara's Declaration of Principles, 1905, is in David Levering Lewis, ed., *W. E. B. Du Bois: A Reader* (New York: Henry Holt, 1995), 367–69; and is discussed in David Levering Lewis, *W. E. B. Du Bois: Biography of a Race* (New York: Henry Holt, 1993), 316–22. For the law on lynching, the classic work is James Harmon Chadbourn, *Lynching and the Law* (Chapel Hill: University of North Carolina Press, 1933). The NAACP relied on Albert E. Pillsbury, "A Brief Inquiry into a Federal Remedy for Lynching," *Harvard Law Review* 15 (March 1902): 707–13; *United States v. Cruikshank*, 92 U.S. 542 (1876); *United States v. Harris et al.*, 106 U.S. 629 (1882);

and *Hodges v. United States*, 203 U.S. 1 (1906). There are numerous undated drafts of Houston's brief in box 163–25, Charles H. Houston Papers, Manuscript Division, Moorland-Spingarn Research Center, Howard University, Washington, D.C.; "Memorandum for the Assistant to the Attorney General," August 30, 1933, file 158260, Department of Justice Central Files, National Archives, College Park; and Roger A. Fairfax Jr., "Wielding the Double-Edged Sword: Charles Hamilton Houston and Judicial Activism in the Age of Legal Realism," *Harvard Blackletter Journal* 14 (Spring 1998): 17–44. For World War II and its impact on race relations, see Neil A. Wynn, *The Afro-American and the Second World War* (New York: Holmes and Meier, 1976); Gilbert Ware, *William Hastie: Grace under Pressure* (New York: Oxford University Press, 1984), 497–530; and Phillip McGuire, *He, Too, Spoke for Democracy: Judge Hastie, World War II, and the Black Soldier* (New York: Greenwood, 1988). I also consulted the *Chicago Defender* and other newspapers, the NAACP Papers, and the William H. Hastie Papers at the Law School Library, Harvard University.

Chapter 5. For Chicago, see James R. Grossman, *Land of Hope: Chicago, Black Southerners, and the Great Migration* (Chicago: University of Chicago Press, 1989); and William M. Tuttle Jr., *Race Riot: Chicago in the Red Summer of 1919* (New York: Atheneum, 1970). For dynamite, see Arthur Pine Van-Gelder and Hugo Schlatter, *History of the Explosives Industry in America* (New York: Arno Press, 1972), 402–30; and Paul Avrich, *The Haymarket Tragedy* (Princeton, N.J.: Princeton University Press, 1984). The *New York Times* reported numerous bombings, and I relied on its reporting and Thomas J. Tunney as told to Paul Merrick Hollister, *Throttled! The Detection of the German and Anarchist Bomb Plotters* (Boston: Small, Maynard, 1919); and the anarchist newspaper, the *Blast*, which I found at the San Francisco State University Labor Archives. See also Michael Klarman, *From Jim Crow to Civil Rights: The Supreme Court and the Struggle for Racial Equality* (New York: Oxford University Press, 2004); and Robert K. Murray, *Red Scare: A Study in National Hysteria, 1919–1920* (Minneapolis: University of Minnesota Press, 1955). For Gandhi and his methodology, see Krishnalal Shridharani, *War without Violence: A Study of Gandhi's Method and Its Accomplishments* (New York: Harcourt, Brace, 1939); and Richard B. Gregg, *The Power of Non-Violence* (Philadelphia: Lippincott, 1934). For Birmingham, see Charles E. Connerly, *"The Most Segregated City in America": City Planning and Civil Rights in Birmingham, 1920–1980* (Charlottesville: University of Virginia Press, 2005); Andrew M. Manis, *A Fire You Can't Put Out: The Civil Rights Life of Birmingham's Reverend Fred Shuttlesworth* (Tuscaloosa: University of Alabama Press, 1999), 79, 108–9; J. Mills Thornton III, *Dividing Lines: Municipal Politics and the Struggle for Civil Rights in Montgomery, Birmingham, and Selma* (Tuscaloosa: University of Alabama Press, 2002); Glenn T. Eskew, *But for Birmingham: The Local and National Movements in the Civil Rights Struggle* (Chapel Hill: University of North Carolina Press, 1997); and Howell Raines, "The Birmingham Bombing," *New York Times Magazine*, July 24, 1983. See Lynda Dempsey Cochran, "Arthur Davis Shores," MA thesis, Georgia Southern College, August 1977, 11–41. Cochran interviewed Shores over several years, and her thesis is virtually a primary source, recording her valuable oral history interviews with Shores. The Birmingham Public Library is an essential stop for researchers interested in civil rights violence: see surveillance files, Birmingham Police Department, Birmingham Public Library. See also William A. Nunnelley, *Bull Connor* (Tuscaloosa: University of Alabama Press, 1991); Aldon D. Morris, *The Origins of the Civil Rights Movement: Black Communities Organizing for Change* (New York: Free Press, 1984); and Ben Green, *Before His Time: The Untold Story of Harry T. Moore, America's First Civil Rights Martyr* (New York: Free Press, 1999). I consider Michal R. Belknap, *Federal Law and Southern Order: Racial Violence and Constitutional Conflict in the Post-Brown South* (Athens: University of Georgia Press, 1987), essential reading for this period. See also Arnold R. Hirsch, "Massive Resistance in the Urban North: Trumbull Park, Chicago, 1953–1966," *Journal of American History* 82 (September 1995): 522–50. My account of the Emmett Till lynching comes primarily from Whitfield's superb book, *A Death in the Delta*. For grassroots organizing in Mississippi, I consulted Charles M. Payne, *I've Got the Light of Freedom: The Organizing Tradition and the Mississippi Freedom Struggle* (Berkeley: University of California Press, 1995); and John Dittmer, *Local People: The Struggle for Civil Rights in Mississippi* (Urbana: University of Illinois Press, 1994). There is a thorough and complete account of the Parker lynching: Howard Smead, *Blood Justice: The Lynching of Mack Charles Parker* (New York: Oxford University Press, 1986). J. P. Coleman Papers, Mississippi Department of Archives and History, Jackson, are particularly valuable for the 1950s in Mississippi. Use in conjunction with Orley B. Caudill interview with J. P. Coleman, Mississippi Oral History Program, University of Southern Mississippi, volume 203 (1982).

Chapter 6. For Goldwater's fiery speech in San Francisco, see Barry Goldwater with Jack Casserly, *Goldwater* (New York: Doubleday, 1988), 185–86; and *New York Times*, June 5, July 17, 1964. For the backlash, see Michael W. Flamm, *Law and Order: Street Crime, Civil Unrest, and the Crisis of Liberalism in the 1960s* (New York: Columbia University Press, 2005); Dan T. Carter, *The Politics of Rage: George Wallace, the Origins of the New Conservatism, and the Transformation of American Politics* (Baton Rouge: Louisiana State University Press, 1995); Peter Brown, *Minority Party: Why Democrats Face Defeat in 1992 and Beyond* (Washington, D.C.: Regnery Gateway, 1991); and Thomas Byrne Edsall and Mary D. Edsall, *Chain Reaction: The Impact of Race, Rights, and Taxes on American Politics* (New York: Norton, 1991). For Ronald Reagan's speeches on crime control, Ronald Reagan Library, Simi Valley, Calif., kindly provided me with the essential texts. Nicholas Laham, *The Reagan Presidency and the Politics of Race: In Pursuit of Colorblind Justice and Limited Government* (Westport, Conn.: Praeger, 1998); and Charles Fried, *Order and Law: Arguing the Reagan Revolution—A Firsthand Account* (New York: Simon and Schuster, 1991). See also Philippa Strum, *When the Nazis Came to Skokie: Freedom for Speech We Love to Hate* (Lawrence: University Press of Kansas, 1999); Valerie Jenness and Ryken Grattet, *Making Hate a Crime: From Social Movement to Law Enforcement* (New York: Russell Sage Foundation, 2001); and Joyce King, *Hate Crime: The Story of a Dragging in Jasper, Texas* (New York: Pantheon Books, 2002). For free speech, see John P. Roche, *The Quest for the Dream: The Development of Civil Rights and Human Relations in Modern America* (New York: Macmillan, 1963), 1–102; Richard Polenberg, *Fighting Faiths: The Abrams Case, the Supreme Court, and Free Speech* (Ithaca, N.Y.: Cornell University Press, 1987), 197–284; David M. Rabban, *Free Speech in Its Forgotten Years* (Cambridge: Cambridge University Press, 1997), 129–380; and Paul Murphy, *World War I and the Origin of Civil Liberties in the United States* (New York: Norton, 1979). For the Supreme Court and hate speech, see *Brandenburg v. Ohio*, 395 U.S. 444 (1969); and see *RAV v. City of St. Paul*, 505 U.S. 377 (1992), for the Court and hate crime. I also cover the rise of hate crime in place of lynching in Christopher Waldrep, *The Many Faces of Judge Lynch*. Robert D. Putnam's *Bowling Alone: The Collapse and Revival of American Community* (New York: Simon and Schuster, 2000) remains useful for understanding American social life after World War II.

Index

About the Author

Christopher Waldrep is Jamie and Phyllis Parker Professor of History, San Francisco State University, and the author of *Vicksburg's Long Shadow* and other books and articles.